Fiction and Philosophy in the *Zhuangzi*

An Introduction to Early Chinese Taoist Thought

ALSO AVAILABLE FROM BLOOMSBURY

Chinese Philosophy: An Introduction, Ronnie L. Littlejohn
Daoist Encounters with Phenomenology, edited by David Chai
Doing Philosophy Comparatively, Tim Connolly
Philosophy of the Bhagavad Gita, Keya Maitra
The I Ching (Book of Changes), Geoffrey Redmond
The Qur'an: A Philosophical Guide, Oliver Leaman

Fiction and Philosophy in the Zhuangzi

An Introduction to Early Chinese Taoist Thought

Romain Graziani

BLOOMSBURY ACADEMIC

LONDON · NEW YORK · OXFORD · NEW DELHI · SYDNEY

BLOOMSBURY ACADEMIC
Bloomsbury Publishing Plc
50 Bedford Square, London, WC1B 3DP, UK
1385 Broadway, New York, NY 10018, USA

BLOOMSBURY, BLOOMSBURY ACADEMIC and the Diana logo are
trademarks of Bloomsbury Publishing Plc

First published in 2006 in France as Fictions philosophiques du "Tchouang-tseu"
by Romain Graziani, © Editions GALLIMARD, Paris, 2006

First published in Great Britain 2021

English language translation © Romain Graziani, 2021

Romain Graziani has asserted his right under the Copyright, Designs
and Patents Act, 1988, to be identified as Translator of this work.

For legal purposes the Acknowledgements on p. vii constitute an
extension of this copyright page.

Cover design by Holly Bell
© Illustration by Radiocat, Shutterstock

A catalogue record for this book is available from the British Library.

A catalog record for this book is available from the Library of Congress.

ISBN: HB: 978-1-3501-2432-5
       PB: 978-1-3501-2431-8
       ePDF: 978-1-3501-2433-2
       eBook: 978-1-3501-2434-9

Typeset by RefineCatch Limited, Bungay, Suffolk

To find out more about our authors and books visit www.bloomsbury.com
and sign up for our newsletters.

CONTENTS

Part Three   Human versus Heaven

FOREWORD

While many early Chinese texts are adduced, quoted or alluded to in this essay, my primary concern is with the *Zhuangzi* (pronounce Juang-dzeh), which is the first repository of fictions, narratives, fables, and tales developing a way of thinking that came centuries later to be labeled as Taoism.

This book requires no knowledge of China or Chinese. Almost all notes and comments on the translation of early Chinese texts or on the textual history and editions of the *Zhuangzi* have been removed from this new version. The only language-related remarks that remain directly contribute to the understanding of the stories presented and commented on the following chapters.

The *Zhuangzi* is an early Chinese text named after its supposed author, Zhuang Zhou (*c.* 356–286 BCE), who is said to have lived during the Warring States period (481–221) about 150 years after Confucius (551–479 BCE). Its title could more aptly be translated as *The Writings of Master Zhuang*. In addition to chapters and tales written by Zhuang Zhou himself (their precise identification is an issue still dividing specialists and is a debate likely to continue to do so for many years), it also contains texts from the hands of an undefined group of emulators, companions, and followers. This packet of writings was revisited, reorganized, and edited some five centuries later, forming the work as it is known today. Thus, the name "Zhuangzi" can refer, depending on context and assumptions, to the original author—incomplete data allowing only the vaguest conjecture about the man—to the title of the collection of anonymous texts bearing his name, or to the eponymous personage, who, whether he be real or fictional, appears in many of the episodes scattered among the thirty-three chapters that make up the book.

Most of the stories presented and interpreted in the following pages are taken from the first seven chapters of the *Zhuangzi*, known as the "inner" chapters because traditional commentators generally agree to attribute them to Zhuang Zhou himself. Some persuasive scholars in China and in the Western academic community claim that even parts of the inner chapters are from the hand of different authors, thereby complicating our understanding of how the different layers of the book were composed. Knowing which stories are from the historical Master Zhuang and who is behind the remaining chapters and when they were written is likely to remain anyone's guess. I have here also selected several stories from the "outer" and "miscellaneous" chapters. These are as much the product of inventive genius as the stories contained in the first seven chapters. Whether they are by Zhuangzi or by equally talented followers is of little importance. Such a question may even seem pointless, given the fact that texts were composed in early China in the absence of anything resembling the modern concept of authorship.

This book is a revised, updated, and partly rewritten version of a book originally written in French and published in 2006 by the publishing house Gallimard for a general readership under the title *Fictions philosophiques du Tchouang-tseu*. Barely half of the original work remains unaltered in this present version.

While several English and American translators have worked on this manuscript (my gratitude goes in particular to Mrs. Clare Perkins), I have ventured to modify and expand the version they handed me considerably, adding new material and ideas as years went by. I bear sole responsibility for the errors or lacunae that may remain. For the present version, my gratitude goes before all to Haun Saussy and Roel Sterckx, for the powerful inspiration, the friendly support and the tireless help they provided at every stage of this book. They are among the best persons I have ever met, within and without the Chinese field, *fang zhi nei* and *fang zhi wai*. I should also like to thank Guo Jue who refined and redefined in the noblest way the notion of a close colleague, someone in the company of whom you can stroll while culling along things of interest to both in a shared environment, even when reconnoitering the boundless territory of death.

Four of the six chapters of this book draw on previous academic publications in English, Spanish, and French that were originally published, in different versions, as book chapters or articles in journals of Chinese studies.

1   "When Princes Awake in Kitchens: *Zhuangzi's* rewriting of a Culinary Myth," in *Of Tripod and Palate. Food, Religion*

and Politics in China, ed. Roel Sterckx, Palgrave Macmillan: New York, 2005.

2 "Ascesis por un tumultuo," in *La palabra transgresora: ensayos sobre Zhuangzi*, ed. Albert Galvany, Madrid: Trotta, 2006.

3 "Combats d'animaux. Réflexions sur le bestiaire du *Zhuangzi*," *Extrême-Orient Extrême-Occident*, no. 26, 2004.

4 "Un monstre, deux morts et mille métamorphoses. Une brève fiction philosophique du *Tchouang-tseu* pour en finir avec la mort," in *l'Infini*, no. 90, 2005.

The transcription of Chinese names continues to be a bone of contention among sinologists and a puzzle to lay readers. I have reluctantly adopted the international system of transcription of Chinese names (the pinyin system) created in the People's Republic of China in the 1950s. This system is quite counterintuitive for Anglophones, flouting many basic notions of English phonetics and spelling (this is how "Chuang-tzu" ended up as "Zhuangzi").

While offering extensive translations of and commentaries on the stories of the *Zhuangzi* presented in each of the following chapters, I sometimes found the occasion to present a same passage in two slightly different translations of mine, thereby emphasizing aspects or subtleties that were sometimes forced to linger in the shadows of the first English version. In a word, I had the rare chance to expand the overall dimension that the translator is unfortunately forced to reduce and betray in order to deliver a version readable at once. The purpose of my commentary is not only to clarify the translated text; it must also reflect the shift on the gauge, as it oscillates between the notches on the slide-rule of discontinuous terms, before it comes to rest, for the requirements of the translation, at a certain spot. This is why, in my commentaries, rather than reproducing the translation used in the text, I propose certain variants and for certain key terms (the Tao for example) suggest other equivalents in English that offer, in this or that context, a more adequate contour of meaning.

A final point: I have used *Zhuangzi* in italics to refer to the work. "Zhuangzi" (the honorific title of Master Zhuangzi) and "Zhuang Zhou" (his family and given name) are used interchangeably to refer to this singular and multiple author who is both revealed and concealed by the book traditionally attributed to him. When I mention Zhuangzi, I only use the term as a metonym for the extant text revised long after his death and for a body of ideas, sometimes irreconcilable, that are attributed to him as one of the *Master*s of the Warring States. "Zhuangzi" is not even a concept, it is a conceptual shorthand, just as Homer has been for the Western world.

Introduction

And all my words could be called riddles. Perhaps, after ten thousand generations, a great sage will appear who can solve them, but that would be fluke and nothing else.
ZHUANGZI, CHAPTER 2, "ALL THINGS ON A PAR"

The goals that the authors of the *Zhuangzi* set themselves are more or less the opposite of what is commonly called Chinese wisdom. Far from the exhortations to cultivate agreeable behavior toward others, revel in the study of ancient texts, or thrive on the pious observance of ritual, they come across as dedicated disparagers of moral virtues, they reduce the sayings of saintly rulers of the past to the likes of fossilized excrement and improvise with the darkest irony on the self-defeating schemes, the moral delusions, and fierce tyranny of men. Many tales and episodes in this work stretch language to its utmost, breaking free from the dulling effect of common phrases and everyday perception, determined to shake and shock people out of their inauthenticity. The role of this book in Chinese history is aptly encapsulated in Haun Saussy's series of paradoxes: "The *Zhuangzi* has been the bible of eccentrics, the roadmap leading away from the highways of worldly success, the classic of anti-classicism, the norm of abnormality."[1]

The reader is likely to be taken aback by the offbeat direction and erratic tone that puts the *Zhuangzi* apart, even if such topsy-turvydom might seem less offensive to our current age, well accustomed to valuing countercultural inversions. Once the legions of paid-up scholars and priggish impersonators of virtue have been given short shrift, then an even more ferocious offensive is undertaken against the core of the political authority, eventually extended to all forms of social structure. The *Zhuangzi* is the only book from the Warring States period (481–221 BCE) to flout not only bad rulers, but the very notion of rulership, inveighing against the fallacious concept of order and the idea that humans should submit to a single and unified source of authority, a principle that was shared by all schools of thought at the time (they only disagreed on the best means to achieve such an aim). Rather than tagging along with scribes and masters busy sanctifying the monarchical rule and redefining social hierarchies, as did so many of his contemporaries who were trying to solve the problem of the erosion of royal power and the institutional crisis of the late Warring States territorial rule, the *Zhuangzi* creates strange and striking encounters between historical characters and fictitious people, unspools into tangled skeins of parodic variations on classical scenarios such as the edifying conversation between a masters and his disciples, or advice given to a ruler by his sage minister. Far from providing instruction or satisfaction, the words that the *Zhuangzi* puts in the mouth of its contrarian characters demolish or trouble their interlocutors, who often emerge dazed, undermined, and struggling. To a man formerly trained by the legendary Emperor Yao and moulded by his narrow moral education, a sarcastic recluse responds: "If Yao has already branded your forehead with the iron of Justice and Benevolence, if he has already cut off your nose with the pincers of Right and Wrong, then how can you now stray freely like a wanderer along the meanders of the winding way?" (Chapter 6, "The Primordial Master").

We need to view Zhuangzi as an author of philosophical fictions: neither as an ancient sage, nor as a simple artist of language. His texts are not mere flights of fantasy or amusing literary divertissements. His tales about escaping the entanglements, constraints, and duties intrinsic to life among other people is tied to his ambition to deconstruct all axioms, maxims, paradigms, and paragons current in the Zhou dynasty, and of showing the harm we inflict on ourselves and our milieu, and, finally, the catastrophe towards which we are marching, driven by our obsession with name and fame, health and wealth, self-image and the preservation of our individual identity.

Even the Zhuangzi's praise of the unanimously admired skill of clairvoyance, although not completely frenzied, takes on an eerie dimension; intrigue permeates so-called rational considerations, and under the cover of witty fables, a violent indictment rages against the concealed norms of so-called wise sayings. The authentic lives that emerge from the carnival procession of his characters bear a touch of the impossible, the bizarre and the dangerous. With its reasoned defense of deformity and the shapelessness; with its ardent search for a state of blissful confusion and masterly unknowingness; with its pathos-averse attitude towards death, with its monadic and nomadic vision of happiness (an ecstatic flow-like roaming in distant spaces), with its aggressive summons to give up any intention towards benevolence or service to other human beings, the *Zhuangzi* marks a path to all possible transgressions, whether worldly, cognitive or moral.

Where the likes of Confucius (traditionally dated 551–479) or Mencius (fourth century BCE) both aspired to official posts from which they might deploy their skills for the enlightenment of the sovereign and the moral instruction of the people, Zhuang Zhou dismisses such aspirations entirely. He rebukes the two emissaries from the powerful state of Chu who were sent to entrust him with the government of the kingdom. With fishing rod in hand and not even bothering to turn round to address them, he treats the envoys to a maliciously candid parable that expresses his choice not to wield power but rather to go freely with the flow of the water and "drag his tail in the mud," as he imagines the celebrated sacred turtle whose relics are worshipped in the ancestral hall of the palace would probably have preferred to do (Chapter 17, "Autumn floods"). Another tale in the same chapter portrays Zhuang Zhou engaged in discussion with his old sparring companion Hui Shi, the famous sophist and logician whose impeccable political career led to his becoming a minister in the State of Wei. Hui Shi is on his guard when Zhuang Zhou comes to visit, suspecting that his real purpose is to unseat him from his post. Zhuang Zhou snidely reassures him with another animal parable: he cannot covet a ruling position in the State of Wei any more than a bird nourished on the subtlest of refinements would peck the rotting carcass of a rat that could barely make an owl's mouth water. Zhuangzi's baroque parlance is suited to such skirmishing and whiplash quips: when an envoy from Song, returning triumphantly smug from a profitable meeting with the King of Qin, struts about before the hundred chariots bestowed to him by the sovereign, Zhuang Zhou stands before his counterpart like a proud pauper, starving and shabbily clad, wearing the straw sandals he has plaited himself. Having listened to the envoy's swaggering words, Zhuang Zhou congratulates him on his therapeutic devotion to the King of Qin: when one realizes the king rewards with one carriage anyone who lances his abscess, or offers five to he who would treat his piles, one can surmise that the generosity shown in this instance must have been prompted by a pandering willingness to lick the royal hemorrhoids.[2]

For Confucius, and much more so for his troupe of glum and dour devotees who lack their master's finesse, a man can only fully flourish in the public role that he carries to perfection, always being tactful, timely, and mindful of what the present situation requires. The uprightness of the true gentleman (*junzi*), never far from uptightness, obliges him to play his part immaculately in a social choreography mapped out with a thousand invisible hedges of decorum. The authors of the *Zhuangzi* insist on showing how illustrious or legendary individuals exalted by tradition fell in fact prey to all types of inner adversity. We see mythical sovereigns or holy hermits striving and struggling in whichever way they can to be released from their inner fetters and shackles. Other characters confess to their powerlessness or are reticent about playing their part in society; they often fail in their attempts to elevate themselves to the level of the Tao. Zhuangzi's "Black Paintings" omit nothing, they portray physical monstruosity and mental illness, frightening agonies, lepers giving birth in the dark, amputated criminals, the miserable loneliness of kings, and the fate of pariahs. This is what makes the *Zhuangzi* in part a tragic text. Tragic, indeed, to the extent that it lays bare in texts that were bound to circulate far beyond the milieu of courts and palaces, the rift that had appeared since the later Spring and Autumn Period (722–481) between the norms dictated by the political-ritual order and the genuine aspirations of individuals. Tragic too because, as Zhuangzi's revisionary figure of Confucius puts it in a discussion on the rules defining human society, "those who live inside the rules and those who live beyond the rules can never meet" (Chapter 6, "The Primordial Master").

One of the reasons for Zhuangzi's lasting reputation for superior literary talents lies in his invention of a virtuosic style that freely juxtaposes anecdotes, didactic narratives, parodies and comic scenes, palimpsests of myths, general considerations, fables and verse: he canters through the various literary genres of his time, breaking away from the formal, edifying notations of the court scribes and from the academic prose style that had developed in the various textual traditions during the Warring States period. The reader of these pages is bound to wonder where the *Zhuangzi* belongs. Is it an erratic collection of texts, albeit with strong moments of structural coherence, or just a capricious composition following no rule but anarchy, a mosaic laid down haphazardly by different editors and the vagaries over the passing centuries? In the received version, most of the thirty-three chapters of the *Zhuangzi* have a splintered and fragmentary form, showing no overall plan. Early on, the name of Zhuangzi became the consensual default label for an unknown number of unidentified writers over several generations. The result is a protean text that takes as its author (in the Latin sense of *auctor* "originator, source, and authority") the profile of a master whose identity and personal contribution can be no more than fragile conjecture. The work's disjointed form appears to stem as much from reasons intrinsic to the ideas brimming in the *Zhuangzi* as from its editorial tribulations over the ages. Because the sequence of such dissimilar episodes appears to be arbitrary, many passages give the reader the disturbing impression of an obstacle course, an uneven pathway and an arduous track where the only constant is a broken line. From story to story, from chapter to chapter, some questions are resumed, motifs echoed, enquiries reiterated with minor variations. The tales in dialogue form retain the flow and the surprising turns of live conversation; they pay close attention to the profound reactions that such speech may produce. We can see a character experiencing different frames of mind, suddenly becoming mute, disappearing and then reappearing later on in another story, picking up the remark that silenced him, and then losing himself in the narration of a pivotal experience. In this way, the recurring characters in the *Zhuangzi* cannot be locked into a single role for purposes of proof, edification or persuasion. Their rhetorical and didactic functions change at will. Sometimes, the disciple or the servant subjugates the master or makes the sovereign change his mind, as does Yan Hui, who surpasses Confucius so conclusively that the latter begs to be accepted as his disciple's disciple.

The polyphonic dimension of the *Zhuangzi*, equally evident in its introduction of new types of human beings, corresponds to the foundations of what, by default, one may call "Zhuangzi's thought." But the anecdote, the tale, the parable or the fable is never the lesser relative of philosophy. An endless variety of expression is for Zhuangzi a means to give shape to a valid critique of language, its categories, its shortcomings, and its distortions. The reader may be tempted to see this as Zhuangzi masking a theoretical inability to achieve his intentions, entrusting poetic style with the task of expressing ideas in the form of muddled prophecies, sometimes contradictory and brilliant, but maddeningly elusive. In fact, it becomes rapidly obvious when reading the eponymous work that Zhuangzi never intended to write a treatise, a master's discourse or a series of wise lessons. To what extent then, or in what sense, does the title "philosopher" apply to Zhuangzi and the co-authors in his wake? In Jean-François Billeter's clear and simple description: "A man who thinks by himself and takes counsel from his own experience; a man who ponders over what other people say and uses language deliberately."[3]

Rather than developing a reasoned apologia of naturalness in human beings, which would risk turning into a homily or a sermon, Zhuangzi sets himself and his thought in the constantly changing depiction of the particular, by alternating voices, locations, characters, and tones. His style of composition is clearly in tune with his purely philosophical intentions. He expresses the infinite capacity of Nature to create diversity, and when we notice that he pays particular attention to all forms of dissonance, that he portrays all manner of ugly, deviant or unconventional creatures and that he suggests sheltering and promoting them beyond the reach of the hierarchies of the human world, the ethical dimension in his chosen modes of expression becomes easier to grasp. It is as if the intuition of the equal worth of each creature in the infinity of space and time favored and fostered the invention of a similarly vertiginous diversity of discourses and styles. The idea that the vital stuff forming and animating everything in the universe, known as *qi,* can successively inhabit any available body or thing, becomes a mobilizing principle of literary imagination. The book's tone swings between the theological, enthusiastic, teasing, sophistic or elegiac. Nature, being radically amoral and unconcerned by our ideas of order, produces living forms as an efficient cause, without design or finality. There is no providential plan or divine pattern. "Death and birth: the affair of fate. That the two alternate as surely as day and night, is the affair of Heaven. That therein lies something man cannot grasp is part of the intrinsic reality of beings." There is nothing to add, for the world exists without question. Creatures may appear beautiful or ugly, lucky or unfortunate, but all are perfect in that each one has the form that it should have. "No-one lives longer than a stillborn child and the patriarch Pengzu[4] died prematurely" says Chapter 2, meaning that the maxim of "All things on a par" is endowed with a cosmic dimension. A human being is a plurality of forms undergoing repeated metamorphosis. "When one undergoes change, can one know what escapes change? And when nothing changes, can one know what has already changed? In the end, you and I have never so much as begun to wake from the dream that we are... Finally, can I really know if that with which I connect myself, is not in fact part of me? One day you dream that you are a bird soaring in the sky, another day you are a fish diving deep down in the abyss, but when you speak to me, do you even know if the one who speaks is dreaming or awake?"[5]

The accepted cartoon cliché of Zhuangzi portrays him as an apolitical, if not anarchist, thinker, a sublime aesthete, who considers all official responsibility an insufferable burden. His case is more complex than that. His repeated challenges of prevailing norms of morality, his diatribes against figures of the highest standing, his disapproval of his contemporaries and the methods they use to join the entourage of the ruler, cannot be construed as a refusal to cope with the harsh political reality of his time or regarded simply as the ineffectual brilliance radiating from a subversive wit. His political conscience tries to address the question of the necessary evil that is represented by any form of political authority. Power is not bad because it is poorly or perversely enacted, it is evil in its very principle. Unlike the supposedly provocative literature of our contemporaries, which nimbly responds to the demands of an audience tuned in advance to the wavelength of outrage (an audience that finds scandal less shocking than its absence), the reader will not find in the *Zhuangzi* the slightest hint of gratuitous provocation by a privileged scholar in search of easy targets. Zhuangzi's work is written at a time when the Zhou dynastic project succumbed to the rise of powerful territorial states struggling against each other in a deadly race for hegemony; that era witnessed the first historical attempts to impose on a giant scale a centralized power structure with its subjugating administrative system backed up by a frightening array of repressive laws, to muster the population into huge rival armies deployed in endless military campaigns while imposing relentless drudgery on the anonymous mass of non-free workers.

To understand what guides Zhuangzi's critique, let us make a first directive hypothesis. Aspects as diverse as the reflection on the pitfalls of language, the damage of willful and assertive action, or the delusional power of discursive reasoning to regiment our lives, all hark back to the loss of the immediacy of living, the loss of the original state of non-distinction between self and surroundings, between personal identity and pervasive perceptions. The human civilizing process, i.e. the history of his forced domestication within a power structure, derives from an even stronger barrier between his "constructed mind" (*cheng xin*) and the natural within him, which is, at its core, pure activity, pure mobility, pure opening towards change. Spontaneity, which Zhuangzi calls "the natural trigger," is never immediately given but, rather, something long-lost and hard to regain in moments of grace that are few and far between.[6] It is constantly scrambled together or hampered by our consciousness, that is, by "the Human part that acts within us." Indeed, what seems primarily to interest *Zhuangzi* is neither stylistic prowess nor aesthetic innovation, but the way language organizes knowledge and structures our perception of the world. When used with prudence and shrewdness, language that turns against its own reifying tendencies can transfigure life by mustering all the resources of a dynamic imagination. It ignites or incorporates unsuspected powers in a discourse on things or events usually conceived as only tragic or negative only (such as extreme poverty, distress, illness, physical deformity, agony or death). We cannot stress enough that the *Zhuangzi* is the only work of its time to have understood with such lucidity the barriers and inhibitions that exist not only in institutionalized forms of subjection, but also in the way humans (with a few exceptions bearing the name of sages or of "ultimate men"), have become subservient to the diktat of their own conscious mind. Zhuangzi's approach, which challenges so many diverse trends and other doctrines of his time (the ritualism of the Confucians, the utilitarianism of the Mohist school, the escapism of virtuous recluses, the technical or strategic intelligence of persuaders and political advisers), is as much an inventive meditation on the political and moral future of the kingdom, on the fate of bodies taken over by the political order, as on the chances that a few men might create, amid the human community, a lifestyle that could escape the oppression inherent in any form of social structure.

The *Zhuangzi*'s critical thrusts are finally directed against the ascendancy of the power structure that infiltrates the core of the language and the representations it conveys. The authors perceive the props of authority hidden within language and its accompanying institutional forms of servitude. For the world cannot be apprehended as it exists, independently of the structures of language through which it is directly presented as having a strict and hierarchical order. This order seems to legitimize distances and oppositions established between things as soon as we put them into words. "Who can use non-being to make his skull, use life to make his spine and death to make his arse? If there is someone who understands that death and life, subsistence and destruction, are one and the same, I'll take him as my friend," exclaim the four masters in the jolly quartet brought together by the common aspiration to free themselves from the common pathology of human sensitivity. Indeed, "things, it is when they are given a name that they become such," Chapter 2 notes. Whence the difficulty of an exclusively discursive critique of power, for the world as it appears shaped by language is one of the most deeply interiorized consequences of political authority to detect within us. If we cannot escape the pitfalls of language by using it with utter freedom, we cannot attain the authentic form of experience which the *Zhuangzi* associates with nature's quickening within us. Constraining, by its very nature, a dynamic apprehension of reality, the uncritical use of language tricks us into alienation and distortion. To make language the vector of personal emancipation, it was necessary to dissociate it from the structures of political authority, at a stage when the Chinese language still obeyed, on account of its origins in the milieus of diviners and scribes at Court, a religious and administrative order. The authors of the *Zhuangzi* all undertake in various ways a radical critique of the very tools we use to shape our world and forge our vision of a supposedly natural order. Through short narratives, dialogues or allegories, this critique lays bare the main factors of human alienation: the desire for possessions, the worshipping of utility, the constant forcing of the diversity of phenomena into a set of logical propositions, the narrowing effects of individual perspective, or the violence underlying apparently noble efforts to establish social harmony. In the stories of death and agony presented herein, the *Zhuangzi*'s lesson is, in the end, less a reflection on human finiteness as it is part of a broader enterprise to disavow recourse to the usual disjunctions of language between being and not-being, between identity and otherness, between brevity and longevity. Indeed, in the words spoken by Master Lai on his deathbed "that which made my living good is also that which makes my dying good" (Chapter 6, "The Primordial Master").

Rather than aiming at an in-depth characterization of the competing strands of thought championed or debated in the Zhuangzi, or doing justice to its richness and ambiguity, the exegetical tradition more often than not attempted to stamp the person Zhuangzi with a character that has over time become an accepted convention. He was often reduced to a single figure: that of a magnificent, sovereign and solitary protester whose writings could tempt any scholar-servant of the Chinese empire, once day was done, to drift at will in a space reserved for his free untrammeled spiritual journeying, thereby gaining some mental distance from his everyday responsibilities, from the ritualistic rigors of state service and the subjugation to the imperial ideology ringed round by the scriptural canons of the Confucian school. During the collapse of the empire and the rise of political chaos at the dawn of the Chinese Middle Ages in the third century CE, Zhuangzi spoke to the basic aspirations of the scholar longing to become a private recluse in search of a natural life, in order to transcend the frontiers of this futile restricted world. However loaded with prejudice this vision may be, however opportunely convenient as a *modus vivendi* for a scholar at the time of the Six Dynasties and beyond, the rift it created vis-à-vis Confucian orthodoxy, the doctrinal linchpin of imperial ideology, reinforced a separation that is still evident today. The Zhuangzi therefore became the antidote to the willing servitude of the scholar in service to the ruler, the panacea for the hypocrisy of those who govern others, the rallying point for an intellectual elite freeing itself from the responsibilities, the prejudices, ambitions and the conflicts inherent in any closed society. Leaving aside technical commentaries flourishing in Taoist alchemical milieux, this is roughly the profile of Chinese exegesis on the Zhuangzi for the past 1,500 years. Although more difficult to appropriate than Laozi, who was deified by Taoists, and already partially reclaimed by Han Fei—the theoretician of absolutist monarchy in the early stages of the unification of the Chinese kingdoms—Zhuangzi inspired, via deliberate mis-readings and distorted interpretations, part of the cosmological discourse of imperial China. For an author who displayed the fundamental aporia concerning the ultimate origin of things and the absurdity of the zeal to classify the infinite and immeasurable realities that make up the universe, this is quite a paradox. The imperial reading of the *Zhuangzi*, which can be found for example in the *Writings of the Prince of Huainan*, has no *raison d'être* today. There is also the ingenious exegesis that the commentator Guo Xiang (d. 312) appended to the *Zhuangzi*.[7] Before signing and circulating his commentary, Guo Xiang took it upon himself to rework and organize the text to his taste—the extent of his changes is still unknown—to bequeath what became *the* canonical *Zhuangzi*, in the absence of any alternative version. Guo Xiang can indeed be disparaged, his commentary denounced for its piecemeal reading and blame laid on his editorial dishonesty and interference. As criticism of this sort is still well underway among sinologists,[8] I will only add my voice to say that his commentary is a model of audacity and inventiveness that offers paradoxical homage to Zhuangzi's sense of ambiguity. Though the commentary by Guo Xiang is fragmented and partial, there is no gainsaying its rich perspectives for the interpretation of such an open-ended work. If Guo Xiang had not saved the work, the *Zhuangzi* might never have come down to us other than as a few more or less faithful quotations, scattered about in various historical accounts and anthologies from late antiquity.

If the *Zhuangzi* bequeathed to posterity a store of expressions for the future delight of scholars and artists, it does not allow speech to have the last word. As is emphasized in Chapter 2, where the author develops a magisterial critique of language and discursive consciousness, "words lose themselves in their own profligacy." Zhuangzi shows the reader what happens when we are in a state of knowing and social awareness, adhering to accepted manners with things and beings. He also depicts what happens when we succeed in untying the discursive threads linking us to the world.[9] He points out that when we remove ourselves from the visible world brimming with shapes, colors, and words, through silence and inner retreat, and when we break away from the alienated vision of life as the existence of an individual self in surroundings that are reduced to a collection of external things, then, decisive, eye-opening, and long-resonating changes may occur. In such moments, we are no longer "companion to Man" but "companion to Heaven." Zhuangzi notices that when we hide the outside world behind a screen of neat categories, we see only objects and we block out the dynamic forces which travel through them and drive them to transform into their opposites. The tales and dialogues examined from various angles in the following chapters use this motif of the clouding of the mind, the blindness to natural forces, and the destructive logic of a sensibility unaligned with the way things are.

Though bedridden and drawing their last breath, Master Yu and Master Lai still take pleasure in the thought of their future transformations, having liberated themselves from the anxiety of disappearing or the horror of physical deformity. The *Zhuangzi* considers the different stages in the ever-increasing separation of humans from the realm of natural life: first, we have come to conceive of mankind as separate from other forms of life; next, we have conceived of individual beings as separate from one another; then we have envisioned individual things, "thises" and "thats," ontologically distinct from each other. Finally, we have made incredible progress in the differentiation of consciousness: we have devised abstraction and analysis to distinguish qualities and properties in the objects we have carved and hewn out of a "blooming buzzing" continuum of phenomena. What we now need is to learn to cooperate with forces that are not directly under our control or within our reach; we need to think in terms of integration, and to recognize the self-defeating efforts of human will when driven by the urge to maintain things as we see them from the perspective of our individual identity.

Buffeted about by external forces, warped by outside constraints, we may nonetheless, if adequately guided, endeavor to direct our psychic energy towards a state of effulgent spontaneity. But how can we *work* on spontaneity? How do we cope with the apparent paradox of endeavoring towards non-action? How can we hone and fine-tune the skills of carving out the experience of effortless and graceful activity without letting the whole enterprise be doomed by the very intention and effort to do so? It seems we are then grasping for powers that are beyond our reach, that are not within the purview of the will. How can we ever attain, more fully, a state that has previously been experienced in a precarious, fleeting, and contingent way? Should we rely on exercises, on meditation techniques, or on the propulsive power of habits?

Allusions to meditative and breathing practices abound in the *Zhuangzi*, but we never see them formulated as technical exercises. Their sketchy descriptions are constantly subject to the inventive dynamics of literary imagination and are quite unavailable as didactic indications or universal recipes. It is not even clear to what degree the reader is meant to take at face value the descriptions of ecstasies and enlightenments that crown certain ascetic practices. The language, the terms, the metaphors keep changing according to the various characters and the type of narratives in which they are embedded. The *Zhuangzi* displays no interest in the possible political exploitation of strength gained from a type of physiological or spiritual exercises that may help a man to qualify for command. In this regard, the *Zhuangzi* radically differs from the straightforward, impersonal, and didactic texts produced in self-cultivation milieux (as in the *Writings of the Prince of Huainan*, or in the four famous and seminal chapters on "Mental Techniques" collected in the *Writings of Master Guan*), dealing with the storage, the channeling and refinement of vital energy (*qi*) toward its final conversion into a form of spiritual energy that grants health, longevity, immunity, and political supremacy to the devoted practitioner.

The quest for long life and the preservation of the vital principle have been constant obsessions in China since earliest times. They form one of the great aspirations of self-cultivation practices as these developed in the *Zhuangzi*'s time during the Warring States period. Dietary rules, the art of using breathing and sexual organs, and even later on calligraphy, were seen as possible methods to prolong life, to maintain the energy principle that animates us and to prevent our atrophy. The *Zhuangzi* even devotes a chapter ("Engrave in the mind," "Ke yi") to the critical description of the adepts of these methods, who force themselves into laborious exercises with the aim of "nourishing the vital principle." The position of the *Zhuangzi* regarding these practices is ambiguous; in the end it seems only to reject the most fastidious, technical and instrumental forms. Excessive devotion to oneself proves a self-defeating attitude, just like excessive self-abnegation, however admirable. A sarcastic anecdote of Chapter 19, "The Full Comprehension of Life" illustrates the point:

In Lu there was Shan the Leopard—he nestled in a hollow on a cliff, drank water exclusively, and had no truck with other people. He lived up to seventy years, keeping the complexion of a young child. Unfortunately, he ran into a famished tiger that killed him and ate him up. And then, there was Zhang Yi—

whether humble doors or noble gates, there were nowhere he would not go and pay a visit. At the age of forty, he contracted a fever and died. Shan the Leopard was concerned with nurturing his inside and was attacked on the outside by a tiger, whereas Zhang Yi, who was concerned with providing for his outside, was ruined by illness from the inside.[10]

On the other hand, many narratives in the *Zhuangzi*, even when playful in tone, shows how the authors were keen to elucidate the interior transformations of vital activity when it turns in on itself. The kind of meditation reported by Crookback Woman (Nü Yu), discussed in the fifth chapter of this book, leads to the direct and perhaps frightening perception of the dynamic principle of nature, as we learn to "place the world outside of oneself" only to "put being outside of oneself" and finally to "put life outside oneself." When one has erased everything that the mind has in view or in expectation, everything that pollutes the perfect efficiency of flow-like activity, when "the old twinning of thought and words is undone,"[11] what is there left to see? Zhuangzi gives us the answer in the form of riddle: "Calm in the tumult, because it is only through tumult that things are accomplished."

Another facet of this enquiry deals with the virtuoso gesture, or more precisely, the bodily dynamic prompted by an unobstructed perception of one's actions. From this perspective, in the first chapter I consider the virtuosity of an activity so perfectly mastered that it is unaware of itself, like the actions of the memorable butcher who, in his task of dismembering a bullock, chops up the political order that is held together by sacrificial offerings and the hierarchical distribution of cuts of meat. When maneuvering his blade across the muscles, meat, and bones of the sacrificial animal, the butcher reaches a Heavenly mode of action, guided no longer by his sight, only by the *élan* of the Spirit. The coarse task of killing for the benefit of ritual officers becomes a spiritual practice that directly nurtures the self in motion. In the butcher as in other hidden sages, Heaven takes for a while precedence over the Human.

Heaven and the Human: this is perhaps Zhuangzi's central intuition and his most fundamental one, because it expresses the double foundations of human life. The distinction between the two is the starting point of one of the most salient through-lines in the development of the book but is at the same time the root of many difficulties. It is not indeed the matter of a theoretical distinction between two well-defined concepts; the intuition seems to preside over a system of oppositions never fully explicated as such: the spontaneous and the intentional, the necessary and the arbitrary, instinct and intelligence, profound incitement and superficial excitement, unknowingness and conscious reflection. The main difficulty lies in understanding how these forces or how these modes of functioning alternate, antagonize or work together within us. And here we are up against yet another difficulty, namely, to resist the temptation to ascribe once for all contrasting values to the Human and the Heavenly modes. Rather than go with the tendency to praise the Heavenly and condemn the Human mode, we would do well to stay in a position of neutrality, which might allow us to choose which mode we should use and when, depending on when we are facilitating and when we are hampering our own efforts.

One may well ask whether or not the *Zhuangzi* makes dogmatic use of the notion of Heaven. His constant, almost obsessive, recourse to Heaven, or to the Tao—the key word in his critique of humans—might indicate the limits of a largely rhetorical and insufficiently thought-through usage. Indeed, Heaven itself might well be a dogmatic invention, a notion standing as a universal value but insufficiently probed. The reader must ask whether Zhuangzi interrupted his critical diagnosis with a simple valorization of Heaven or of the Way (Tao). Because Zhuangzi's thought proceeds mostly in a narrative form, ideas only taking full shape in the guise of fictions, I have reserved the most theoretical considerations on the two sources of life in *Zhuangzi*'s work for the final chapter, which offers a sort of edifying portrait of the authentic men of the past, a distant, unlocalized past that is in fact the most convenient horizon for present and future actions.

PART ONE

Humans versus Animals

1

Carving up a Myth in the Kitchens of Power

Here is the famous tale of the encounter between the prince and the butcher in Chapter 3 "The Key in nourishing one's vital principle.

> Butcher Ding was cutting up an ox for Prince Wenhui. As he seized the beast with a *clap!* he shouldered its weight and stood firm with his knees braced against it; his knife replied with a melodious *chop!* to a rhythm that seemed to echo the ancient dances of Mulberry Grove, responding to the dynastic tune of "The Lynx's Head."[1]
>
> "Ah! how admirable!" exclaimed the Prince. "To say that one can attain such heights in technique!"
>
> Putting down his knife, the butcher replied, "What your servant values in his task is the way things work, beyond pure technique. When I was learning my trade, I only had eyes for the ox. After three years, I stopped seeing it as a whole. Now I perceive it by the spirit, without using my eyes: knowledge of the senses is brought to a halt and I give free rein to the powers of the spirit, which finds its way around the inner structure of the beast. My knife slices between the intervals, runs through the cavities following what is inherent to it. The blade moves without ever catching in the veins or the arteries,[2] in the ligaments or the tendons, or of course in the bones. A good butcher changes his blade once a year because he cuts. An ordinary butcher changes his blade every month, because he chops. The knife you see here is already nineteen years old: it has carved thousands of oxen and

its blade is still as sharp as if it came straight from the whetstone. The thing is, there is a space between all the joints, but the knife-edge itself has no thickness. If you penetrate these empty spaces with a blade that has no thickness, then it has the freedom to move around inside: you even have room for maneuver! That is why although I have been using my knife for nineteen years, it is still as good as new. Nevertheless, when I get near a complex joint I consider how the difficulty presents itself; I stop still, observe attentively and proceed, step by slow step. I ply the knife with infinite care, and *slap!* the cuts of meat fall to the ground like clods of earth and the ox passes from life to death without even realizing what has happened![3] Then I remove the instrument, stand up straight, look around, elated and fulfilled, and clean and sheath my knife."

"Excellent!" said the Prince. "By listening to the words of Butcher Ding, I have learned the art of nurturing life."

This story is still one of the most popular ones in Chinese culture, though people never agree on what exactly makes it so pleasant. Moreover, oddly enough, the internal structure of the story has never been unpacked (unlike the butchered ox). It draws on four main points: the culinary activity in question, namely the dismembering of an ox, a sacrificial animal *par excellence*; the political and ritual values of food and their synthesis into the theme of "nurturing the vital principle" (*yang sheng*); the supposed location of the scene, probably in the kitchens of Prince Wenhui[4] or perhaps on sacrificial hallowed ground; and finally, superimposed upon the account of the animal's dismemberment, the joyful dismantling by Zhuangzi of a political fable based on a cliché that circulated during the Warring States period, namely the scenario of an edifying encounter between a king and his master-chef, whose evocative discourse introduces the sovereign to the "recipes of power."

The culinary and sacrificial background, which is infused with political overtones, is generally neglected by readers and scholars who tend to select only certain morsels, that can then be served up with a ready-made sauce created for similar pieces about fabled craftsmen in the *Zhuangzi*, in particular the story of Bian, the wheelwright. The chosen elements then become side dishes to accompany personal ruminations, leaving aside the less noble segments, such as the carving of the meat or the restoration of the body, which give this its most singular flavors. It is time to enjoy every part of the ox, reaching the heart and the goodness, instead of lapping directly at its philosophical coating.

Rather than reducing this story to a pleasant lesson for living by means of a craft analogy, I recommend a second reading of the aggressive dialectics which associate it, as is the case with all great writings of the Warring States, in an overt or covert fashion, with questions of government and domination.

Although the reader is in the presence of two characters who represent, in an extreme form, the structural polarity of society, namely its highest station and lowest rung, it is easy to see how these two men represent two types of sovereignty: one over the subjects of a state, and the other over the interior state of the subject. Here, as in many other similar tales in the *Zhuangzi*, a servant reveals the secret of inner strength to his so-called master.

To reposition this commonplace scenario, which would otherwise run the risk of simply reiterating a well-worn theme in Chinese philosophical literature, i.e., inner wisdom versus outer royalty (*nei sheng wai wang*)—let us pause for a moment to consider the fact that the meeting between the two men begins with the topic of food preparation. Butcher Ding is cutting up an ox, which we can presume is destined for the prince's table. However, the illustration of social hierarchy through culinary activity is deliberately distorted here. As a butcher, Ding is supposed to nourish his prince, but the gestures he uses to carry out the work contribute to the nurturing of his own vital principle and thus liberate him from the servitude of his main task, which becomes the occasion, rather than the goal, of his activity. This activity carries him far beyond the task of satisfying his master's appetite. The rhythmic beat of the movements and postures used for handling the animal, the joyous atmosphere emanating from the *pas de deux* with the body he is carving, give this exacting, strenuous, and bloody task the wider dimensions of a healing and inspiring spectacle. Even if Ding fulfils his role by preparing nourishment for the prince, he is not preoccupied with his master's stomach, unlike the prestigious *shan fu*, the royal steward in charge of preparing tasty and dainty dishes for his lord. When Prince Wenhui questions him enthusiastically, Ding confesses in plain terms that he is not interested in the technical aspects of his task but in the modus operandi of reality itself, or the Tao. Contrary to the various officials assigned to oversee the diet of their sovereign, the butcher has no need for niceties to morally transform his interlocutor. Rather than rehearsing the common theme that carefully prepared foodstuffs exert a moral influence on the body of the sovereign, the *Zhuangzi* portrays a character who affects the mind of his master directly by using the description of his work as a butcher.

The tale of the butcher freeing himself from the servitude of his social status affirms the true independence of the individual from the mechanisms of subjection through food. It would still be improper to say that the butcher is enjoying autonomous activity *in spite of* the drudgery he is assigned: rather, he uses the very task of carving as a springboard toward emancipation.

The meeting between the butcher and the prince is all the more striking for its blithe disregard of all the usual social and ritual mediation between these two extremes of the hierarchy governing culinary activity. The butcher was one of the lowest professions in the long chain of activities that began with the slaughter of animals and culminated in sacrifices to honor ancestral spirits. Many texts relating to the organization of culinary activities at court and sacrificial rites assert the need to isolate the cook and those involved in the preparation of food from the servants in charge of the ritual ceremonies. This division of tasks, as stipulated by convention, situates the cook at an impossible distance from his prince. In this passage, however, the conversation is informal and Ding launches confidently into a speech on the subject of acquiring his art.

Among the officers in charge of catering for the sovereign, Ding is charged with the lowest of material activities; his task is also the most deadly, as he has to dismember an animal rather than cooking and flavoring its parts. And yet, this craft as practiced by Ding has a dynamic and a subtlety unseen elsewhere. While cutting up the carcass, the humble butcher acquires spiritual potency and is able to find the vital nourishment that the officers of the royal household are trying to instill in the body of their sovereign.

In other words, the tale of butcher Ding should be read as a polemical re-writing of a literary classic of Zhuangzi's era: the interview between the sovereign and his head cook. The manner in which Zhuangzi recycles this theme discreetly awakens the tensions between ritual values and spiritual values, which in many moral tales appear in continuity. In early literature, the character of the cook is often presented during an encounter with his sovereign, where he delivers a discourse of a political nature on the art of feeding oneself the reader will find the best introduction to the political meaning of stories about cooks and butchers in Roel Sterck's book "Food, Sacrifice and Sagehood in Early China" (2011), chapter 2 "Cooking the world". Simply by virtue of his discernment, the cook is then promoted to high office or entrusted with ministerial responsibility. At a time when rival heads of State were vying to attract talented men in all domains to their courts, from military strategists to jesters, the theme of the gratifying interview between the cook and the sovereign honored the meritocratic ideal that a man of humble background could rise in the world on the strength of his talents.[5]

Given the symbolic value of the portioning of food and its offering to the ancestors in sacrificial religion, but also due to the lack of a clear distinction between the cosmological, dietary, ritual, and purely nutritional values of foods, from a very early date the figure of the head cook was associated with royal power. The story of the exceptional career of the head cook Yi Yin, promoted by Cheng Tang, the founder of the Shang dynasty (c. 1765–1122 BCE), to a ministerial post after having demonstrated his political acumen, is a good example of a narrative that pairs the art of government with the art of cookery. Since different versions appear in various works from the late Warring States and Han periods, the story most likely already circulated in Zhuangzi's time, during the first three decades of the third century.[6]

Unlike the legend of Yi Yin the cook, the story of butcher Ding[7] is not used as a transparent analogical prop for ruling the world; it does not take the task of perfecting the bodily self as preparation for governing men. Instead of seasonal harmonies of flavors contributing to the equilibrium of the kingdom, the carving of an animal directly influences the prince's vitality and inspires in him the true art of nourishing the self. As these were the edifying themes circulating in the different traditions of thought during the Warring States, it is significant that the speech of butcher Ding does not mention the meaty delicacies prepared for the pleasure of the prince.

Confucian gastronomy and the re-appropriation of the slogan "nurturing life"

The polemical meaning of the encounter between the prince and the butcher becomes clearer if we compare it to an episode in the *Mencius* the author probably had in mind when writing this tale. It concerns a discussion between the eponymous philosopher and the sovereign Hui (self-proclaimed king of the state of Wei during the twenty-sixth year of his reign), about issues of supplies and resources. An illustrious figure during the Warring States period, Hui was born in 400 BCE, the son of Lord Wu of Wei, and he enjoyed an exceptionally long half-century reign (369–319 BCE). He was thus a contemporary of Mencius and also of Zhuangzi, who was probably born around 369 BCE. After Hui had established himself as sovereign of the most powerful of the states, he suffered a series of crushing military defeats, first by the rival kingdom of Qi and then by that of Qin, forcing him to form alliances with his enemies; he subsequently abandoned his ambitions, adopted a more humble stance and dangled generous stipends to attract the best minds of his time to his court, such as Zou Yan, Chun Yukun and of course, Mencius himself.[8]

The *Mencius* opens with a famous interview between the renowned philosopher and King Hui of Liang (another name for the state of Wei after the transfer of the capital to Daliang).[9] The king swears he has used up all the resources of his mind (*jin xin*)[10] and adduced all possible means to manage his kingdom in the best possible way but is sorry to observe that, for all his efforts, the number of his subjects has hardly risen. He then asks Mencius how to find ways to enrich his state, assuming that the words of the prestigious court adviser might be profitable. But Mencius immediately delivers a moral harangue, admonishing him to abandon the search for personal benefit (*li*) in order to cultivate the virtues of humanity and justice (*ren yi*). In fact, Mencius' entire speech refers to the correct way to manage supplies and foodstuffs by practicing the virtues evoked above. In this way Mencius makes the theme of nurturing life (*yang sheng*) his motto: he gives the discouraged sovereign recommendations on the management, development and use of vital resources (fish, grain, wood, husbandry) in order to satisfy his subjects' needs. He then vehemently reproaches King Hui for keeping good fat meats in his kitchens and for feeding his pigs and dogs with food intended for his people, who die of hunger by the roadside because the granaries are kept locked. In short, Mencius bluntly accuses the sovereign of murdering his own people, not with the sword, but with his style of government. King Hui receives only sermons and reprimands. On leaving the interview, Mencius even confides to his disciples his low esteem for the king.

In the fictional encounter staged by Zhuangzi,[11] although the concern for "nurturing life" is implicit in the core of the discussion, the focus of attention is removed from the issue of population growth and food supply to the question of increasing one's own vitality. The theme of *yang sheng* ("nourishing life," an expression that Mencius also uses in addressing his sovereign) is interiorized by Zhuangzi, and its reference to the problem of external government erased. In this way, Ding can act freely on the moral state of his king, lighten his burden of responsibility, free him from subservience to the desire for wealth, and avoid a sermon which would plunge him into a moral dilemma (having to choose between the benefit of personal interests, *li*, or Humanity and Justice).

The prince's ears are assailed with descriptions of lumps of meat falling to the ground like clods of earth: Ding spares him no detail about how to slice the flesh. With its raw and rough elements of meats and bones, this philosophical tale contrasts with the sophisticated combinations of flavors evoked in ritual texts, and with the highly ritualized atmosphere of ceremonial banquets. Zhuangzi presents here an uncommon description of the nurturing of the self. Yet, in the course of transforming an animal into cuts of meat, the butcher manages to recreate the festive and gracious atmosphere typical of a ritual ceremony.

Ding has elevated the mundane activity he is tasked with to the level of an art. In this sense, the thing upon which Ding exercises his transforming action is as much his own body as that of the animal. The knife, so proudly described by Ding, is not so much a tool but, rather, the vehicle of his vital energy, playing almost the same role as the brush in the arts of painting and calligraphy.[12] Yet, in the wielding of the knife Zhuangzi also finds the aesthetic perfection of ritual gestures in a ceremonial context. Plunging into the compact mass of the meat, sullied by the smell and flow of blood and in stark contrast to the purification and fasting required from ritual officials in sacrificial ceremonies, this knife calls for an elegant choreography harmonizing the movements of knees, arms, feet, and shoulders with unmatched ease. The body in motion as a whole becomes the agent, the instrument, and the purpose of its activity. For Confucius, or for Zhuangzi's contemporary Mencius, the idea of a technical activity that requires a tool is of little value and has no role whatsoever in their thought. Actions involving instruments and gestures directed toward the outside world that result in the transformation of material object, have nothing to do with the enrichment of personal experience. For Zhuangzi, what matters is the manner. The making of something (as evinced in many other stories illustrating various crafts and skills) refines the awareness of the body, fine-tunes the way motions and movements are fashioned. A new somatic style is developed within; the body comes to know itself more intimately and gains a know-how that is experienced as a deep and personal source of satisfaction.

When Zhuangzi describes the graceful movements of Ding's body and the rhythms recalling the ancient tune of Mulberry Grove[13] where the ox seems to be in the role of a dancing partner, other prestigious elements of official ceremonies are evoked, namely dance and music; Ding conjures them up as he takes the carcass under his knife. The transformation of a sacrificial animal into meat, an evocation of dynastic melodies, the presence of the sovereign, the efficiency of the Spirit (*shen*): all these elements participate in setting up a symbolic arena of social order in the kitchen, where the simple carving up of the ox, a preliminary to any of the ritual activities connected with food, offers an opportunity for a festive dance. But before jumping to conclusions, it should be noted that the location of the action is never mentioned in this tale. It is possible that the encounter takes place in the open, on a sacrificial terrace, during the offering of an ox to a divinity. This is possible in view of the double function of the butcher-cook (*bao ren*), both profane and ritualistic. The subversive effect of the story of Ding is no less powerful because of this double role: it still portrays a person under orders, doing the preliminary carving of the meat, and enjoying, alone and without restrictions at a sacred site, the pinnacle that any sovereign would aim to attain through ritual ceremony: the presence of the Spirit. Such reading of the story is also plausible, but as Zhuangzi (apparently knowingly) maintains uncertainty of place, we can equally use the first hypothesis: the kitchen, as a backdrop.

Drawing on an elegant set of inversions, this tale is devoted to the moral rehabilitation of the kitchen and counters the ritualists' condemnations. There is a material reason why the conversation that follows the chance encounter between the prince and the butcher does not take place in a throne room. Ding did not receive an invitation from his lord; he is, one might say, *on his home ground*. The prince is a guest there and the discussion has none of the formal or constricting formalities of an audience. A lord, however, is not expected to visit his kitchens. To fully appreciate Zhuangzi's provocative presentation of the meeting between the prince and the butcher, the reader must return to the *Mencius* and the narrative that follows the initial conversations between King Hui and the visiting sage. The decision to display a dismembered ox in the presence of the king echoes an episode where King Xuan of Qi (r. 319–301) finds himself face to face with an ox being taken to the kitchens by one of the servants in preparation for the consecration of a ritual bell with the fresh blood of the animal.[14] The king cannot bear to see the terrified look in the ox's eyes, and, feeling uncomfortable and guilty, he orders for a sheep to be sacrificed instead of the ox. Hearing of the event, Mencius used it as an opportunity to show the active presence of the virtue of humanity in the king's reaction and enjoins the sovereign to cultivate this moral disposition with his subjects. Although it is used here to awaken the king's moral conscience and then to offer suitable guidance, the encounter with the ox is no less trying. Mencius even recognizes that if a gentleman has seen an animal alive, he cannot bear to see it die.[15] This is why he should stay away from the place where the animals are slaughtered. Princes are not supposed to run around in kitchens.[16] One should insulate one's spirit from interior troubles and from the guilt connected with the blood slaughter, even in a sacrificial context.

In contrast to this show of excessive sensitivity and moralizing overtones, Prince Wenhui in this story is delighted with the faultless work of carving the ox. The description of how Ding plunges his blade into the beast and how he runs it through the carcass, fires his imagination instead of disturbing his conscience. "I use the knife with infinite care, and *slap!* the cuts of meat fall to the ground like clods of earth and the ox passes from life to death without even realizing what has happened."

The butcher operates in such a fashion that the animal is spared the suffering of being carved up (even if this is only a side effect), and at a flick of Ding's wrist it finds itself in pieces on the ground. Unlike Mencius' ideal gentleman (*junzi*), Ding seems elated by his chores in the kitchen. With Zhuangzi, we are thrown headlong into an amoral environment, where we spare ourselves the hypocrisy of substituting one animal for another in order to salve our guilty conscience. The kitchen is no longer a gloomy slaughterhouse as in the *Mencius* (*si di*), the sight of which is enough to put anyone off their meat;[17] for Zhuangzi it is a sort of workshop for self-cultivation, where Ding, through skillfully maneuvering his knife in the flesh of the dead animal, experiences the untrammeled quickening of his *daimon* (*shen yu*). This is how Zhuangzi transfers the Spirit (*shen*) from the altar to the kitchens, where the prince is pleased to be in the company of a butcher surrounded by heaps of dead meat.

The notion of nurturing one's life by preparing meat seems even more appetizing when one realizes that Zhuangzi is exploiting the religious values of the foodstuff in question. In early religion, the ox was the most prized sacrificial animal, and as an offering it nurtured and regenerated the bond between the living and the dead. The deceased, who have acquired the status of Spirits or Manes (*shen*), have the power to increase harvests, and so to nourish the bodies of the living and to guarantee their health and longevity, but the beneficiaries of these favors must ensure in return that the Spirits have their share of food. During the sacrifice, the ox was thus the material accessory for communication with the Spirits, who delighted in the roasted flesh and its heaven-bound aroma. With the tale of butcher Ding, the efficiency of the Spirit is revealed during the transformation of animal to food, appearing not as a transcendent Spirit invoked by the sacrifice, but as an optimal experience of the "inner workings" of the self.[18]

Aristocrats and officers were known as "meat eaters" (*rou shi zhe*), not because they were the only ones to enjoy such food (although it was probably a rare and costly commodity for ordinary people), but because of its defining role in establishing the identity and recognition of members of the aristocracy during the sacrificial meal. The notion that the butcher cutting the meat enjoys the efficient power of the spirits is in itself a subversive re-appropriation of the monopoly of favors granted by the invisible world to the nobility, their legitimacy being founded on the performance of sacrifices in ancestor worship. The question of material food is therefore both abandoned and preserved. Content with describing how he transforms an animal into food, and without the slightest morsel being consumed, Ding shows his prince a powerful vision, immersing him in the pleasures of dynamic imagination.

The course of the blade is guided by a superior state of clairvoyance, reducing the intervention of the senses to a minimum. This optimal state is expressed by analogy with the visitation of the spirit in the body of the medium, who removes himself from his physical and sensorial existence to allow the powers of ancestors to transfuse. From the origin of sacrificial practices during the Zhou dynasty until their re-appropriation in the *Zhuangzi* beyond the strict sphere of religion, the *shen* is "nurtured" but in two radically distinct ways: in the first case the *shen* refers to an ancestral spirit; in the second case, it is not regarded as a transcendent entity, but as the optimal efficiency of the body's inner activity. And the distance between the two meanings of *shen* in early China can be explained by the development of "practices of the self" (often referred to by the generic term "self-cultivation") with all the physiological reflections on vital energy that were then current. Here, the butcher acquires knowledge of the *shen* by working with food, the *shen* being perceived as an internal force that makes him proceed in an infallible and necessary manner; it is no longer the *shen*, seen as a divinity, that is nourished with the offering of food. The context of food preparation here allows the transfer of meaning between nourishing the spirits and nurturing the vital principle.

The discovery of a new form of self-cultivation

The knife that never becomes dull, gliding smoothly through the empty interstices among muscles and tendons, suggests that Ding has mastered the art of preserving his vital energy when he works through the knots and the difficult places.[19] The animal ceases to resist him in the form of an object (*objectum*, in the sense of an opaque encumbrance to the visual field, where its weighty mass makes a difficult task exacting), and Ding can disregard the external forms of the animal. By gradually integrating incomplete movements, which become increasingly delicate during the various stages of the dismembering, Ding can override the obstacles inherent to sensory perception.

It should be noted that Ding's speech to his lord has nothing didactic or doctrinal about it; he makes no recommendations, nor does he give advice. He simply describes personal experience acquired by mastering the use of a tool. Even so, Ding makes the strongest and deepest impression, helping the prince to see something he had never considered before. Ding's intimacy with the way things work, the Tao, comes via a certain technique. A technical procedure gives access to the natural process. But in this tale, we find an original way to apprehend the nurturing of life, one that lies beyond the frameworks provided by the different groups of adepts of self-cultivation in Zhuangzi's time. These practitioners used various techniques (respiratory, dietary, gymnastic or sexual) based on prescriptions originally formulated in medical circles.

One such description can be found in the treatise "The Inner workings" ("Nei ye"), which probably dates from the end of the fourth century BCE. It recommends a range of postural and respiratory techniques to refine the vital energy (qi) found in its raw state in the body and to use it as the physiological foundation for a quasi-divine state of inner potency and perceptual acuity. The authors of this treatise, anonymous scholars from the Jixia Academy in the state of Qi, succeeded in eliminating nearly all material elements from the nutritional and therapeutic techniques. They preserved only the core concept of absorption of vital energy, which, having been correctly channeled through the body and converted, after attaining a state of deep calm, into a subtler dynamic as "essential energy" ($jing$) transmutes in its final phase into spiritual energy ($shen$). As mentioned earlier, Adepts of these longevity techniques, some of whom practiced stretching and contraction exercises imitating birds or bears, are described by the *Zhuangzi* in a bantering tone in Chapter 15, "Engrave in the mind" ("Ke yi")[20]: these exercises rely on a collective repetition of prescribed and artificial movements demanding laborious execution using willpower in order to arrive at what can only be reached by leaving an assertive attitude aside. The striking element in the butcher Ding story is his ability to blend tiring daily toil with the uncommon practice of vitalizing the resources of the body as a gateway to the Spirit. Here Zhuangzi is reconciling different spheres of experience which were hitherto mutually impermeable: the closed sphere of ritual ceremonies where the Spirits appear after offerings of meats in a joyous and festive atmosphere; that of the practitioners of self-cultivation engaged in technical exercise; and that of tiring, servile, repetitive labor, represented here by the carving of a gigantic piece of meat.

In these three different spheres of experience, the practice of nourishing the Spirit can be found, but they are so clearly distinct as to be well-nigh contradictory. The milieu of practitioners of self-cultivation serves as a common ground with the other two. It allowed for the redefinition of the Spirit, starting with the discovery of the internal dimensions of the human being. In self-cultivation, the Spirit no longer means a transcendent, volatile, capricious entity that is to be lured by the delicious aroma of meats and the offerings of alcohol, but becomes an optimal form of energy, which endows its recipient with charisma, acumen, and authority. Zhuangzi "imports" as it were the efficacy of this Power into the body in action, not by the offering of food, nor by the practice of askesis as in self-cultivation but by simply chopping up a sacrificial animal. While the butcher's act is the primary, primitive, workaday basis of the other practices involving the Spirit, Zhuangzi inverts the usual course of elevation from matter to energy. It is the butcher who receives the Spirit, not the Spirit who is nourished by the offerings of meat. Zhuangzi breaks free from the limited framework of self-cultivation, showing that the possibility of exalting the vital principle is not reserved for a group of practitioners devoted to technical exercises, transmitted in a language understood only by a few initiates. The humblest of activities, engaging with the objects to be fashioned, can make the body the operative locus of spiritual potency.

While his intimacy with the fundamental stimuli of active life carries the butcher beyond his lowly condition of food provider, the admiration that he provokes from his lord does not bring about any change or promotion in his status. The *Zhuangzi* portrays a butcher who is indifferent to any external profit, and who is content to relate his art and his personal satisfaction while his prince looks on entranced. Although he plays a genuine role of adviser by enlightening the prince, and by transforming his attitude to life, unlike Yi Yin, he is not appointed minister at the end of the story. Ding's work is not guided by the idea of pleasing his sovereign or benefiting the kingdom; he frees himself from the constraints of his task by raising it to the level of an *art* of living per se. The interesting thing here is the author's refusal to dramatize the political virtues of the loyal servant or the social recognition of hidden talents. Unlike Yi Yin who, before his political acumen was recognized, made seventy requests for an audience with King Tang,[21] Ding does not ask his lord for anything. It is the lord, won over by Ding's talents, who comes to talk to him. Ding appears as a model of disinterestedness. He is the one who *promotes* the prince, by relieving him of his social personage and arousing his enthusiasm. Indeed, if Prince Wenhui only speaks twice, and very briefly, at the beginning and at the end of the encounter, this is enough to show that he is no indifferent spectator of this state of playful dynamics described by Ding: he cries out in admiration for the wonderful rhythmic carving dance, then at the end he joins in the butcher's contentment, carried away by the vivid description of his know-how.

The spirit of this story could not be further from the court literature that used this sort of encounter not only as an opportunity for an edifying lesson on the art of government, but also as a lesson on the potential profit for the underling who serves well his lord. The *Zhuangzi* never discusses the central question of state power, nor the strengthening of the power base or the consolidation of the military machine, but, instead, turns to a reflection concentrating on personal inner dispositions. The most illustrious works of the Warring States period such as the *Mencius*, the *Xunzi* (*Master Xun*), the *Guanzi* (*Master Guan*), or the *Four Treatises of the Yellow Emperor* (*Huangdi sijing*) endlessly discuss security and peace in the kingdom, the means to enrich the country and to reinforce the army, while for the authors of the *Zhuangzi* the only brake remaining on the machine as it runs out of control towards endless accumulation and absolute power, is the call to the king's nature to recognize the pleasures that he might draw from his own life, like those the simple artisan experiences when his craft frees him from lowly service and allows him to access his *ingenium*, or his *daimôn*.

Conclusion and overture

Against a background of moral tales classifying techniques of government on the model of food preparation and praising the promotion of talented commoners to the rank of minister,[22] the free and easy words from the butcher and the delighted words of approval from the prince emerge in startling relief.

In works taking up the theme of self-cultivation, the theme of food giving access to the efficacy of the Spirit had already been abstracted from its material ingredients and all reference to ritual procedures such as banquet, sacrifice, ceremonial, hierarchical sharing of meat, communion with the ancestors. Drawing on the widespread idea developed in self-cultivation milieux that the Spirit can be the result of nourishing one's vital energy, and making the carving of a sacrificial animal the occasion for it to take full possession of one's activity, the *Zhuangzi* illustrates for the first time the immanence of the Spirit in the human "form." The question of food itself, the edifying images of the enjoyment of taste and flavor, the political model of royal gastronomy no longer have their place in this striking encounter between the butcher and the prince. Within the prince, it seems that the gap between his social persona and his vital activity has been bridged; he touches on something intimate and nourishing that remained ordinarily obscured by his awareness of his own standing and role. Attitude dictated by hierarchical etiquette are bracketed for the duration of the encounter. Both parties engage in a relationship with neither social nor moral constraint, without an intention to gain benefit.

The description of the butcher's movements as he cuts and carves the animal evokes, for the reader, as for the prince, the feeling of physical satisfaction that can be drawn from working on materials with appropriate tools. The meat to be cut inspires inventive gestures of the hand, overcoming the resistance, the inertia and weight of objects. The images that Ding's description of his task brings to mind—such as that of the route through the cavities of a carcass seemingly so compact viewed from the outside, of the fluid passageway between the nerves, the tendons, and the bones—all have a power of suggestion which gives access to the internal resources of energy that a person spontaneously musters when immersed in her work. The prince feels his imagination awakened; far from remaining at the level of purely mental representations, these images uncover the potential powers inscribed in the human body and the experience of will in motion guided by the physical acumen of the body.

However, the butcher's description of his carving is limited. The vital force that inhabits Ding in his work cannot be delegated to anyone else. Prince Wenhui can only be vicariously pleased about the work process of his servant rather than effectively enjoying it. As

Zhuangzi offers his reflection on the symbolic values of food in the form of a striking encounter, he is in effect attuned, albeit implicitly, to a much more modern idea, namely, that the real source of personal flourishing lies in working on material objects, however humble, rather than simply in the possession of such things or the privilege of consuming them. Ding's satisfaction has nothing in common with the pleasure of rest that restores or relaxes the artisan: through the craftsman's consummate skill, labor itself becomes an exercise of liberation. In this regard, this story offers a counterpoint of sorts to Hegel's conceptual narrative of the dialectic between the master and the slave in the *Phenomenology of Spirit*.

Zhuangzi is also suggesting a powerful counter model to the idea of happiness construed as leisure and contemplation, familiar to us from the invention of the *vita contemplativa* in ancient Greece. Conceived as the highest and purest activity of the thinking being, the metaphysical aspirations of Western philosophy were crystallized in this way of life, meaning that contemplation is the only activity that deserves to be cherished for its own merit (unlike political, civic or military action). Because contemplation (*theoria*) is the only type of activity that draws pleasure from its own exercise, enjoying complete independence from other modes of existence, being its own end, it alone deserves to be called divine by Aristotle.[23] In the end, however, the gap between the active and the contemplative life can create divisions between people, a hierarchy of their natures, or a justification of the existence of a servant class (the question of theoretical life, the pinnacle activity and the highest way of life placing man on the same footing as the gods, is closely linked with slavery in Aristotle[24]). The *Zhuangzi* shows how the individual can resolve this chasm, namely the alternative between toil and contemplation, the alternation of leisure and work, the polarities of pleasure and pain. Within the narrow space and time of narratives such as that of butcher Ding, fixed roles in society are transcended, hierarchies become meaningless and the violence inherent in relationships between dominant and dominated evaporates. It is enough just to want to give up banqueting with the Spirits to concentrate on one's own vital resources and hidden potentialities.

Perhaps the values of contemplative life itself are challenged in this story, if we carry its lesson out to its full extent. Butcher Ding's story indirectly shows the superficiality of an attitude that limits itself to a visual dissection of the world, in other terms to an *analysis*, and does not rise to the challenge of solid and compact matter; it can be called superficial insofar as it precludes access to a practical intelligence of the material world and deprives itself of the lessons of the hand, the clairvoyance of the gesture—in a word, cuts itself off from the resources of the body in motion.

This story's most interesting philosophical contribution may be the exposure of the initial subject/object dualism in a mobile and dynamic relationship. Contemplation presents a superficial and static gateway to the world, a view that prevents active perception. Philosophy is a visual craft, particularly as regards the actor. Visual perception conceives of objects by their outlines; it reflects upon the ties that inextricably interweave the object with its background. The mind analyses how an object appears, but the philosopher never eradicates the distance separating him from the object. Instead of emulating a perfectly integrated activity, such as butcher Ding or the waterfall swimmer at ease in whirlpools (portrayed in Chapter 19), a professional thinker tends to remain seated at his desk, describing how to designate or represent to himself the tiling of his swimming pool seen through the casement or the red tint of the vase beside his table. He ponders or describes an object facing himself, but this object is only a mirage for the body, it offers no resistance, at best a certain degree of opacity. A philosopher is absorbed by the intentionality of this relationship, but cannot experience the excitement aroused by the concrete resistance of matter. Reality thus loses all its dynamic, becoming for the contemplative mind a set of names or conceptual items that it tries to classify by group, and segment the world into areas. Thought has an intentional object, but the agent lacks an *object-complement* sufficient to arouse its vital force.

This is one of the *Zhuangzi*'s strongest intuitions: that we reach our deepest vital resources in depth only through an active relationship with the world and, if not with tool in hand (a pole, a mallet or a chisel as in other stories in the *Zhuangzi*), at least with something *to do*. The relationship between the object and the subject does not form a secondary object offered up for speculation. It is an opportunity to trigger an internal dynamism. As soon as we confront matter, the object transforms us through the imagination that it elicits as much as we transform it by applying our energy to it. The matter/hand dialectic constitutes the hub of the duality between the gesture that manipulates and the object that resists, a dualism quite different from the classical object/subject dualism, which in its contemplative form inevitably leaves the subject to its physical inaction and the object to its inertia. The hand that carves acts as an accelerator of the psyche; it has an effect of traction, inspiration, emergence of unsuspected efficient forces, which the author calls spirit (*shen*), in opposition to "my" mind, in the sense of the reflexive conscience (*xin*, heart/mind). We can only find the root of these hidden but all-powerful forces in ourselves only by a material confrontation with something *outside* ourselves. Such confrontation is a sort of continual therapy, a *cura sui* of the actor, "a nurturing of life," a restoration of vital forces, which transforms the relationship we maintain with the world. In its traditional form, psychoanalysis, perhaps because it places the subject in a seated or reclining position (but in both cases immobile) and involves him in the conscious representation of his acts and words, fails to achieve the integration of his activity; neither can it make the patient recover the vigor and strength needed to take action. The imaginary ox, seen from the couch as a mere representation, leaves the hand indifferent. But as we approach the real beast, cleaver in hand, it unmistakably galvanizes the will to act. If the stuff of objects seen through the eye is inert, the real becomes dynamic again in the process of extraversion through workmanship.

One can imagine in what terms a psychoanalyst would be tempted to decode the butcher's delight at being watched by the prince while he carves the bullock. The psychoanalyst would remain within the limits of a strictly social interpretation, where using tools on objects is a substitute for repressed action against authority (the superego as we would say today). Such a reading would forget that the human dimension is not limited to the polarity between the basic instincts and the social aspects of the person; it would come down to forgetting that we live in a world of forms and forces and that the apprehension of the real can only exist via the exercise of dynamic imagination. Butcher Ding's dynamic will, linking imagination and cheerful excitement, can be put to full use without his being obliged to adopt an aggressive attitude (unleashing his tool in hand against matter), or feeling the half-angry, half-joyful thrill at flesh that has been cut open and attacked. The images of the material penetration of the carcass, far from suggesting the disguised expression of a sexual instinct or an offensive and inappropriate act against the superego, reveal a dynamic that is composed of virtuosity, tranquil contentment and cautious insinuation. Ding's feelings of victorious satisfaction when he has finished carving do not indicate a vainglorious sense of manly bravery such as one associates with the work of the blacksmith or the stonemason. Ding's knife does not work against the hostile compactness of the material but cooperates with its most intimate configurations. He does not confront the material's resistance, he sidesteps it and diverts his way through the empty spaces, guided by the innermost sinews that give the animal its coherence.[25] To him, the worker's sense of pride in dominating his materials or gaining enhanced manliness from his blade cutting into the matter at its very heart, is beside the point. A phenomenology of the body in action is sketched out in this story, centered on the metaphor of the intact blade effortlessly working through compact matter. As a distorted echo to this topic, let us quote by way of conclusion this amusing observation from the father of phenomenology about his obsessive art of sharpening: "Husserl himself was aware of his tendency to repetitive compulsions: he used to tell people that, as a boy, he was given a pocketknife as a present and was delighted, but sharpened it so obsessively that he wore the blade away entirely and was left with nothing but a handle. 'I wonder whether my philosophy is not unlike this knife', he mused."[26]

2

Zoocide: Zooming out for the Wild in the Zhuangzi

One of the steles erected at the apex of his power by the First Emperor of China (r. 221–210 BCE) recalls for posterity the widespread effects of his rule and how his influence and favors reached out to all beings, even oxen and horses. This florid commemoration of his accomplishments, sited on a remote mountaintop, is echoed more accessibly by an inscription engraved above a town gate during one of his tours of inspection.[1] Viewed as a product of the imperial propaganda machine, this detail about the sovereign's influence on animals may well seem either absurd or insanely megalomaniacal. And yet, the idea that a ruler's moral and martial virtues are manifested by the submission of all forms of living beings was fairly common at the time. Within this frame, the obedience of wild and exotic creatures was a sign of the ruler's sway over the remotest regions under Heaven. The First Emperor sets himself up as a paragon of wisdom, peace, and benevolence for his subjects, radiating forth his teachings for the benefit of all living beings under Heaven.

In the writings of the Warring States period, the animal theme is almost invariably associated with a type of domination that the sage ruler can—or should—exert upon the world. In edifying or fantastic tales of early imperial literature, we frequently find descriptions of the taming of birds and beasts as part of a triumphal act of universal sovereignty by the Son of Heaven. While drawing on earlier tales of direct physical control over savage creatures, this discourse on the moral transformation of the wilds was an important guiding theme in the attempt to "naturalize" political power and conceal its *de facto* brutality. Just as Barbarians (whose tribes were often given animal names) can become moral creatures through education and the practice of ritual, animals should be receptive to the virtuous influence of the sovereign. By issuing these commemorative inscriptions, the First Emperor was thus re-establishing one of the tenets of his omnipotence over the ritual, religious and political order.[2] At the moment when such representations were crystallizing into a solid ideology of monarchical power, the *Zhuangzi* stands as the only notable exception to the widespread conviction that peace and harmony require the establishment of an absolute power ruling every form of life.

Indeed, the animal stories in the book muster a variegated fauna along with imaginary creatures in order to undermine the moral and ritual structures of society. When one becomes sensitive to the inventive distortion that the *Zhuangzi* authors exerts on these ideological themes, one also becomes aware of the scope of the *Zhuangzi*'s reproof to the ambitions of political authority and the desire to control and govern the whole world.

Zhuangzi's bestiary—seventy-five species of animals are referred to throughout the book, ranging from tiny etc., from tiny insects to giant whales, not to mention mythical creatures and hybrid beasts— can be seen as a massive riposte to the forceful incorporation of all living beings into the political order, an idea that culminated in the aforementioned self-laudatory phrases of the First Emperor stele's inscription. When the *Zhuangzi* promotes the idea of a primeval community between humans and animals, it never portrays the animal kingdom as receptive to human morality. Instead, it emphasizes that humans are characterized by a deep incomprehension and a feral violence towards other beings. Situated at a latitude considerably distant from our usual moral climates, the true or authentic Man (*zhen ren*), "whose Virtue has remained genuine," like the mythical chief of the Tai clan, "sometimes considers himself as a horse, sometimes as an ox."[3] The Old Master, Laozi himself, reminds a crusty and cantankerous would-be disciple: "I feel I have already freed myself from the category of people held as skilled, knowledgeable, spiritual or wise. Yesterday, if you had called me an ox, then I would have considered myself an ox, and if you had called me a horse, I would have just considered myself a horse."[4]

When reading this line, one should not be puzzled by the assertion that a man in a position of command can liken his inner disposition to that of a horse or an ox: this is not a Chinese form of *cynicism*, but a rhetorical turn devised to celebrate the uncorrupted nature of someone who sees beyond the fallacious boundaries between humans and animals and does not recoil at the prospect of undergoing a deep change, without wishing to cling to a former and fixed identity. Many animal stories in the *Zhuangzi* converge on the idea that social norms, bookish learning, and technical inventions at the service of uncontrolled appetites, inflict damages upon our original nature parallel to the harmful effects of lacquer, ink, glue, hammer and T-squares on the animal realm. Most men end up misled by social virtues, shackled by ritual, quartered by kindness, and branded by justice.

By ascribing new roles to animals—the same creatures that contemporary texts had turned into meek creatures and docile symbols of political authority—the *Zhuangzi* can tackle the consensual ideology of monarchy, mock its magico-religious aura and expose the extent to which man harms himself in the course of his supposedly "civilized" life. Animals stand at the frontline of this rebellion against this ideology of early Chinese cosmic monarchism.

Sacrificial, divinatory, and ritual uses of the animal realm

Means of transport, tilling tools, treats of meat, sacrificial victims, messengers of the Spirits, sacred omens and tamed companions, decorative emblems, icons of authority, and objects of worship: from the outset animals fulfil in China innumerable roles and functions. These can be economic, religious, pedagogical or aesthetic, relating them to man in multiple ways, and this was already the case well before the emergence of written records that mark the beginning of history. As in many early civilizations, the ritual slaughter of animals during ancestral sacrifice unified religious and political power. An important network of diverse activities— war, hunting, agriculture, ritual—gave animals a major role in the economy of early society. From ancient times, a rich and imaginative animal iconography was projected on every inch of the royal domain: beasts and birds adorned bronze vessels, the shafts of chariots, drums and bells; they appeared on blades and spears, emblazoned banners and armored coats, and were carved on ceremonial jades.[5] Painted, inlaid, embossed, embroidered, or bled, interred, quartered, or decapitated, animals were used to express both the real and the symbolic domination of humans and, above all, of the sovereign over the natural world, turning fauna into a vast supply of devices for communication and exchange with the invisible world.

The use of animals for religious purposes has been traced back to the Neolithic period.[6] Evidence of sacrifices to royal ancestors and to various natural powers, sometimes involving hundreds of beasts, has been uncovered from the Shang era (c. 2000 BCE); though it is unknown whether the sacrifices were made on a regular or exceptional basis, it is apparent that animals were burned, buried whole or drowned by the dozen in rivers. Although reduced to a less extravagant scale around the eighth century BCE—as a response to clear signs of a reduction in the presence of fauna and the indiscriminate destruction of their habitat—animal sacrifices were still among the dominant dynastic institutions of the Zhou dynasty, along with divination.

For the purpose of divination, too, great numbers of animals were slaughtered. Turtle shells and scapulae of cattle and sheep were used as media on which were inscribed the responses of deities and ancestral spirits invoked by the royal college of diviners; these bones, neatly prepared as a means of communication with the invisible world, also served as archives recording the context and the content of mantic procedures.

Later, over the course the seventh and sixth centuries BCE, the old practice of oath-taking, a decisive element in territorial expansion in a context of feudalism and internecine struggles, took the form of a ceremony where lords sealed their alliance by invoking Spirits as the guarantors of their pact while smearing their lips with the blood of a slaughtered animal.

In sum, animals were the instruments of cohesion between the visible world and the invisible realm of Spirits through the political and religious practices of sacrifice, oath, and divination.

Torturing turtles and
gainsaying soothsaying

As early as the Shang dynasty (*c.* 1500–1050 BCE), the first war chariots were used by an aristocratic elite in battle and for hunting. While the horse was enrolled in campaigns for territorial expansion and pacification of the wilderness, the turtle was caught in a network of sacrificial religious ceremonies; used for divination, progressively loaded with symbolism from the Shang dynasty onwards, it came to be regarded as a miniature replica of the universe. The ventral side of the shell represented the square of the earth, while the hemispherical dorsal part referred to the vault of heaven. Although certain myths and apocryphal texts make the turtle one of the sacred animals that revealed the presence of signs and writing in the natural world that proved pivotal in the process of civilization, the authors of the *Zhuangzi* for their part see in the turtle's superior usefulness the very reason for the maltreatment it has been condemned to suffer ad infinitum.

Keeping in mind the cosmological symbolism and the divinatory role associated with the turtle, let us read a story extracted from Chapter 26 of the *Zhuangzi*, "External Things."

One night, Prince Yuan of Song saw in his dream a man with unkempt hair peeking him from behind a door ajar: "I come from the deep waters of the Path-of-the-Master. The Spirit of the Bright River sent me to visit the Count of the Yellow River, but on the way I was caught by Yu Qie, the fisherman."

When he awoke, the prince asked for an interpretation of his dream and the soothsayers replied: "The Spirit in question is a sacred turtle."

So the prince asked: "Among the fishermen here, is there one named Yu Qie?"

"There is," replied his courtiers.

"Bring him to the court," said the prince.

The following day, Yu Qie the fisherman came to the court and the prince asked:

"What have you caught recently?"

"In my net," replied the fisherman, "there was a white turtle, measuring five feet in circumference."

"Show me this turtle," ordered the prince.

When the turtle was brought before him, the prince was unable to decide whether he should have it killed or whether he should keep it alive. In doubt, he consulted the oracle and the answer was: "Kill the turtle and use it for divination: sign of good fortune." So the turtle was gutted. Seventy-two holes were bored in its shell and not one prediction was proved wrong.

Confucius observed: "This Turtle-Spirit was able to appear to Prince Yuan in a dream but was unable to stay away from the net of a fisherman. Pierced with seventy-two holes,[7] it responded infallibly but it could not avoid ending up slaughtered. It seems something blocks out intelligence, and even for a Spirit some things stand beyond reach. Although endowed with perfect intelligence, the Spirit fell prey to men's conspiracies. For fear of the pelican, the fish forgets the net. Whoever can free himself from the narrowness of his consciousness will be enlightened by great intelligence; he who dismisses excellence, will of himself excel. To learn to speak, a young child has no need of a great master; he just has to stay among people who know how to speak."[8]

The man with the unkempt hair peeping in at the door during the Prince of Song's dream is a Spirit from the abyss of the Path-of-the-Master who is sent as emissary to the Count of the Yellow River; he was caught, his mission failed. By breaking into the mind of the prince, the Turtle-Spirit is asking to be set free. The dream is an injunction and an enigma for the lord who does not recognize the Turtle-Spirit in a human guise. It is at the least unusual to see a Spirit requesting help of a man. Here the traditional roles of humans and animals in divinatory practices become deliberately muddled. In the morning, the prince's dream is elucidated. The turtle, usually in the role of tool and revelatory agent in mantic practices, reveals its true nature through the act of divination. This shift, seen in relation to regular divination procedures, is particularly noticeable where the prince becomes a surface for the inscription of signs emitted by the Turtle-Spirit, who is using the prince's sleeping state to convey his plea. Roles are reversed, as if the prince were replacing the turtle shells, becoming a receptacle for the inscription of formulae to be deciphered on awakening.

Then, the prince hesitates. Although killing the turtle would allow him to benefit from the numinous powers of the turtle shell and to see into the future, he teeters between two opposite courses of action since the entrapped animal has just begged him for help. Instead of deciding by himself, the prince listens again to his entourage. Absurdly, this second divinatory procedure follows the previous one (the interpretation of the dream), takes as its theme the divinatory animal par excellence, sets as its purpose the possession of a sacred turtle shell, and may be using in this instance another turtle shell as a divinatory tool in order to address the Spirits to enquire about the appropriateness of making one of their number perish. The Turtle-Spirit seems to be caught in a spiral of predation. No wonder that the result of the divination coincides with the interest of the diviners, who cannot but benefit from the enjoyment of such a prestigious turtle shell. "It would be auspicious to kill it and to use it for divination." The turtle shell once dismembered and perforated will be used as the medium to receive responses from the spirits solicited by the prince regarding events important to the court: harvests, hunts, births, expeditions, etc. The exchanges with the spirits all prove conclusive, all the predictions are vindicated by further events.

This tale of capture and sacrifice also suggests another lesson, one about the degeneration of the relationship between humans and animals. Initially, in the Prince of Song's dream, the turtle is the author of a divinatory message with its own life at stake; in the second phase, that of the second divination, it is merely the theme or the topic of this divination; in the last phase, once the divine turtle has been eviscerated, pierced, and burnt, it can only serve as a commodity and a tool for further divinations, perhaps bearing on the opportunity of putting other turtles to death, as could be intimated by the absurd cycle of events depicted in this story. In this cycle, the chain linking production and consumption is continuous, underpinning a self-generating dynamic of destruction that is revealed between the lines, divination providing for its own needs with no other purpose.

If this story depicts a supernatural being caught in the drift nets of human interests, its ultimate meaning may not lie in the consideration of man's cruelty toward animals; the final touch is provided by Confucius in a fictitious (but for once gratifying) portrayal of the master. Confucius extrapolates from this narrative of an unfortunate turtle whose death allows auspicious predictions, in order to expose the limits of human intelligence and the dangers of its exercise. He turns a pitiful anecdote into a moral fable by decoding therein a typical example of human failings.

In early China, one of the most salient signs of intelligence in masters' discourses was the capacity to remain perceptive in all circumstances, to see far into the future, in other words to detect and anticipate change, to deal with things when they are still in the bud, before they reach their full term. In this respect, divination was the royal paradigm of knowledge. It is in this sense that we may compare the form of intelligence valued in early China to that shown by the inspector or the sleuth in detective stories: same gift, same flair, same talent for observing, predicting and preventing.[9]

At the same time, by the end of the fourth century BCE, following on from the *Zhuangzi* and the first writings explicitly dealing with self-cultivation, there was a move to discredit divinatory practices in favor of personal perspicacity, perceptual acumen, and the ethical independence of individuals (one can easily imagine the disagreements between court diviners and the milieu of intellectuals and wandering scholars). As is affirmed in the book of Laozi, foreknowledge is merely an "excrescence of the Tao," "the antechamber of foolishness." In the foregoing story, the turtle is the emblematic victim of this folly and its misdeeds.

The moral judgment voiced by Confucius thus leads us to understand the story not only in terms of a denunciation of the absurd practices of divination and the perverted ties between spirits, men, and animals, but also as an appraisal of the harm inflicted on one's life by narrow forms of intelligence, when the activity of the mind is reduced to schemes, plots, and intrigues. Seen in this new exegetical light, the turtle is not so much the epitome of all the victims of human predatory instincts, but rather a convincing allegory of the faults and failings of the human mind, whose perception is always biased, whose understanding is beclouded, whose great capacities go along with a destructive blindness about one's current position in the world. The *Zhuangzi* exposes the cycle of sterile and destructive consumption to which men condemn themselves by their practice of calculation and prediction. The turtle, especially once dead, excelled at fathoming distant events but when alive neglected its present state: the sly procedure which allowed it to winkle out a nightly "audience" with the prince by sneaking into his dream, exposed it to danger and did not permit it to escape the machinations of the ruler's entourage. Human intelligence[10] can get caught in the same sort of snare.

Ordinary human intelligence, which the *Zhuangzi* calls "narrow consciousness" (*xiao zhi*), is made up of self-principled calculations and illusory speculation. It beclouds the limpid view of things and ignores the traps along its way. One might also ask whether the turtle's initial mission as emissary between the two spirits, one from the abyss and one from the river, might not have already condemned it from the start to the trap of the fishing net, since it had already embarked upon a mission implying migration and message-carrying, playing thereby the role of ambassador just like these masters, expert in various skills, arts, and techniques, who traveled through feudal states and mingled with the mighty, constantly risking their lives.

The story can also be understood in the light of another tale, one of the most memorable in the *Zhuangzi* despite its striking brevity. It recounts the murder of Humpty-Dumpty (*Hundun*[11]). This uncanny creature is an embodiment of original Chaos, resembling a gourd without apertures, like the fruit of the calabash tree, or like a hermetic bag of skin closed in on itself. Humpty-Dumpty lived in a happy state of autarky, at the very center, while every now and then hosting the two emperors from the Northern and the Southern Seas, Zippy (*shu*) and Zingy (*hu*), whom he treated with consideration. The two guests, hoping to reciprocate Humpty-Dumpty's favors, decide to render him "normal," by piercing his skin to create the seven orifices that will give him a human face (eyes, nostrils, ears and mouth), and so they set out to pierce one hole a day. On the seventh day, their unfortunate initiative causes the death of Humpty-Dumpty. We can detect in this eerie tale a parody of the archaic myths of the dismembering of an original totality.[12] This initial murder is the necessary pool of blood upon which society is built, the primordial sacrifice that must be concealed.[13] The turtle itself is also a symbol of totality, and that is why it ends up pierced through, to give way to the multiple activities of men. Before the start of any enterprise, men must cut, dismember, divide, and separate, and the turtle pays the price for its lack of prudence.

> To learn to speak, a young child has no need of a great master; he just needs to sit among people who know how to speak.

The final phrase of the story sums up the gist of Confucius' remarks: what is at stake is the switch from the critique of divination as an institution to the critique of divination as a model for knowledge. With Confucius as the paradoxical go-between, the author puts forward the decisive idea that the acquisition of authentic abilities is a question of surroundings and not of means, a question of passive and quiet exposure rather than active speculation. The child has no teacher and is guided by the natural and unconscious resources of the body, progressing imperceptibly from silence to babble, from babble to language, not knowing what he is doing, without pondering over his actions, without passing like the Prince of Song through the hands of experts in hermeneutics. The child displays an intelligence that almost entirely escapes its consciousness. It allows itself to be guided by his inner workings without intentionally seeking the aptitude for speech. One can see here how the critique of divination is related to a deeper critique of those traditional ways of acquiring knowledge, which requires the intervention of a teacher, the type of education of which Confucius appears, in canonical texts, as the venerable patron, and, in this episode of the *Zhuangzi*, the penetrating gainsayer.[14]

The brief commentary on the fate of the turtle by Confucius could lead to another development, because it touches upon certain essential questions constantly returned to in the *Zhuangzi*. The authors indeed pay special attention to the fact of highly important mental episodes that tend to elude or bypass consciousness, and which remain enigmatic for it. The tale of Humpty-Dumpty makes a pair with the anecdote with the centipedes and the snake in Chapter 17, "Floods in the fall":

> Kui, the one-footed creature, said to the centipede: "With my one leg, I hop along, with much effort and little progress. But you, how on earth do you manage to work these hundreds of legs?"
>
> The centipede replied: "That's not how you should see things. Surely, you've already seen a man spit? He hawks up saliva and it all gushes out, some drops big like pearls, some fine like a drizzle, and they fall on the ground all jumbled up as a countless shower of particles. I put in motion the natural spring in me without knowing how the mechanism works."[15]

The author suggests through a deft analogy with the act of spitting that most actions, words and gestures, when they are spontaneous and efficient, are fueled so to speak by a part of ourselves of which we remain unaware: most of our expressions branch out from a continuous dynamic driven by unknown forces within us. Anyone who pays attention to what happens when we speak is able to notice how, with each phrase constructed, things get said that were not pre-formulated; clauses and expressions form themselves without us mentally supervising their construction as if a dynamic impulse toward a meaningful expression progressively traces out speech and ensured the continuity of the flow. Our natural capacity to improvise and extemporize draws on bodily resources of which we are hardly aware. That is how through every sentence and gesture we move toward what consciousness has not yet perceived, and seamlessly circulate between the known and the unknown, the intentional and the spontaneous. This shows to what extent knowledge, along with all our conscious capacities and deliberate mental operations—all of which the *Zhuangzi* subsumes under the Human mode (*ren*), is deeply rooted in unknowingness and is constantly nurtured by the natural workings or Heavenly mode (*tian*) which surpasses our power of awareness. And that is how, to come back to our story, an infant, as Confucius recalls, gradually learns to speak, just by being where people are talking: "He who understands the workings of Man uses what his conscience and knowledge (*zhi*) understand in order to nourish what they do not understand yet.[16]" As for the turtle, both alive as an emissary and dead as a means of communication with the invisible, it remained sadly subservient to the logic of divination. Absorbed in its blind attempt to fulfil its diplomatic mission and see beyond the present moment, beyond the flux it was paddling through, it found itself enmeshed in a situation it had overlooked. And the turtle's death only served to foster the predatory cycle of predictions it fell prey to.

Governing in music

Animals in early China also lent themselves to the ideological regimentation of the natural world. Ritual and philosophical texts of the pre-imperial and early imperial period (that is, from the third to the first century BCE) single out certain creatures which display on their skins and hides meaningful signs[17] that inspired the legendary sages' major cultural innovations, such as the trigrams in the *Book of Changes* (*Yijing*), the elementary marks of writing, but also music sounds, dance steps, colors, and garments. However, as Chapter 14, "The Turning of Heaven," warns: "if one forces a monkey into the Duke of Zhou's clothes, it will certainly get its teeth into them, pull them around and tear them and will not be satisfied until it has removed them all. The difference between the olden days and the present is comparable to the dissimilarity between the Duke of Zhou and a monkey."[18] An infuriated monkey here is comically arrayed in the accoutrements of one of the most eminent founding fathers of the Zhou dynasty, referred to by Confucius himself as a paragon of perfect virtue and considered in the literary tradition as the tutelary icon of ritual order. Obviously, the sacrilegious nature of this analogy must not have gone unnoticed at the time this text began to circulate. Unlike the monkey pitting the fighting instinct of wild animals against human restrictions, people do not even try to writhe out of their moral clothing. They just cope with an inner straitjacket, even if they forget how to breathe.

In stark contrast to this rebellious image of nature defying the civilizing process, many authors harp on the idea that humans can transform the wild world through gentleness rather than by force or technique, using among other things music as a moral vehicle. By transforming airs and customs, music exerts a deep and invisible influence in the same way as climate and atmosphere. Various writings from the Warring States period and the Han era link the origins and the practice of music to the observation of sounds, movements, and rhythms in the animal realm. They hammer home the idea that music, far from being a purely human creation, is just the fully achieved expression of inborn inclinations and tendencies to be found everywhere in the natural world. According to the chapter "Music of the Ancients"[19] in the *Springs and Autumns of Sir Lü*, an encyclopedic work written by a group of courtier-intellectuals under the auspices of the chancellor Lü Buwei of the powerful state of Qin at the end of the Warring States period (481–221 BCE), the twelve notes of the musical tubes were derived from the sounds produced by the male and the female phoenixes (six each). But without the transformation of these basic sounds into musical notes, and their combination into melodious sequences, animals themselves would have no moral experience of music (and how tragic that would be!).

The association of animals with the recursive analogy drawn between music and the art of governing enables the latter to apply seamlessly to the political realm and to the natural world. The recurring combination of musical notes and animal sounds offer a vast reservoir of images that serve to celebrate a harmonious sovereignty. It is from this perspective that one should read the recurrent narratives describing famous music masters whose astounding performances bring animals into submission. At the tinkling of Hu Ba's lute, fish would leap from the water the better to listen to it, while Bo Ya's virtuosity on the zither enchanted horses to the point that they forgot their fodder. The melodies performed by Kuang, music master and player at the court of Duke Ping of Jin (sixth century BCE), could inspire a dance in two rows by eight black cranes.[20] The chapter "Record on Music" ("Yueji") in the *Book of Rites* acclaims the fruitful influence of music, whose resonance in the natural world grows horns and antennae, puts wings in motion, brings insects back to the light and makes mammals thrive.[21] As a sociopolitical force, music disperses its natural bounties to the furthest and wildest lands and gives resonance to the moral authority of the sovereign worldwide. Music instructs and controls by gently transforming (*jiao hua*) predatory instincts in men and beasts, in contrast to legal violence and physical coercion. I will refer here only to one example, for its instructive difference with another story from the *Zhuangzi*. It is a rhapsody by the Han dynasty poet Lu Qiaoru (*c.* second century BCE) in which are evoked 翯 cranes crossing a marsh at a ford, probably in the parklands of a king. The virtuous conduct of the ruler is all that is needed to inspire a moral disposition in all living creatures, and to placate their wildest instincts. The following lines suggest that despite their natural propensity to flight and to reach for the sky, the cranes prefer to dawdle on the banks of the lake:

Thus, we know that these wild birds, these wild tempers,
Have not escaped from their cage.
Entrusting themselves to the magnanimous love of our king,
Although they are wild creatures, they cherish his goodness,
And bound, hopping and dancing,
The scarlet hurdles bringing them joy.[22]

The very instruments of enclosure and boundary—hedges, fences or cages—are, for these wild creatures (the author insists heavily on this point), a source of effervescence and the cause of their deliberate stay in the royal domains. The same ideological notion of a civilizing force wielding its magic influence on the wilds is used by the poet-courtier to acclaim the aura of royalty[23] surrounding the sovereign: although the poem is posterior to the *Zhuangzi*, the rich corpus of writings describing the influence of music in the transformation of the animal kingdom suggests a general official acceptance,[24] to differing degrees, of such an idea by the greater part of the philosophical intelligentsia during the Warring States period, and under the Qin and Han dynasties. Chapter 18 of the *Zhuangzi*, "Supreme Joy," already ridicules the socio-centered vision of the moral influence of the sovereign on birds by reporting a fictional episode from the life of Confucius. The story can be outlined as follows: an exhausted seabird falls from the sky on the outskirts of the state of Lu. The lord of Lu takes it to the ancestral temple, treats this guest to sacrificial wine and meats and finally deafens the poor bird with ceremonial music performed in its honor. On the third day, deprived of the right food, the bird starves to death. So much for the magic transformations caused by music and ritual offerings. The music played in the ancestral temple is a cultural creation with no relevance to the sounds of nature, in the same way as alcohol and sacrificial meats are the worst possible food for a seabird. By wishing to please the bird, the prince is flaunting his considerate generosity. In the same way Zippy (*shu*) and Zingy (*hu*) were doing Humpty-Dumpty a favor by piercing his body, making him look like themselves, the prince inflicts a prolonged agony on the bird while believing he is honoring it. "He nourished it as he would nourish himself, instead of feeding it like a bird.[25]" Far from trying to integrate beasts into the human realm, the *Zhuangzi* reinstates them in their *otherness*, emphasizing their specific needs and desires. The bird is like the turtle of the previous story: once enmeshed in the human world, the bird must serve human interests, and thus perish violently.

Music, which is air filtered by purely human preferences, "plays the wrong tune" as far as animals are concerned. During an imaginary audience narrated in Chapter 14, Confucius complains to Laozi about his lack of success as counsellor despite his assiduous study of the ritual canons and the classics that record and celebrate the virtuous conduct of the sages from times past. The Way seeming beyond his reach, he has no hold over his fellow men. Laozi advises him to leave aside these writings, which are hardly better than fossilized footprints or lifeless traces, and suggests that he starts to become receptive to the invisible workings underlying the formation of all beings, using enigmatic expressions alluding to animal reproduction. Confucius secludes himself for three months and comes to realize, by observing the ubiquitous fecundity of the animal world, the internal dynamic of things and the continuous engendering and transformation of life forms. In short, he has grasped the Way. Transformation is everywhere in the air: reproduction is carried out by the wind, acting as a generating agent dispensing with physical contact.[26] Here the *Zhuangzi* plays on the ambivalence of the word *feng*, wind, which in the Confucian textual tradition, particularly in the *Book of Odes*, a repository of ancient songs and hymns praised by Confucius, also refers to the airs of music sung in the various parts of the kingdom and the moral climate that permeates their inhabitants. As opposed to the stultified signs to be found in sacred texts, likened in another anecdote to excrement left by the sages of old, the author proposes the meaning of *feng* as a spontaneous force for generation, a fertile breath whose dynamic permeates the air all around.

This wondrous revelation sparked by his long solitude gives Confucius a felicitous reconnection with the life force that underlies the ever-rising profusion of this world. Here the sage does not observe the patterns and the motifs on animal bodies or the traces they leave on the ground, in order to derive writings or omens for the human community. On the contrary, Confucius is rapt with admiration at the animals' instinctive mode of reproduction, and captures the vision of natural dynamics in its native state. The workings of nature have no need of music. Confucius can now be sensitive to the flow, to the signals and to the silent communications between creatures who call to each other and engender each other.[27]

Who needs to "frighten the horses"?

Many other activities involving a cooperation between humans and animals, such as driving a chariot or grooming and harnessing a horse, were used as exemplary images of the art of ruling.[28] Both in philosophical works and in technical handbooks, these activities emphasized peaceful conciliation with animals, coercion being viewed as entirely unnecessary. A treatise on military strategy, traditionally attributed to the general and minister Wu Qi (*c.* 440–361), stipulates that the rider and his horse should maintain a close relationship. The charioteer should follow the movements of the animal rather than manipulate it. When the mind of the driver is in harmony with the horses, the horses will likewise be in agreement with the vehicle. Going beyond the denunciation of the extensive and endless maltreatment of animals, many of the stories in the *Zhuangzi* lead the reader toward the idea that in the process of establishing their cultural status, men are also responsible for alienating, mutilating, and torturing themselves.

The theme of separation of men and animals in the *Zhuangzi* appears particularly meaningful when we observe in what way it stands in opposition to other social and political projects circulating during the Warring States period. In these programs, we find two rival conceptions of the original condition of humanity. The first emphasizes the antagonism between incompatible species and the moral superiority of human beings who, by way of various institutions and inventions (education, agricultural techniques, writing, ritual, laws, and measurements) provided by the cultural heroes and saintly sovereigns of a remote past, raise themselves from their primitive state of confusion and hostility. The second perspective, present in the *Zhuangzi* and later taken up in Taoist-tainted writings, depicts a blissful primitive age of peaceful cohabitation between men and animals, when neither sought distinction through value or strength. Here the birth of 'civilisation' initiates a process of decadence when Man, to quote John Florio translating Montaigne, "selecteth and separateth himselfe from out the ranke of other creatures; to which his fellow-brethren and compeers he cuts out and shareth their parts, and allotteth them what portions of meanes or forces he thinkes good."[29]

The different accounts of the creation of humanity, whether they insist on physical separation from animals or on moral instructions dispensed by early sages, intimate that there is no ontological difference between man and other living beings, and that only moral principles and technical invention can emancipate humans from the wilderness. The legends concerning the first sages are tied to narratives evoking humanity rising from hostile surroundings where each and every being was in confrontation with other species, and where every being was prey to its own bestiality. While these myths about sages elevating humans above their own nature were being formulated, each philosophical tradition, according to its specific political agenda and moral values, was enumerating the decisive changes and inventions that allowed people to attain a proper level of humanity.[30]

The major Legalist writings such as the *Book of Prince Shang*, the *Han Feizi* and the *Guanzi* recall the time when the sages and kings of ancient times separated humans from animals and codified laws, created hierarchies and imposed units of measurement. The writings of Master Mo and his disciples, the only thinkers in early China who offered a logical analysis of language, describe an original state of chaos, wherein each man made a personalized and peculiar use of words, thereby destroying the possibility of establishing community of any sort. This linguistic confusion relegated men to the level of wild animals. The early sages were thus obliged to define criteria for evaluating and distinguishing truth and falsehood, in order to allow the existence of moral judgment and common meaning of words. As one might expect, the Confucians[31] for their part celebrated the invention of rites and rules of propriety to regulate behavior and establish a code of duties. The *Book of Rites*[32] says: "A man without rites, though he may possess the ability to speak, does he not have the heart of a beast?" Mencius, as noted by the historian Mark Edward Lewis in his reflection on legal violence,[33] described the three stages by which man can escape the animal realm and reveal his authentic nature: physical separation, technical invention, and moral education. After the separation took place, reconciliation with the natural world, based on the political idea of harmony, is understood in the Confucian discourse as the moral transformation of animals and their integration into a civilizing order, and not as man's return to the animal sphere. For Confucians, what is in a rough or wild state is always something awaiting transformation or civilization, and must eventually under the aegis of a wise ruler join the realm of a *cultural cosmos*.

Confucius' endeavors were directed at all the elements that could educate man and elevate him above bestiality and barbarity: rites, manners, etiquette, ceremony, music, recitation, and exemplary moral behavior. He was the first to remould the sense of social relationships in the aesthetic form of ritual, while enjoining people to cultivate the virtues of benevolence (*ren*), justice (*yi*), or loyalty (*zhong*) which allow one full access to one's true humaneness. The authors of the *Zhuangzi*, for their part, diagnose man as an alienated being, suffocating and crippled by textual training and social taming, fettered by rites and branded by the irons of customary virtues. They describe the ravages of being torn away from nature, they struggle to uncover a life-force whose free play within us would not be hamstrung by traditional knowledge or debilitated by the fallacious categories that underlie our perception of the world. The *Zhuangzi* proposes a distinct form of education, free from book learning, an education that rebukes and humiliates professional masters and experts in social manners. The uncanny Confucius featured in the *Zhuangzi* is a complex crystallization of both these criticisms and ideal stances. We see him in one episode leaving his disciples and friends in order to start a new life in the company of wild animals by a swamp, feeding on acorns and chestnuts, wearing fur and unadorned clothes of coarse fabric, but in peaceful unison with the birds and beasts all around. Just as if the author of this anecdote were responding to the historical master, who in the *Analects* chased off his frustration with his lack of success in the human world by threatening to go live among the barbarians, by sending him to actually live in the wild and mingle with barbarous beings:[34]

> The master expressed his desire to wander out the wild East and settle among the Yi tribes. Someone observed: "These people are so uncouth, how can you bear it?" The master replied: "If a gentleman settles there, what uncouthness would there be?"

The text at the beginning of Chapter 9, "Horses' hooves," is dedicated to the contentious relationship between natural condition and human government. Behind the history of free and happy horses who suddenly had to undergo the cruelty of men and survive the hardships of dressage, the reader cannot but imagine the tyrannical exploitation of creatures whose fate is similar to that of men hobbled by rites, tamed by rules, and weakened by music and other inventions introduced by the so-called sages. In the idyllic days of old evoked in the "primitivist" chapters of the *Zhuangzi*,[35] everyone had the same simple, artless needs, desires and activities. Inequalities, greed, and competition arose with social division, the polarities of servitude and power, the imposition of rules for every kind of public interaction and the strict observance of hereditary hierarchies that decide on the place and the fate of each and everyone.

In Chapter 24 ("Xu Wugui"), the hermit Xu Free-From-Daemons meets with the glum lord of Wei, who lapses into smouldering silence after being told about his harmful way of life. But right after making him dig in his heels, the astute hermit, drawing on his expertise in sizing up dogs and horses, defuses the situation by setting lose a stream of bewitching images which succeed in drawing the ruler out of his prickly isolation.

> Xu Free-from-Daemons: I know about horses and I can tell you that those who run straight forwards, as if on a plumb line, and those who can revolve following a line like a hook, take a corner at right-angles and turn in circles like a compass. They are nothing but "horses for the kingdom." Their worth is far from that of the "horses for the world," which by nature are perfect. They are wild and disorientated as if they had lost all awareness of themselves; they are made that way so as to outpace all other creatures, abandoning them to the cloud of dust left by their galloping hooves. No one knows where they reside.[36]

The flurry of deft animal descriptions echo more or less consciously in the ruler's mind as judgments on life-styles in general, including his own. The main difference between the two kinds of horses is due to the specific spatiality and mobility that define their daily life: the horses for the state or the kingdom, once sufficiently broken in and beaten, are able to execute strict geometrical figures; they are an apposite image of the subjugation of natural dynamism. The hermit then evokes the blissful lightning gallop of horses always engrossed in a dreamy mood, knowing no borders in their infinite roaming. The lord of Wei upon hearing this description feels the benefits of imaginary expansion in space. These images make the prince (and the reader) aware of the extent to which animals, livestock, and draft animals that were domesticated, underwent deep changes in morphology, were rendered docile, submissive, meek, and yielding. Humans were affected by a similar process, through corralling and crowding, by changing patterns of physical activity and social organization, and the ensuing narrowing of the perceptual and experiential horizon. To go back to Chapter 9, "Horses' hooves," the following description also hints at how much we, as humans, have strayed from the natural course of things.

> Horses have hooves that can tread snow and ice, a coat that protects them from wind and cold. They graze and drink, they gambol and frolic: such is their true nature. Were they given spacious stalls in vast stables, they would find no use for them.[37]

The author is simply considering horses in their natural state: what they have, what they are and what they do, free from human subjection. The enduring power of adaptation of the horse allows it to live anywhere, especially in an environment hostile to men. It is equipped by nature and has no use for the habitat men provide, unless it has been weakened to the point of needing to shelter from the weather. Horses are just one example of the fate of domesticated animals, which were caught, tamed, milked, shorn, and shod. First, they experienced a restriction of space: they were no longer free to go wherever they pleased. They became captive species and their diet was modified along with their mobility. Horses and cows, sheep and pigs, were confined together in enclosures under constant human supervision. Humans likewise became a domesticated flock, oblivious of the behavioral traits of their free-living untamed ancestors. The pervasive theme in the *Zhuangzi* of an unencumbered roaming across wild tracts of lands or boundless stretches of space can be seen as a moment of acute awareness of the harms of domestication and the will to break free from this political dispensation.

In the following part of this short narrative, the maltreatment of horses and the death of the restive ones is used to reveal even more clearly how men govern themselves and to illustrate the mutilation they inflict on their own natural abilities. Degrading practices lies at the foundation of the social reorganization of the natural world.

> Then one day appeared Bo Le, who declared himself expert in the art of training horses. He submitted their coats to the blade and to fire, clipped them, cut them, branded them and shod them, then he bridled them and put them into halters and shut them in stalls. One third of them died. So then he made them hungry and thirsty, made them trot and gallop, walk in file and in line: plague of reins and snaffle at the front, fear of the whip and the stick at the rear. More than half of them perished.[38]

As groom to the semi-legendary King Mou, Bo Le is traditionally presented as the archetypical horseman, the equestrian connoisseur *par excellence*. His ease and mastery in the domestication of animals illustrates the concept of enlightened government. A bamboo-slip manuscript describing the physiognomy of a horse unearthed at the archaeological site of Mawangdui detects a geographical outline of the earth in the lines and curves of the horse. A handbook dating from the Tang dynasty (618–907) on the physiognomy of horses indirectly testifies to the literary fortune of the political symbolism of animals, firmly implanted in China since the end of the Warring States. This handbook decodes the outlines of a moral and political order from the shape of animal bodies. Its author draws an analogy between the anatomy of the horse and the organization of the state and again gives Bo Le the starring role as the finest connoisseur of the natural world. The different parts of the body are explained through the categories of the politico-administrative order, as:

> Bo Le says: "The head of the horse is the king. Thus, it should be square in shape. The eye is the minister-counsellor, thus it should be clear-sighted. The spinal column is the army general, thus it should be robust. The belly is the citadel, thus it should be wide and spacious. The four feet are the commanders, thus they should be of elevated status."[39]

In his pioneering monograph *The Daemon and the Animal in Early China*, Roel Sterckx has thoroughly analyzed the textual process whereby corporal reality is made subservient to moral order during the Warring States and Han periods. It is probably in reaction to such administrative projections and the way they deform the view of natural needs that, in Chapters 9 and 24 of the *Zhuangzi*, horses trained so harshly as to behave like remote-controlled puppets are contrasted with those whose apparently wild and chaotic behavior intimates the overflow of an unrestrained vitality. Here we have a privileged literary standpoint to observe the breach created between Heaven and Man, between the natural realm and civilizing order, whose deceptively seamless continuity conceals the mistreatment of natural life. Authentic men, as portrayed in the *Zhuangzi*, reveal a disturbing closeness with these horses that wander cheerfully, frolicking through the world without ever reaching the end of their ride. In fact, Bo Le doesn't know how to manage horses because he doesn't follow their nature, he only knows how to force them and train them, condemning those who refuse to be docile to a premature and violent death. When the horses are groomed, they are burned (*zhao*) and incised (*ke*) at the hoof: these verbs are also used in referring to the sacred turtle that is put to the tests of divinatory fire and incision. The title "Horses' hooves"("Ma ti"), judiciously chosen for this chapter by the editors of the *Zhuangzi*, provides a view of the tension between the innate capacity of horses to move about freely ("tread snow and ice") and their forcing into step: the hoof is an emblem for the tortured and debilitated body, a synecdoche that directs the eye to the place where the most notable actions of subjection to humans are concentrated. Men cut and shoe the raw hooves which formerly allowed the horse to travel freely through the world and adapt to all different types of terrain.

It is the downfall of human nature, kneaded and shaped by the inventions of tyrannical brutes called sages, that should be read between the lines of this story. All the more since a horse-drawn chariot is one of the most common images of government in early literature. The implicit conclusion is that there is only a small difference between a bad and a good government, since any form of political organization implies a process of conquest and violent subjection, breaking the natural spring (*tian ji*) in all living creatures. "Governing the empire is not any different from herding horses: you just need to get rid of anything that can harm them, that is all."[40] Such is the wise advice reluctantly given by a young boy, almost blind, in the moorland when asked for guidance by the Yellow Emperor, unsure as to how fulfil his mission as a ruler. Against the hypothesis of a chaotic state of nature advanced by political thinkers to legitimate their vision of an orderly society, the *Zhuangzi* calls forth a herd of various creatures to reveal the damages brought about by the domestication of nature. It is the only text from early China that depicts the pristine state of nature as the age of absolute perfection, the end of which proved an unredeemable catastrophe for animals and for men. Unusually, however, its authors do not make a naively Utopian use of the past and the state of nature: they do not hanker after a lost Golden Age in a distant past, against the subsequent and common history of human corruption; rather, they locate the distinct features of a possibly superior way of life within the human community in a fictional non-political state. Such descriptions of a pre-state life do therefore not attempt to present a historical truth concerning early times but merely put into perspective the present human situation and reveal its damages in a magnified form. They give a hint of what our present condition could have been if only history had left people intact. The *Zhuangzi* is more interested in the naturalness within us than with the description of a state of nature to be situated on a historical timeline. Much in the same way, the "authentic men of ancient times" depicted in Chapter 6 are merely conceptual figures allowing the reader to imagine the possible shape of the optimal development of the self, in counterpoint to the observation of the sorry plight of common men.

When the founding sages appeared in the world, the havoc they wrought on animals can retrospectively be seen as the harbinger of a major disaster for human life. In the critical discourse of the *Zhuangzi*, those who established civilization, arts, techniques, and institutions on earth were nothing more than a bunch of violent and despotic masters, all hungry for power, heedless of the reputation they would leave to posterity. In its most anarchist vein, the *Zhuangzi* counterposes, as the two extremes of the human condition, the spontaneous concert of living beings, driven by the unrestrained use of their native powers, and the forced harmony of rigid conduct secured by the permanent inculcation of ritual norms and legal strictures.

In Chapter 9, "Horses' hooves," the description of the process that leads the animals from their natural state to the pitiful condition of subdued, weakened, and shackled creatures suggests that the political training of men depends on the creation of needs and desires that are completely superfluous to their state of nature. This is how political authority keeps its subjects under the yoke, just as the trainer holds the horse in check by means of the bridle and bit. The trainer breaks restive horses, exhausts those who survive dressage and forces them to become dependent on the warmth and shelter of the stable.

Like fish out of water, dribbling to survive

In the *Zhuangzi*, the account of how man became cut off from nature and brutally groomed to fit into a political dispensation based on absolute domination leads to a reflection on the possible ways of *sticking* together. By virtue of a negative comparison, the spontaneous community of animals shows that organized society is a means for men to survive outside their natural element. Society is a space where its members may survive, but breathe with difficulty and in no way achieve fulfilment:

> When a spring tarries, fish find themselves together on dry land. They blow on each other to stay damp, wet each other with their saliva, but life is nowhere near as good as it was when they could ignore each other in lakes or rivers.
> Fish move together in water and men move together in the flow of things. As they move in the water, fish penetrate the depths and hollows where they find sustenance; men, who move in the flow of things, can secure their lives by staying in a carefree idleness. That is why I say that "fish forget each other in lakes and rivers, men forget each other in the flow and ebb of things."[41]
> Rather than eulogize a great emperor like Yao and denigrate a tyrant like Jie, surely it is better to forget them both and ignore the traces they have left behind.

The central issue of finding the way to a free and unfettered life is imaged in the watery traffic of the fish. The Tao as a waterway remains one of the most influential images bequeathed by the *Zhuangzi*. Rivers and streams are to fish what the Way of nature once was to humans: a flow, a stream, a current, a nurturing milieu inspiring permanent movement in every direction.[42] Each fish follows its own course, is carried along by the flow, without harming the indistinct throng of its frolicking companions. A school of fish has no pilot, they are together yet at the same time unaware of one another, without having to learn rules or restrict their desires, fully committed to their "natural enjoyment." This togetherness dispenses with the need to physically signal their intentions to others, it is free of the social semantics that suffuses ritualized behavior; there is no need to act out conventions or duties in order to affirm the will to be together and form a group. In other words, fish are not tied to each other by a shared representation of the body they collectively form, as their community is not the result of a deliberate organization. In this idealized illustration of the world beneath the waves, what differentiates the community of fish from the society of men is that the aquatic denizens form a silent and effortless sphere that does not have to create and propagate an image of harmony to bind its different parts together; their mutual understanding seems to arise spontaneously, and this form of peaceful and mutual empathy becomes the favored image of optimal relationships in the *Zhuangzi*.

Then we see the fish forced out of their element, gasping and "drowning" in the air. Defined mainly by the cultivation of benevolence, altruism and sense of reciprocity, worshipping loyalty and devotion, the Confucian "gentleman" (*junzi*) is the paragon of those whose nurturing spring has run dry, those who unknowingly suffocate and suffer a slow sclerosis, while trying to orchestrate a docile community of fellow-creatures. Stranded outside their original element, they are now obliged to worry about one another in their own interest. Lying on dry land, forced to huddle and dribble on each other to survive, the desperate fish parallel a society based on forced promiscuity, a desperate exchange of spit and saliva, a writhing swarm of suffocating creatures pushed to the breaking point. The threads of dribble laid by one fish over the other foreshadow the necessary ties connecting the scattered multitude which seeks makeshift solutions to alleviate distress. Ritual is like the saliva preserving this sick community's existence. In Chapter 5, "Signs of Complete Virtue," the promises and contracts made between men are described in the same vein: "Which is why the Sage has in him the capacity to roam and travel freely [. . .] He knows that promises and agreements are only so much glue [. . .] The Sage does not carve out anything, why should he need glue?"[43]

However helpful social virtues may prove in a survival situation, however meritorious a master like Confucius may have been with his social ethics and his struggle against chaos and violence, the *Zhuangzi* objects that mutual assistance and charitable actions are only poor remedies in an age of decay, they will never equal the golden age of carefree wandering across the flow of things.

> Rather than eulogize a great emperor like Yao and denigrate a tyrant like Jie, surely it is better to forget them both and ignore the traces they have left behind.

The two figures of Yao and Jie were used at the time as a sort of conceptual dyad to refer to good and bad government. The best thing to do is to transcend the simple alternative, move beyond the bounds set down by the imprisoning binarism of Yao, the mythical sovereign and paragon of virtue for the Confucian school, and Jie, the last king of the Xia dynasty (c. 2000–1600 BCE), depicted as a cruel and depraved oppressor.

The praise of the good ruler and blame of the bad one both express an attitude arising from the same level of comprehension of existence—the level of conventional morality, from which all opposites and alternatives arise. The *Zhuangzi* retorts that in comparison with a pre-state community, political authority is always bad and brutal, and that all rulers were oppressors, whatever their individual legacy. Other texts in the *Zhuangzi* extend this objection, in which Yao and Jie are placed on an equal footing, the reviled sovereign and the venerated emperor being both unworthy, having shown their fundamental faults in the battles they waged, in their murderous conquests and their will to dominate the people. One of these texts is the long standalone narrative of Robber Zhi (Chapter 29), which recounts the pathetic efforts of Confucius to win over to morality a powerful feral warlord who sheds blood and terror wherever he goes. Zhi's forceful tirade in response to Confucius' admonition offers a very unsettling vision of the past, in which good and bad rulers are all thrown in the same basket. The sacrosanct figures of political authority of the Golden Age spilled blood like the others and ushered in an age in which the majority abused and oppressed the minority. The so-called sages' appetite for power turned them against their own inborn nature, and is held responsible for destroying a primeval state of harmony, rendering men wicked and violent. In this political satire all the ideological cornerstones of Zhou moral values seem to dissolve, while Confucius ends up brain-addled, defeated, and frightened.

All the passages in the *Zhuangzi* lumping together the historical figures that were traditionally seen as antithetical, declare that the commonly accepted opposition of Yao and Jie does not touch the heart of the political structuring of human society; it merely castigates its most scandalous elements because its aim is to prevent condemnation of the system itself. The only ones to be blamed and reviled by posterity are those who, like Jie, by their corruption and cruelty transgress in the most brazen way the ideal of a great and united political family or the ideological fiction of the ancestral community. Hence, with its parable of the fish, the *Zhuangzi* suggests that when men have been flung in the inferno of a political community, the principles of moral conduct can at most appear as a survival strategy. The reassurance provided by mutual assistance and attention is only a remedy once existence has been arrested in its untroubled course. A correct line of conduct that is beneficial to the community has nothing of the positive joy to be found in the easy, random progress of each creature, set free-wheeling in its own direction.

The reflection on the right way to be together, without injury or prejudice, is continued in Chapter 24, where the three species of animal symbolize three different ways of living in a group:

> The inspired man (*shen ren*) detests seeing people gathering together in a crowd. When they gather, he does not frequent them, nor does he seek to gain from them. This is why he does not approach anyone, nor does he over-distance himself either. He retains his inner potency, preserves balance and goes with the world. Such is the authentic man: he rejects the ants' perception, moves with fish and dismisses the sheep's good will.

On the one hand—in the light of the previously discussed passages—the parasitical activity of the ant, attracted by the strong odor of the sheep and a comfortable nesting place even at the risk of immolation by sacrificial fire, denounces the behavior of courtiers attracted by the rancid whiff of saintliness reeking from mythical sovereigns like the Emperor Shun. On the other hand, the powerful but involuntary attractiveness of the sheep, who is the victim of its own odor, and who, in spite of itself, hosts a myriad of congregating insects, illustrates the moral charisma of the sage who, to the detriment of his health and well-being, brings the burden of people and power upon himself. Clearly, the *Zhuangzi* does not mould the animal realm into one indivisible entity in order to put forward one ideal archetype in contrast to humans who have been misled and corrupted by civilization. The authentic man knows instinctively how to position himself at a safe distance from his gregarious fellows and foils the stultifying alternative of "being with" or "being without" others.

Animal myths, nascent fiction, and the ideology of the sage

The last narrative that I will cite in this context, the story of the fish changing itself into a bird, portrays a gossiping pair of small-minded creatures and their picayune way of disparaging a splendid and solitary being.

"In the northern darkness there lives a fish whose name is Kun." The cosmic journey of the mutant animal, placed as an overture in the first chapter "Roaming, rolling, roving," offers one of the most memorable scenes in Chinese literature. It tells the metamorphosis of Kun the fish, a sea creature so huge as to exceed the power of mental representation, into a no less gigantic bird who in its fury rises above the sky. Its flapping wings resound through the whole of space, from ocean to heaven, from the darkness of the North to the darkness of the South, to the reservoir of Heaven (literally: *tian chi*, "Heaven's Basin," an expression that combines, like the fish-bird, both airy and watery elements). The morphing bird leaves the limbo of the universe and returns to the darkness of the confines. "And when he rises up and flies far off, his wings are like an endless trail of clouds lingering in the sky." The image of the mythical mutating animal surpassing every reference and every scale reveals a world incommensurable with the categories of the human mind. And no one knows what will become of the bird, or whence the giant fish comes.

By directly addressing the reader's imagination and skirting the borderlines of representation, forcing the mind to picture this uncanny mutation, the *Zhuangzi* guides the reader along the course of an unsettling story devoid of familiar landmarks or reassurance. Such a scene is far more than an allegorical prelude: it expresses the necessity of an inaugural fracture in narrative forms and norms. While in this single scene, the *Zhuangzi* is bringing the potency of fiction into the heart of philosophical discourse and enriching the early Chinese literary mind with the new notion of the fantasy tale, it can also be seen as a critical offensive against the ambitions of moral reform nurtured in the different schools of thought in the pre-imperial era. This nonsensical and unprofitable tale of bird and fish quotes an imaginary old treatise, the "Universal Harmony," in an obvious attempt to poke fun at those who seriously invoke authoritative texts from the past to make their point. This narrative setting flies in the face of the sort of utilitarian and pragmatic discourses which pullulated in the entourages of princes, ministers and powerful merchants, encouraged by the increasing trend toward a stipend system between patrons (*zhu*) and clients (*ke*) underlying literary production and intellectual exchange during the Warring States. With this opening passage, Zhuangzi "took an almost suicidal satisfaction in reminding the reader that the story he was telling was only, after all, make-believe."[44]

No wonder that the *Zhuangzi* retains a distinct position in Chinese philosophical literature: it is the first one that from the outset yanks the reader out of any social or historical context and into the pure realm of imagination. The dreamlike images of metamorphosis are unrelated to any daytime experience or to any meaning in one's daily life. Suffice to compare it with the opening passages in the works of celebrated masters: Confucius extolling in the *Analects* the value of a studious existence and the happy feeling when finding oneself in the company of friends from afar; in the *Mencius*, the eponymous philosopher meets with King Hui of Liang and exhorts him to the cultivation of justice and benevolence toward others. In the *Mozi*, Master Mo affirms directly the vital necessity for a kingdom to protect and preserve worthy men and to ensure the well-being of servants of the State. Master Sun in *The Art of War* establishes the supremacy of war among affairs of state and human lives and redefines it as an exercise of intelligence. And the pattern is filled out by the moralizing speeches and fictitious dialogues in historical chronicles such as the *Discourses of the States* (*Guoyu*), almost entirely devoted to the audiences of sovereigns, ministers, and counsellors in their various domains between the tenth and the fifth centuries BCE. Each and every one of these opening pages is situated in human history and claims to offer worthwhile instruction for the cultivation of the self, for the moral conduct of rulers or for the affairs of the state. Set against the singular stance of the *Zhuangzi* and its position in the intellectual landscape of its time, all these inaugural passages of masters' literature[45] reveal a family likeness. Putting the *Zhuangzi* next to other roughly coeval works commonly perceived as rival texts reveals underneath the prima facie diversity of the latter and their common basic assumptions about men and society.

Later in this first chapter, a dove and a cicada, talking animals as if taken from one of Aesop's fables, snidely mock the fabulous Peng-Kun creature.

The cicada and the little dove laugh at this, saying, "When we make an effort and fly up, we can get as far as the elm or the sapanwood tree, but sometimes we don't make it and just fall down on the ground. Now how is anyone going to go ninety thousand *li* to the south!"[46]

Unable even to rise above the trees, the two incredulous animals are only capable of making denigrating comments about other beings beyond their potential. The comments made by the idle duo drag the reader back to the heart of a socialized world, where common and categorical judgments rule. They offer a picture of ordinary men face to face with the authentic man who appears now and again throughout the book; not only do they echo the contrast between sophists and rhetoricians such as Hui Shi or Gongsun Long who stand as foils to the character Zhuangzi in certain episodes, but they may also illustrate the position of contemporary readers, who, reading the story of this solitary voyage across the universe, would be tempted to sneer at such an improbable and pointless scene.

In the end, we may wonder indeed if we occupy the position of the cicada and the dove, alarmingly blind to the movements of the world, or if Zhuangzi is merely raving and mystifying his readers. The theatrical metamorphosis of the fish into a bird taking flight, followed by the deprecating comments of the two petty cronies, puts the reader in an uneasy position: to trust the story of the metamorphosis would be absurd but to disbelieve it means joining ranks with the small-minded and the malicious. Is it precisely their kind of petty and slanderous talk that accounts for the initial fury (*nu*) of the bird taking flight and leaving the world?[47]

Conclusion

Unlike its contemporaries, The *Zhuangzi*'s use of the animal world does not serve the purpose of moral edification: it is on the contrary a vigorous attack on the social practices and moral values that passed for common standards. When the *Zhuangzi* touches upon the civilizing labor of the wise sovereigns of the past, it replaces the theme of the moral influence of royal virtue on the wild world with the notion of the destructive contamination by technical and moral artifices at every level of nature. Sovereigns who claim to impose their authority and laws on the whole world do not express a form of civilizing generosity but rather a hyperbolic egoism that reaches far beyond the boundaries of the human sphere. "So, this is how chaos prevails, obscuring the light of the sun and the moon above, arresting the vigour of mountains and rivers below, and upsetting the cycles of seasons in between. Insects that crawl and slither on the earth, creatures that fly and flutter, each one loses its nature: that shows how great is the chaos in the world caused by the quest for intelligence!"[48]

The rhetoric that holds that graphic inscriptions, musical sounds, and rhythmic movement are intrinsic to nature and, in consequence, far from having arbitrarily been invented by men, were simply derived from the animal world, was omnipresent in the Warring States' philosophical and political writings. These animals sonic and visual patterns were refined, ordered, and broadcast with a calculated echo-effect towards all living beings, thus morally affecting animals and taming man's bestial behavior. It was one of the stoutest arguments in support of the idea that absolute monarchy was a natural, necessary and beneficial institution. The *Zhuangzi* counters this discourse of legitimation by denigrating the attempts to infuse cultural and moral principles into the physical attributes of animals, reaffirming the irreducible otherness of the fauna, even as they fall prey to men's predatory appetites.

The bestiary of the *Zhuangzi* opens a perspective on political societies, but that is not all, nor is it merely a collection of obvious and overt allegories of human shortcomings. It shows how the themes and theses produced by all the different schools of early Chinese thought always come back to the same propositions about governing nature and the barely veiled need for violence to control the wild. The *Zhuangzi* is unique in its rejection of the socio-centric vision of the world and its attempt to imagine relationships between humans and animals from the standpoint of animals. From this perspective, the harm done to animals and the deformation of human nature shackled by standards of collective existence are inextricably entangled.

PART TWO

Humans versus Death

3

One Monster, Two Mortals, and Myriad Metamorphoses

"If I were a scribbler, I would produce a compendium with commentaries of the various ways men have died. Anyone who taught men to die would teach them how to live."[1] If this consideration of Montaigne from his first book of *Essays* can be taken for wise, then one has to admit that right from the start, most Chinese thinkers lost their way by parrying and denying death.

Confucius, traditionally regarded as the first of the masters, dodged the issue. "If you don't even know what life is, what could you possibly know about death?"[2] While Plato invented a philosophical approach to death with his description of the final hours of the condemned Socrates, pairing death with philosophy as one and the same art of liberating the soul from the body, the disciples and followers of Confucius reported that their master did not address questions concerning the afterlife, the supernatural or the strange and kept the spirits at a safe distance.[3]

The reluctance to take death seriously as a guide to life was shared by adversaries of the Confucian school. The Mohist school had much to say about death, but in a negative fashion: they railed against extravagant spending on funeral rites, demanded the abolition of the three-year mourning period owed to parents, argued in favor of the existence of ghosts and the survival of consciousness after death, and exhorted grave-diggers to bury corpses in deep cavities to prevent toxic emanations from rising to the surface and infecting the living. Despite these funeral obsessions, reflecting on the meaning of death as a personal event that affects daily decisions and actions was not on the agenda. Even the widespread interest in self-cultivation, which brought together the adepts of meditation, breathing or sexual techniques that were later folded into the precursor forms of Taoism, was focused entirely on the quest for increased vitality, inner strength and longevity. As for the supporters of authoritarian monarchy, traditionally referred to as Legalists, they were mostly addressing death from the perspective of punishment, exploring and exploiting the instinctive horror inspired by the perspective of suffering or dying in order to provide the ruler with an efficient means of mental pressure on his subjects.

From this vantage, it seems that in early China, the question of death as a personal event was to a great extent repressed. Yet, familiarity with death was inescapable, since the foundation of political legitimacy and the rationale of religious practices was the cult of the dead and the maintenance of mutually profitable relationships between the visible and the invisible. Many a member of the nobility supervised the building of his funerary chamber and kept his coffin at close range during his lifetime. In this regard, what matters most in death is the ritual transformation of the deceased into an ancestral spirit, the correct expression of grief according to one's social position and family relationship to the defunct person, and, accordingly, the construction of a consistent lineage uniting the living and the dead through an uninterrupted chain of sacrifices and duties.[4] In ancient religion, one never really dies as long as one is properly nurtured by one's descendants: the real disaster is to die unattended, to lack proper burial, and so to wander like a ghost in the obscure recesses of the world.

Although philosophical thinking appeared in China as early as the sixth century BCE, and then flourished throughout the Warring States era, the *Zhuangzi* was the first text to address the issue of death and the trials of existence—illness, mental anguish, exclusion, physical deformity—from the standpoint of the individual, bringing them together in spectacular portrayals and philosophical tales. The *Zhuangzi* teems with episodes concerning sickness, agony, ugliness, funerary rites or burials. In these stories, for the first time, death is discussed as a personal issue.

The richness of the conversations with the dying and the deformed provide accounts that recall Montaigne's obsessive, if not Christianly morbid, curiosity about death: "and there is nothing about which I inform myself more happily than the death of men: what words, what looks, what expression they had; nor episodes in histories to which I pay more attention." Let us consider for a moment the precision of Montaigne's terms: they may serve as a first foothold in the exploration of the Chinese discourse (and this in spite of Montaigne's Christian perspective which radically diverges from the *Zhuangzi*'s take on death). The author of the *Essays* writes that he was in the habit of having, "not only in the imagination, but continually, death on his lips"; he experienced "the need to digest this resolve to die" and the wish that death should "lodge in the mind of a man of understanding."

Subject to a similar fascination with death as Montaigne, and also suffering from the same preoccupation with finding a way to confront it, to be reconciled with the inevitable and to relieve its tragic implications, Zhuangzi comes at it from all sides through stunning dialogues between the living, the wounded, the dying, and the dead. No writing in China had ever gone so far in the attempt to bring the reader so close to death as a personal experience. It was surely the strongest response there had ever been to the question until the introduction of Buddhism several centuries later. Now let us discover what these tales are really all about:

Master Si, Master Yu, Master Li and Master Lai were chatting together, all wondering: "Who can make his skull from non-being, his spine from life and his arse from death? He who understands that death and life, subsistence and destruction are one and the same, I'll have him as my friend!"

The four then looked at each other and burst into laughter; seeing that they kept nothing from each other, they became friends.

Not long afterwards, Master Yu fell ill and Master Si came to enquire after him. Yu said to him: "Wonderful! Now the Creator is making me into this bent and squat thing!" There he was, warped, crippled, hunchbacked, his guts tangled up, his chin buried in his navel, his shoulders overlooking his head, the bones of the neck pointing skywards and his Yin and Yang wandering all over the place. But his heart was at rest, unfazed; he staggered over to the well, and looking down at his reflection exclaimed: "My word! So, the Creator is making me into this bent and squat thing!"

Master Si asked him: "Don't you feel any aversion?"

"Of course not! What cause would I have for aversion? If he gradually changes my left arm into a cockerel, I'll use it to announce daybreak; if he changes my right arm into a crossbow, I'll use it to dine on roast barn owl; if he changes my buttocks into wheels and my spirit into a horse, then I'll have them as a mount: no need for a carriage! What one gains in this way depends on the moment; when we lose something, we are only following the course of things; when we remain peaceful in the moment, taking part in the course of things, neither affliction nor joy can make their way in us: it is what used to be called "letting go of one's ties" and if one cannot let go, then one is shackled by things. But the fact that things cannot prevail over Heaven is something we have known all along: why would I feel any aversion?"

Not long afterwards Master Lai fell ill; he was gasping, panting and about to die. His wife and children were weeping by his bedside. Master Li appeared, seeking news of his friend and cried: "Shoo! Off with you! You're disturbing the transformation!"

He leaned against the door and began to speak to Master Lai. "Marvellous, this play of moulding and remoulding! What will he do with you next? Rat's liver? Bug's leg?"

Master Lai answered: "A child always obeys his father and mother, North, South, East or West, he goes wherever they tell him. But does one not owe even more to the Yin and the Yang than to one's father and mother? If they put me at death's door and I pretend not to hear, it is only unruliness on my part, no crime of theirs! The earth—this great clod—burdens me with a body, tries me with life, relaxes me with age, rests me with death: that which made my living good is also that which makes my dying good. So, if a master founder working with metal in fusion should see the metal leap up and cry out: "I must be made into a legendary sword!" for sure, the founder would take it to be a truly inauspicious metal. Just because once, by chance, we found ourselves taking a human shape, we started yelling: "I must remain human, human!"—surely the Great Transformer would consider us to be a very inauspicious someone. But if we consider the universe as a huge furnace, and the play of transformations like a master founder, where couldn't we go?"

Forthwith he fell asleep, and suddenly awoke.[5]

It is worth pausing to reflect on the remarkable change that was taking place at this point in the history of the representation of death in China with this short philosophical tale, one of the most perplexing in the *Zhuangzi* (also one of the most transgressive). By picking over all the details of this story, one can find several of the themes familiar from Western traditions of thought: the happy and unconditional affirmation of becoming, forgetfulness of the self in favor of the intuition of one's vital activity, an aesthetic of the shapeless and the monstrous, or the pre-eminence of forces over forms, or of nothingness over being. Lastly, there is the primordial idea that death, deformity, and meditation follow a common pattern, since all tend to disunite or detach the spirit from the physical self.

A disconcerting accord

A quartet of like-minded fellows are having an amusing discussion opening with a question that is poised between metaphysical eloquence and bawdy humor: "Who can make his skull from non-being, his spine from life and his arse from death? He who understands that death and life, subsistence and destruction are one and the same, I'll have him as my friend!" This initial question is not raised to test the level of knowledge attained by each of the participants, but rather to seek in one another a readiness to *organize oneself* according to the understanding of the working of the vital principle in all things; a way of *constituting oneself* by integrating the forces of generation and destruction working inside the intimate texture of every breathing being. The four friends are asking themselves who among them can transcend the customary duality of life and death and grasp the intuition that both are intertwined from the outset in the contexture of all things. As Montaigne has it: "Death is one of the attributes you were created with; death is a part of you; you are running away from yourself; this being, which you enjoy, is equally divided between death and life."[6] The challenging question raised by the four is thus suggesting a way of putting oneself back together again, of joining up with the forces that escape us in the visible world where substance, stability, and solidity appear to hold out against the forces of mutation. "Make his skull from non-existence" is a playful wording for intimating the possibility of freeing oneself from the perspective imposed by individual consciousness; it is an invitation to remain open to the dimension of emptiness that underlies the constant creation and transformation of things, to take oneself to a state of non-thought, of absolute unknowingness (a practice the *Zhuangzi* calls "fasting the mind."[7]) Human life is viewed as a phenomenon of condensation of vital energy into a particular form, and is associated with the spinal column as the central, most solid and concrete element of the human body, in contrast to death, itself viewed as a phenomenon of dissolution of energies, therefore associated with excretion and vacuity ("make his arse from death"). This builds up what the next part of the tale enlarges upon: the primacy of non-being and the sovereignty of the Void over the visible world.

It is meaningful that the inaugural question in the present story is not attributed to any one particular character. This should even be taken as a decisive element, although it almost necessarily escapes notice at a first reading. It is a question posed by the four in chorus, arising from the spontaneous unison among them. Unlike the collections of wise sayings produced by other philosophical traditions and put under the name of one or another eminent master, here there is no one particular master preaching to his entourage and indirectly to the readers; only life-style companions who have entered into the friendly reciprocity of a collective being-there.

Neither is it a coincidence that this first statement about life and death subordinates this "universal truth" to a call for friendship: "He who understands that death and life, subsistence and destruction are one and the same, I'll have him as my friend!" By first couching the proposition in a tone of rowdy questioning and then making it an occasion for friendship, the *Zhuangzi* avoids using the sententious tone in these observations on life and death. "The four then looked at each other and burst into laughter; seeing that they kept nothing from each other, they became friends." There is neither response, nor any debate among the masters. The result of their spiritual complicity is not expressed in words, but in shared laughter.

It is, as we shall see, the personal life of each of these masters that confirms their unison. The two events that follow, the terrible deforming illness of Master Yu and the agony of Master Lai, are critical in that they vindicate their likeminded and daring views on life and death.

As if this question posed in the guise of philosophical badinage also contained an element of self-fulfilling prophecy, two of the companions then undergo a radical change, both introduced in the same fashion, using the same stylistic temporal abbreviation with the effect of bringing these two crucial events closer together. "Not long afterwards, Master Yu fell ill," then "Not long afterwards, Master Lai fell ill." These two rapid ellipses immediately concentrate the spotlight on the death scene, recording "live" by the bedside, reporting "on the spot" how it feels to pass away.

The vitality of agony

The two friends, Yu and Lai, incarnate in the literal sense the good-humored philosophical stance that sealed their first meeting. Their two companions, Si and Li, each have a role as witness. But far from adapting themselves to the ritual attitudes and codified expressions expected at the moment of death, their manner is jovial and detached, showing that they hold on to their shared understanding of life and death, and that they have organized their thoughts and moods accordingly. The four friends, the dying and those in attendance, desocialize death, dismiss its funerary and macabre dimension, treating it merely as a universal power of transformation.

Master Yu is the first to fall ill. His body becomes deformed in a spectacular and appalling way. He is bent, twisted, withered and compacted by the grip of forces conspiring to generate new forms of life at the expense of his shattered body.

> There he was, warped, crippled, hunchbacked, his guts tangled up, his chin buried in his navel, his shoulders overlooking his head, the bones of the neck pointing skywards, his Yin and Yang wandering all over the place, but his heart was at rest, unperturbed.

With this surprising panoramic shortcut, the *Zhuangzi* evokes all the ills of age and sickness. The travails of disfigurement and necrosis are raised to heights of horror and burlesque in an arresting illustration of the aforementioned idea that life and death, subsistence and destruction, form one whole. The fundamental structures of corporeality are violated in the most humiliating manner through this hyperbolic and accelerated transformation. Master Yu, whose vital breaths are freeing themselves from his body to take on another form, exclaims twice in astonishment at what is happening to him. "He staggered over to the well, and looking down at his reflection exclaimed: 'My word! So the creator is making me into this bent and squat thing!'"

The crucial moment when the sick Master Yu trudges toward the well[8] and glimpses the hideous creature he has just become does not alter his *amor fati*, nor does it undermine his fascination with the life-process. When Zhuangzi gives his character a repeat phrase before and after the "test of the mirror," it may be to indicate that while receiving glaring evidence of his new monstrosity, he has successfully tested his ability not to be affected by events, radical as they may be.[9] Personal experience of a rapid physical deformity may well be the supreme ordeal to gauge the extent of one's unconditional assent to life when it gives precedence to force over form, event over structure, symptom over substance, or metamorphosis over personal identity.

One of the friends, Master Si, comes along to seek news of his companion, and, after offhandedly dismissing the family standing in tears by his bedside, riled as he is by all this noxious pathos, he doesn't show any compassion or sympathy for his dying friend. He has emancipated himself from any sense of obligation to display affection or affliction, and he questions his dying friend with curiosity. "Does that disgust you?" Whoever remains in a state of ordinary consciousness, whoever is subject to feelings that separate death from life, can only feel hate and horror for this monstrous ending. Master Si tests his companion's capacity to face the challenge that forms the basis of their friendship ("making his skull from non-being, making his arse from death, understanding that subsistence and destruction are one and the same"). And it appears that in its most violently disfiguring phase, one can still remain quiet, and even provokingly witty.

Let us consider how Master Yu's deformity is described: his back hunched, his guts protruding, his chin in his navel, his shoulders higher than his head. These extravagant effects of physical degeneration recreate a curved posture, curling the invalid into an almost fetal position. The beginning of human life at its embryonic stage and the end of individual existence, with deformity all round, coincide in the image of Master Yu's amorphous body. Even so, he does not try to resist what is happening. Instead of wanting to maintain what little human shape he still hasn't lost, he blissfully anticipates the feel of his future outlines:

> What is horrible about it? If he gradually changes my left arm into a cockerel, I'll use it to announce daybreak; if he changes my right arm into a crossbow, I'll use it to dine on roast barn owl; if he changes my buttocks into wheels and my mind into a horse, then I'll have them as mount: no need for a carriage!

By making clownish conjectures about his future metamorphosis, Master Yu shows himself determined to behave in a resolute manner whatever his new shaping. Instead of resisting destruction, he seizes this very critical moment which would exacerbate pathos in most men, as a time to manifest his unswerving assent to life to the detriment of his individual self. In the process of becoming monstrous, at the same time Yu is freeing himself: "his Yin and Yang wandering all over the place, but his heart was at rest, unperturbed." Not only is he expelling all preoccupations related to his earthly shape, but he also appears elated and ecstatic at the idea of contemplating within himself a live performance of the great Founder and to experience the surge of primordial forces that are bearing him away.

"What lives has always lived and always will. The only difference I know between death and life is that at present, you live as one mass, and that once dissolved, scattered into molecules, twenty years from now, you will live in detail," says Diderot[10] who suggests a random mutation in the universe. The *Zhuangzi* likewise makes clever use of conjecture, and infuses the core of its discourse with *imaginary puissance* in order to evoke the infinite proliferation of natural forms. What is at stake here is a shared understanding of how things work in nature, a kind of understanding that can unite two people without binding them to each other simply because it is based on an intuition of a universal law of transformation which operates via alternating states of connection and disconnection. Grieving over the altered body of a dying friend would mean a betrayal of the awareness of the way things function, which was precisely the "cosmic pact" of their merry friendship.

Master Yu's imaginative and humorous riff on the transformations suffered by his body proves that his vitality remains intact. There is something Dionysian in the way he confronts the forces of death: with his exultant repartee, he seems to ride away from the death throes, and settles his final moment not with rational arguments but with striking, jokey images.

Master Yu also evokes certain circumstantial considerations, describing what is happening to him like a dénouement, unhindered by any notion of finality. Surrendering to the law of transformation *is what used to be called "detaching oneself from one's ties"; the person who fails in this regard is bonded by things.* As an illustration of the ordinary human condition, the *Zhuangzi* uses the image of a condemned man, lashed and suspended. This type of punishment, perhaps imaginary (at least it is not historically documented in official sources for the period) shows the extent of the subservience of the mind to the world of external things. Unconditional attachment hamstrings the free-flowing process of natural life, by substituting an ersatz for that immediateness, that immediateness of desire and appetites that hold us and rivet us to things. The exacting logic of sensations, combined with the desire to maintain one's being in the same state, detracts from our capacity to give an unperturbed response to whatever may happen. Death and sickness are then considered as an attack on us. To unfasten one's ties means, on the contrary, to stop holding fast to the *personal life* we have experienced so far, and to let our individual identity be swirled away into a new being. When understood properly, death and meditation always work together, both moving in reverse, leading to the formless, to the stage of the world where there are no shapes, sounds or colors (*wu*), a state of Void embodied by Master Yu as his physical form is gradually annihilated and his mind gradually disencumbered.

Death and the demiurge

Following the description of Master Yu's monstrous deformities, the second scene is a tranquil deathbed sequence with Master Lai surrounded by his family. In keeping with Master Yu's disposition, ready to leave this life, speculating jovially on the grotesque shapes that his vital stuff (*qi*) might take once it has been recast, Master Lai's passing also shows a clear absence of sadness and pathos, which in a similar manner contributes to the de-dramatization of death. We hear no words of solace, no sign of hope for a cure, no expectation of a continued personal conscience after death.

Master Li comes to the bedside of his dying friend. The wife is weeping at his side, surrounded by their children in attendance on the agony of their father. Whether this lamentation only conforms to standard ritual, or means genuine sorrow, the story does not say, but it makes no difference since all such arrangements or ritualized behavior render death unauthentic, viewing it from the angle of an exclusive attachment to a world seen as a collection of individual beings and things. Unlike Confucius, who denounced the distance between true feelings and their formal expression,[11] Zhuangzi considered both attitudes as evidence of the lack of true understanding of change and transformation.

So Master Li suddenly bursts in and expels the family, reproaching them with a "Now then! Off with you! You're disturbing the transformation!" His bluntness may seem shocking and his attitude odious at such a time. This impression of vehemence corresponds to the clash between two visions of death. Where the family can only mourn the demise of the master of the house and the crumbling of the central stanchion of the family, Master Li, leaning cheekily into the room where his friend is agonizing, is curious to observe a fascinating spectacle. He seems to ignore the basic feelings of empathy which make us humans, as if he had completely relieved himself of the perspective of the individual self; that is precisely why in the end he is the only one able to accompany Master Lai as far as the gates of death, whereas the keening of his family aims to retain the dying man, "keeping him on the hook" in this world, with the risk of awakening the feelings that are part of his human form, making him forgetful of the invisible forces that have created his "form"; these lamentations by the deathbed even mean that the dying man might resist transformation just when he should be most aware of the change taking place and receptive to the labors of an imminent metamorphosis.

Just like his former companion Master Yu, in his long rejoinder to the teasing remarks of Master Li, Master Lai relies on an image of a punishment to describe the feelings of a man who refuses to give in to death, as if Nature has decided to terminate him. "If they (the Yin and the Yang) put me at death's door and I pretend not to hear, it is only stubbornness on my part, no crime of theirs!"[12]

At first sight, the text provides generous information about the *Zhuangzi*'s conceptions of the afterlife: in the two dialogues the author even appears to be sketching the outline of a sort of genesis of the cosmos in parallel with a theology. The friends who are together on the threshold of life are invoking all kinds of cosmic powers and agents to describe what is happening to them. Master Yu speaks of the "creative principle" (*zaowu zhe*, literally "that which creates beings"; the indeterminate nature of the agent is knowingly maintained in Chinese by the particle *zhe* which can refer either to a thing or a person). Master Li evokes the expression "creation-transformation" (*zaohua*)—an expression coined by the *Zhuangzi* and long-lived in the philosophical tradition—to describe the process of emergence and annihilation of beings, the immanent dynamic of the universe. Master Lai talks of Yin and Yang, notions that were borrowed from nascent cosmology. He also spins the metaphor of the "Great (master) Founder" (*da ye*), having evoked "the Earth, this great Clod" that "burdens me with a body," in reference to both an entirely immanent process and a transcendent event.

> So, if a master founder working with metal in fusion should see the metal leap up and cry: "I must be made into a legendary sword!" for sure, the founder would take it to be a truly unfavorable metal. Just because once, by chance, we found ourselves taking a human shape, we started yelling: "I must remain a man, a man!"—then surely the Great Transformer would consider us to be a very unfavorable someone. But if we consider the universe as a huge furnace, and the play of transformations like [the art of] a master founder, where couldn't we go?

The evocation of a craftsman god who forges beings is something hitherto unknown and completely unheard of in Chinese thought. This demiurge god could be considered to be a precious link with Greek thought (such as Empedocles' metaphors concerning craftsmen used to describe the demiurgic works of Aphrodite, or Plato's *Timaeus* who, in the evocation of the crafts of casting and alloy, also mentions the divine art of the demiurge creating the world, or Aristotle for whom nature works like a painter or a sculptor). And yet, any attempt to merge the *Zhuangzi* with ancient Greek thinkers from this perspective should be cut short: the figure of a god-person does not "set." It is merely a metaphor with no follow-on, waiting to be swiftly reabsorbed rather than initiate a myth, because this founder of metals is to be immediately assimilated with the impersonal play of the cosmic forces that produce all living things. The figure of the divine artisan-craftsman only stands for an entirely natural process of the Yin and Yang. There is no fundamental analogy to be found between the product of artificial activity and spontaneous production, or between the natural process and human action.

However, these images of the master founder and his furnace merit closer attention, for although they are not the basis of a myth, they are used as a subtle reference to an old story narrating human beings cast into metal forms.[13] In his surrender to the fictile forces that are deforming him, Master Yu behaves like metal in a state of fusion. Instead of seeing himself as sick or suffering, he describes himself in natural terms as being remodeled by nature. Metallurgy, or the art of the forge, offers, in ancient myths of sovereignty, a "creationist" model, and a paradigm of transformation expressed in the union of the male and female principles.[14] In a literal translation, the reply of the enraged metal as it leaps like a flame from a blowtorch would be: "I absolutely must be made into a Mo Ye!" Here the *Zhuangzi* turns the legend of the Mo Ye's sword upside down. So, who is Mo Ye? The legend begins with Gan Jiang, the metalworker, who is unable to make swords because his furnace is not hot enough. His wife, Mo Ye, asks her husband about the reason for his failure and he explains: "One day when my master was unable to smelt iron ore he went right into the furnace with his wife and succeeded in casting the metal... Today I have had no success in my attempts to forge swords. Are we not in a similar situation?" Mo Ye replies: "So your master understood that one must melt a body to obtain the same result."

In one of the versions of this legend, Gan Jiang's wife, Mo Ye, throws herself into the furnace and as he pulls the sword from the fire, he gives it her name. Yin and Yang have mingled their life-breath to activate the casting. Marcel Granet concludes: "Might not the Chiefs be smiths and metalworkers who, by officiating at the mysterious wedding of metals, have gained the command of men and Nature, the power to fecundate the world and survey its wellbeing?"[15] An admirable pioneer in the deciphering of these myths, Granet explains that "tempering a sword was likened to a union between water and fire" (i.e. between Yin and Yang). "Fire is male, water female"[16]. No doubt the author of our story was well aware that with the name of Mo Ye he was reviving the myth of a person who makes possible the creation of a sword by sacrificing her human form. Her personal sacrifice recalls the name of Master Si, whose literal translation is "Master Sacrifice" (Si is not a common name, it is made up for the purpose of the story). Only by keeping this mythical background in mind can the reader rightly interpret the demand cried out by the metal in fusion still clinging to its former condition ("I must be made into a Mo Ye!"). Granet explains that swords, as gender-related metal concretions, are considered to be one of a pair always in search of union and then remaining faithful to each other. "Alloy is the result of an alliance: it is a marriage rite."[17] The recrimination voiced by the metal, apart from expressing both desire for fame and the pretention of giving orders to the creator-transformer about the choice of future existence, can be read as the symptom of a sentimental attachment to a previous form of life, just when the transformation requires that affect and individuality be put aside. "The earth—this great clod—burdens me with a body, then tries me with life, relaxes me with age, rests me with death." The earth, whose cosmic role is somewhat depreciated by the strange expression "this great clod," is as much a body acting on an equal footing with Heaven, like Yin and Yang, as a concretion, like the material objects on its surface. Birth, labor, rest, and re-absorption: this is the order of the natural course of things, continuous, necessary, indivisible and equal from beginning to end. The tragedy is that individual consciousness, riveted to its identity and to the valorization of certain moments in the lifecycle over others, tends to divide, and insulate all these various phases, whilst ignoring the dynamic current circulating through them. "That which made my living good is also that which makes my dying good." That is to say, life and death are the heads and tails of transformation, neither one can be removed without carrying away the other. Subsistence and destruction are woven into the same fundamental fabric of vital energy whose various productions are only phases in the continuous life-process.

The *Zhuangzi* says all this without emphasis, without weightiness, in a vivid and colorful way. The author purposely enjoys confusing the levels of explanation, multiplying metaphors and notions either borrowed from various different domains or invented by himself ("creation-transformation," *zaohua*, or the demiurge figure of the blacksmith). It is as if he wishes to foreclose the establishment of a doctrinal discourse. The intriguing metaphors and forged expressions voiced by the two dying friends turns their last words into lessons full of humor, far removed from wise sermons and moral litanies that normally accompany the moment of death.

Here, for example, is how Master Lai commits himself to death. "A child always obeys his father and mother, North, South, East or West, he goes wherever they tell him. But does one not owe even more to the Yin and the Yang than to one's father and mother? If they put me at death's door and I pretend not to hear, it's only bravura on my part, no crime of theirs!" In a family-centered and hierarchically-structured society as was ancient China, each member of the group had a role to learn and to perform. Rituals taught a person how to be a mother, or a wife, or an eldest son. Children not only had lifelong duties to their parents and to their family including their ancestors, but they were also supposed to maintain these ties of obligation. Community ethics drew directly on these family-centered values. Here, the *Zhuangzi* enjoys providing a "good reason" for dying that reposes on a Confucian-style argument while completely distorting its meaning. Master Lai embarks on a cosmic extension of virtuous behavior dictated by an unconditional submission to parental authority. Thus, submission to the law of transformations is presented as a duty dictated by filial piety: the true progenitors are the Yin and the Yang, the male and female cosmic energies, whose interaction engenders life-forms; a pious and loving son must strictly follow their orders towards the destination they indicate.

The *Zhuangzi* directs its shafts against the guardians of rituals and in particular the school of Confucius, inveighing against a lofty principle that lies at the core of early religion and social norms. Many textual sources dating from the Warring States period clearly show that crippled or disabled people were excluded from ritual ceremonies or political functions. The *Zhuangzi* teems with stories about people who underwent legal amputation and characters with deformed bodies whom it hails as enviable, successful or flourishing human beings.[18] In Chapter 5, a certain Wang Tai, although he has had a foot amputated, as punishment for criminal wrongdoing, attracts as many disciples as Confucius, if not more, so that the master is forced to play second fiddle to him. Another anecdote puts us in presence of Ai Taituo (Chapter 5), whose hideous physical appearance is combined with a mysterious ability to charm women, who declare they would rather be the concubine of such a man than the principal wife of anyone else. In Chapter 4, we meet Zhilishu or Uncle-Distorted, who, having luckily undergone the same deformation as Master Yu, avoids going to war on account of his disability and even receives an allowance from the state. The hunchback Yinqi Zhili Wuchun (Chapter 5), with no lips and twisted feet, is the favourite adviser of Duke Ling of Wei; and Wengyang Daying , who has a jar-shaped goiter on his neck (Chapter 5), is the favorite advisor of Duke Huan of Qi.

Now, to return to our story, Master Yu's and Master Lai's words and behavior imply that it is not necessary to do one's utmost to maintain one's body whole and intact until the moment of death in order to serve deceased parents. The wise thing to do is to accept deformity as a result of the action of our true and authentic progenitors, the natural powers, the Yin and Yang, even when these forces twist and distort a human shape or transmogrify it into a monster. This submission to the order of Nature, portrayed in an episode so closely associating death and monstrosity, also undermines the ethical significance of mutilation as a corporal punishment inscribed in the law, because the physical re-form[19] to mark the condemned for the rest of their lives (amputation of feet, hands, nose or ears) draws its punitive meaning from the aesthetic and moral requirement for physical wholeness. As stated above, the Chinese term for both wrongdoing and offence suffered, zui, crime and punishment, is used by Master Lai to exculpate the natural forces that twist, bend, and dislocate his body in every possible way.

The process of joining up with death, experienced without fear or scandal, has no need for arguments; it is part of the immediate assent to the flux of life. When a man dies, it is not life that is dying, it is only a person saying, "this life of mine," it is the individual saying "me." In these dialogues about disease, agony, and death, there is never any postulating the permanence of a personal identity, no stakes on any preservation of individual consciousness. These would be absurd pretentions, mocked by the image of the furnace where everything will be melted down and then reshaped under the hammer wielded by the master of the forge. Master Yu is even jovially anticipating a further step in the process of transformation that has already turned him into a creeping, crawling monstrosity. He has understood that beings circulate within each other, just as Diderot says, and that every animal is more or less a man, more or less a plant. "To be born, to live, to pass away, this is a change of form—and where is the importance of one form rather than another?" *Le Rêve de d'Alembert* [20] says in echo to this story.

The idea of protecting oneself from death is derided via the description of the absurdly pretentious metal as it remonstrates at not being forged into Mo Ye. With their preposterous imaginings and buffoonery, they prevent the common attitude *against* death from taking hold. Far from trying to resist the outer forces of deformity, they seem to welcome the disintegration of their individual selves and do not cower in fear at the idea of becoming matter and material for new *generations*.

Forms and forces

It is not the perspective of one's personal death, but the demise of a parent, along with the complete array of appropriate procedures that provides the basis of discourses on death in early China. Discussed and codified on a social level, overshadowed in its subjective understanding to the benefit of a convoluted discourse regarding funeral ritual and mourning prescriptions, in the ancient ritual records and in masters' literature, death is a theme for ratiocination on social virtues and display of expertise in liturgy. [21]

The *Zhuangzi* talks about death in a way that neither Confucius, nor the Ritualists who followed in his footsteps were able to do. [22] Dying becomes an experience that reveals the health of one's vital condition, which consists not in the mere absence of illness, but in a healed mind that does not consider sickness or disappearance to be an ill. This presupposes transgressing the framework of a consciousness where there is a clear-cut division between life and death, where death is regarded only as terrifying, sorrowful, and hateful. In the *Zhuangzi*, death is explored as an occasion of a happy intimateness with the source of life; it invents a way of dealing with one's own demise through characters that stoke admiration and perplexity for their ready acceptance of universal change. There is no need to depreciate life in order to accept death, nor to put stakes on the afterlife to find consolation for loss of life. The serene good temper and the self-deprecating mood displayed by the two dying friends is not founded on contempt for earthly existence any more than on hope for salvation of the soul.

Having read this text more closely, the reader is almost sure to have noticed certain tensions, apparent paradoxes and perhaps even a fundamental incoherence. That the law of ceaseless transformations, the law of alternation of emptiness and plenitude should affect every living being is one thing; that a man may anticipate what he is to become as if he were still going to be there after death is something else entirely.

> "If he gradually changes my left arm into a cockerel, I'll use it to announce daybreak; if he changes my right arm into a crossbow, I'll use it to dine on roast barn owl; if he changes my buttocks into wheels and my mind into a horse, then I'll have them as mount: no need for a carriage!"

As careful readers, we naturally understand that the consciousness, the appetites, and the thoughts of Master Yu will no longer be there to enjoy the aptitudes of the beings or things that he will have become: so isn't the *Zhuangzi* evading the question of death in the first person? One is justified in asking whether it is a weakness, or indeed a strength, of the *Zhuangzi*'s discourse on death to shift it from a personal experience to an impersonal and indifferent event. And what should one make of attachment to others, of the feelings of love or friendship that tie us to those who are suddenly separated from us by death? Isn't the author being rather impetuous in his portrayal of these two eccentrics unperturbed by the thought of leaving everything?

The *Zhuangzi* never attempts to impose any definitive discourse on death—it evokes a miscellany of optimal manners with which to approach one's finiteness, an attitude that can neutralize the inborn fear caused by the perspective that one's end is ineluctable. It is not so much about learning to reason with death as about getting ready to transform one's typically human sensitivity and free it from any aversive mood. To accept Master Yu's imaginative soliloquy on the shapes he will be wearing in the future, without being duped by his humor or his self-mocking tone, one must adopt the somewhat counterintuitive perspective in which these masters are placing themselves to face their own death. The one who says: if I am changed into a horse "*I* will gallop with no harness" or if I become a cross-bow "*I* will dine on roast barn owl," obviously is not so much referring to his personal consciousness or his own individual identity, as to the vital energies that are about to take another shape. The future transformation is envisaged from the point of view of Nature as an active principle (*natura naturans*), which the *Zhuangzi* calls Heaven (*tian*), and not of natural things continually produced and bound to disappear (*natura naturata*).

Perhaps more radically, via this fantasia on the "I," Zhuangzi is suggesting the unreality of the individual subject in regard to the only true agent, Nature, as if every individual were a *fiction* understood in the proper etymological sense, a figment subject to the play of moulding and remoulding by the master founder. In a paradoxical turn recurrent in the *Zhuangzi*, lucidity about life and mortality finds its expression in verbal delirium, when the dying master is identifying himself with the endless metamorphoses of this energy, taking sides with the vital force against that of individual form, or, to use another expression in the *Zhuangzi*, that of Heaven over that of Man, always inclined to resist the relentless forces of change.

The *Zhuangzi*'s sense of humor and its understanding of the alternating rhythms of life neutralize the tragic vision of human finiteness. Dying does not signify "the end," any more than a silence or a rest in a musical score interrupts a melodic line; "dying" is just "going," "passing," it is no longer the obverse of life, much rather its reconstituting moment. I see no good reason to believe, however, that the authors were not well aware that the mind is confronted with the fundamental contradiction between primitive unity and individuation, between individual will and universal necessity, between affirmation of life and the suffering of the self as witness to its own passing. They just do not attempt to resolve these contradictions in a broader synthesis, to find a higher unity for them, for there is no need to seek justifications or reasons for life. The so-called reasons evoked by the two dying men are so firmly associated with the "divine delirium" of speech that they are imbued with the same rhetoric as the initial banter of the four companions.

If a person establishes a disjuncture that severs life from death and that places him in a defined order, he will also suffer from a pathological tendency to consider any transformation as aggression and as a personal attack on his individual form. It is not death that should be considered as the opposite of life: it is the self that is the opposite of vital activity, despite the fact that this is the same dynamic that engendered the human being that *I* have been for a time: "whatever makes living a good thing is also what makes dying good."

Beyond the event of death, the *Zhuangzi* focuses attention on the invisible, silent life-force, that has nothing to do with what we call the soul, and that is precisely what will be carried off and become a crossbow or develop into a horse: in truth, in spite of the jocular and rhetorical turn of phrase, it is the cockerel and not Master Yu who will announce the day; it is the horse, and not Master Yu, who will be galloping without a carriage.

Death, illness, and meditation are all occasions to free oneself from the perspectives of individual identity and experience the flow of the unknown forces that are the alpha and the omega of our conscious existence. Although in early Chinese there was still no word to mean liberation, let alone a theoretical notion of freedom, the *Zhuangzi* teems with pioneering images, dynamic actions, and turns of phrases (traveling, roaming, flying, soaring high above, expanding in space) that invent, so to speak, freedom as the supreme existential value, as an optimal state fervently prized and sought by the key protagonists.

This state of freedom is the logical opposite of the human condition described at length in many chapters of the *Zhuangzi* where we see people grunting and panting under the burden of their own minds, launched to no avail in a frenzied race against each other, or restrained as in shackles and manacles by their own limited perspectives on the world, and finally choking and suffocating after squandering their breath or frittering their vitality in useless games. Freedom is discussed in the present story as deliverance, as a capacity to untie one's bonds, a way to remove oneself from "mental cramps," as Wittgenstein so aptly said.

But even before the experience of deformity and death, the *Zhuangzi* suggests how friendship can free one from the limitations of individuality. In the opening scene of this story, it is inextricably linked to the theme of full understanding of life and death. The individuality of the four characters was already absorbed by the way they committed themselves. They are gathered together as a collective presence that speaks for each and every one of them, and are defining a relationship of equality and reciprocity. No one *takes* the floor, the long question and the metaphysical statement voiced in direct speech emanate from their collective presence. And when they talk about life and death, their friendship cannot be seen as solidarity *against* the trials of fate. Their friendship is not to be confused with a fraternity facing a common anguish inspired by the inevitable, or with kinship-based closeness in the face of adversity (like that displayed by the wife and children of Master Lai). The four friends are unanimously inspired by the original resonance between death and life in every breathing being. By its ability to distance itself from the agitation of the heart, "that professional mourner" as Plato called it, by its joyous transgression of the ritual framework of funerary procedures, the *Zhuangzi* advocates the need to purge our minds from its sickly desire for immutability. We are bound to change until the point of loss of identity: there is a sort of fatalism here, but it takes the shape of active approval that places awareness of necessity as the opposite of defeatism, and in direct opposition to a notion of victory over death. In spite of the frightening stream of images adduced to illustrate the intractable process of transformation inside the body, the two agonizing fellows explain why they refuse to flinch at their last moment, as if by speaking in these terms they privately encouraged themselves to go forward.

Much as the many tales of death in the *Zhuangzi* may differ in tone or in spirit, they all attack, from various angles, the many tearful melodramas to be found in texts pertaining to the Confucian tradition. A quick comparison of the *Zhuangzi* stories with passages from Confucian literature can substantiate this: in the "Tan gong" chapter of the *Book of Rites* (*Liji*), Confucius is depicted weeping over the death of his disciple Zi You and kneeling, as if he were the father of the deceased, before those who come to present their condolences. The same chapter also shows Confucius bursting into tears when his disciples tell him that the mound he had ordered for his parents' tomb was washed away by torrential rain as soon as it had been raised. On another occasion, Confucius arrives unannounced in a feudal state where the funeral of a high-ranking official who had once offered him hospitality is taking place; he weeps and wails in sincere sorrow. Elsewhere, Confucius, aware of his imminent death, starts to sing in a loud vibrato, dragging his cane behind him: "Even the greatest mountain must crumble! Even the tie beam must break! Even the sage must waste away!"[23]

The reader has already been amused by Master Li bustling the wife and children away from Master Lai's bedside with a "Now then! Off with you! You're disturbing the transformation!" The end of Chapter 32, probably written by one of Zhuangzi's followers, portrays Zhuangzi himself in the final stages of his agony but still quick to scold the disciples wishing to give him a grand funeral. With sacrilegious panache he responds that Heaven and Earth will be his coffin, that the sun and moon will be his paraphernalia and ornaments and that he prefers to have his corpse left out in the open air to serve as fodder for birds rather than fattening earthworms below the surface. But this touches on another theme, the subject of ritual procedures for taming death, to be taken as the guiding line in the next chapter.

At the beginning of this chapter, I introduced a few themes and theses of the *Zhuangzi* by recalling some of the notable formulations of Montaigne in his *Essays*. There is much that positions Zhuangzi and Montaigne at close quarters: a philosophical and also emotional interest in animals, a common contempt for seriousness, a sense of ridicule, a close attention to the way subjective phenomena organize themselves in us, a sharp awareness of relativism along with a joyous assent of life, but also a persistent concern with the issue of death as a personal event. These all too sketchy parallels are also an opportunity to comprehend how a form of wisdom exempt from all the resources of philosophical reasoning was elaborated in early China.

The young Montaigne, drawing from the arguments of the Epicureans and Stoics, strives by all means to dissipate the fear of death: by scorning life, by calculating the advantages of dying in such and such a condition instead of surviving in another, by making the comparison between the actual brevity of the passage to non-life and the interminable fear of death. He also ponders on the fact that a long life and a short life are equalized in death, or by the consideration of the gradual change that operates in old age and makes the leap from being to non-being less difficult. The author of the *Essays* modulates his rhetoric between *reductio ad absurdum* and virile exhortation: "How absurd to anguish over our passing into freedom from all anguish!"[24] But although Montaigne says, "I want Death to find me planting my cabbages, neither worrying about it nor the unfinished gardening" (p. 99), he is unable to avoid a typically Stoic tension even though he is opting for flexibility; he cannot resist seeing death as an enemy that must deprived of all advantages, an enemy against which "no tempered steel can protect your shoulders; we must learn to stand firm and to fight it" (p. 96).

In the light of these passages—taken exclusively from the first book of the *Essays*—*Zhuangzi*'s singularity appears even more clearly. He doesn't subject death to the ordering of reason, but to the reign of the imagination, hence the constant recourse to fiction and literary jests.[25] Contrary to what these stories suggest at first sight, it seems that the *Zhuangzi* does not bother to develop any serious arguments for protection against the anxiety of finitude, and does not attempt to convince or drive the reader to a certain doctrinal position. Death is not faced or anticipated by one person alone, the death situations are associated with the four friends and then with the two pairs engaged in a dialogue: the joyous acquiescence to transformation only appears in a rhetoric of companionable provocation, and the interaction among the fellows (Master Yu and Master Lai, Master Si and Master Li, Zhuang Zhou and Hui Shi) spark a mood, a disposition, a frame of mind that achieve the process of liberation of the individual self. We are here miles away from the younger Montaigne's constant inner soliloquy, arming himself against the throes of his last hour.

In the *Zhuangzi*, consideration of the advantages that death brings is presented in a humorous mode. Rather than relying on the force of argument to subjugate death, or building up faith in a certain form of survival of the self or the soul, these tales draw their impact from the poetic virtue of dynamic imagery and a shared sense of playfulness, in the spirit of the four friends' initial oath: the point is not to have the last word against death, but to make the mind ready to undergo a radical transformation until the last stage, without demur, when the body turns topsy-turvy and the individual self can smell out its imminent disintegration. We may apply to Zhuangzi and his deathbed characters Maurice Merleau-Ponty's concluding formula about Montaigne: "He sought and maybe found the secret of being simultaneously ironic and solemn, faithful and free."[26]

4

Fun at the Funerals

In the previous chapter, we observed that the *Zhuangzi* brings into full view acts and moments that the Ritualists would discreetly place offstage, sometimes with a peculiar style touching on the grotesque and the outré. In the following stories, the *Zhuangzi* considers the event of death from the point of view of the bereaved.

Two bright sparks play a joke on a bigot

Master Sang Hu, Meng Zifan, and Master Qin Zhang met together and were chatting: "Who can assemble in the absence of assembly? Who can interact in non-interaction? Who can ascend into heaven, frolic in the clouds, leap and spring into boundless space, forgetting self and others for a life without end?" The three of them looked at one another and burst out laughing, and, as they kept nothing from each other, they became friends.

Master Sang Hu died shortly afterwards. Before the burial had taken place, Confucius heard the news and sent his disciple Zigong to attend the funeral. At the event, one of the friends of the deceased was improvising a melody, another was noodling an accompaniment on the zither, and both were singing in concert: "Ah! Sang Hu, ah, Sang Hu! You have now returned to the Authentic, whereas we, still human, must remain!" Zigong came up to them and said: "If you don't mind my saying so, is singing in front of the corpse really good manners?" The two men looked at each other and laughed: "Ha! What can he possibly know of good manners!"

Zigong went off to report to Confucius what he had seen and asked him: "Who on earth do they think they are? No manners and no education, they don't know how to behave and they sing away in the presence of the deceased without a care, it's unthinkable! Who are these people?"

Confucius replied: "Those men move beyond the rules of this world, while we move within the rules. Outside and inside cannot meet, but I was still silly enough to send you to present my condolences! Those men are already mingling with the creator of things, moving within the unique breath of Heaven and Earth; they consider life an excrescence, a protruding wart, and they regard death as the lancing of an abscess, the piercing of a pustule. How could they possibly know in which order one should place life and death? They lend themselves to the diversity of things while at the same time entrusting themselves to their common source; they forget their entrails, ignore hearing and sight, circulate endlessly from finish to start, unaware of either thresholds or frontiers. Indefinite and undecided, they wander beyond the filth and the dust of this world, free to frolic in the workings of non-action. Why would you want them to dull themselves in vulgar ritual, just to flatter the eyes and ears of the crowd?"

Zigong: "But in that case, Master, why would you respect these rules yourself?"

Confucius: "Because I myself am damned by Heaven; in the end, you and I have that in common."

Zigong: "May I then ask you about these rules?"[1]

Confucius: "Fish move together in water and men move together in the flow of things. As they move in the water, fish penetrate the hollows and the depths where they find sustenance; men who move in the flow of things, can secure their sustenance by remaining idle. That is why I say that 'fish forget themselves in lakes and rivers, and men in the way they cope with the flow and ebb of things.'"[2]

Then Zigong asked: "So in that case, if I may ask, what about 'the irregular man'?"

Confucius: "The irregular man is so for men, he is on a par with Heaven. Which is why we say:

Lowly for Heaven, princely for men
Princely for Heaven, lowly for men."[3]

Before interpreting this dialogue, let us summarize its main strands. Three friends are having a cheerful discussion about the possibility of associating without establishing ties, and wondering about establishing a bond of sympathy and friendship without binding themselves. Sometime later, one of them dies and at the wake, to the tune of a zither, the other two are improvising an unseemly song, venting their jealous admiration for the deceased and grieving over their own lot in this world. One of Confucius' most celebrated disciples, Zigong, has been sent to attend the funeral and present his master's condolences. Baffled by what he sees, he questions the two uncouth musicians, who quip back with sneering condescension. He then hurries off to report the situation to Confucius who gives an unexpected account of the two men's conduct and, with an arresting clarity, admits to his own shortcomings.

Using self-negating formulations ("Who can assemble in the absence of assembly? Who can interact in non-interaction? Who can ascend to heaven, frolic in the clouds, bound and leap into limitless space, forgetting the self and others for a life without end?"), the three men discuss how to invent a liberal friendship, maintaining mobile, discontinuous, floating ties instead of fixed, long-lasting attachments. To describe the singular nature of relationships that have been relieved of the ordinary affects that entangle people, the *Zhuangzi* expands the scope of language, forging a series of suggestive and novel expressions that must have appeared, from the point of view of logic, downright nonsensical.

The three assembled masters question their capacity to remain mobile and uninvolved with others and at the same time submerge themselves as one in the flow of things. In the Ritualist view of the world, every gesture and every word should be in conformity with the sense of the correct norms and the right forms. One can with good reason wonder why the *Zhuangzi* chose to resort to a character like Confucius to present the vision of free unfettered existence described in the next part of the story,[4] when we know that the historical Confucius would only talk about being together at a funeral in a ritual context that is formally shuttered, enclosed, and signposted, where the place and behavior of each person clearly define their limits, duties, and the degree of emotional intensity they are expected to display. In doing so, the *Zhuangzi* "saves" Confucius from his narrow-minded disciples, from his textual posterity. He severs the master's thoughts from what was to appear as his doctrinal legacy.

Why try to abandon the usual way of forming ties? Why is attachment felt as something unnatural? Because ties and links soon grow into formal duties and subjective attachments that hamper the ability to change and respond appropriately to what may affect us or happen to others. The readiness in the face of the unknown is constantly put at risk by this deep-seated disposition to form ties, which presents its virtues (loyalty, faithfulness, true friendship, deep affection, etc.) as superior to carelessness and forgetfulness. Nature, viewed as the spontaneous force that produces all things is in this sense the opposite of human nature. In the ways we express our concern towards others, maintain ties of friendships or carry out our duties to the dead, we restrict the action of the dynamic within us, we are moved by parasitic forces hampering the "mechanism of Heaven." The sudden demise of one of the three masters is the occasion in which the ethical attitude they all professed can be tested.

Questionable complaints

> Master Sang Hu died shortly afterwards. Before the burial had taken place Confucius heard the news and sent his disciple Zigong to attend the funeral. At the event, one of the friends of the deceased was improvising a melody, another played an accompaniment on the lute and both were singing in concert: "Ah! Sang Hu, ah, Sang Hu! You have now returned to the Authentic, whereas we, still human, must remain!"
>
> Zigong came up to them and said: "If you don't mind my saying so, is singing in front of the corpse really good manners?"
>
> The two men looked at each other and laughed: "Ha! What can he possibly know of good manners!"

In early China, one of the prescriptions in funeral ritual required the removal from the death chamber of all musical instruments (sometimes including the stand) and abstaining from playing or singing until the end of the mourning period.[5] But the two scoundrels are showing off their envy of the dead man's good fortune, singing about it to him and strumming a zither. As he enters the house, the devout Zigong is faced with this blatant outrage to ritual norms and, in a flush of indignation, he finds himself violating funerary etiquette as well:[6] he fails to greet anyone, forgets to prostrate himself before the corpse and starts speaking before he has been addressed, advising the two singers of their misbehavior. Lack of manners and disregard for etiquette are a moral outrage to someone as scrupulously observant as Zigong (as we see him, for instance, in the *Book of Rites*); no wonder then if the farcical, self-pitying deathbed song, in truth more camp than offensive, stokes his anger. The two men are lamenting the fact that they are still restricted to their bodily form whereas their lucky friend has been able to re-enter the original fountain of life, return to the great void and remove himself from this narrow human world. In contrast to this, Confucius never taught Zigong to reflect upon death itself.[7] Now with the portrayal of this imaginary Confucius, it is as if the *Zhuangzi* were creating an opportunity for the master to finally explain his sentiment about life and death taken as a whole, while also confessing to personal limitations as an educator and admitting to the failure of his own existence.

"If you don't mind my saying so, is singing in front of the corpse really good manners?" We can tell from the way Zigong turns his question that he makes an effort to keep a certain forbearance under the provocation and the impropriety of the two lads. The only response he gets is a cruel jeer, with a laughter that signals, as it usually does in the *Zhuangzi*, a spontaneous expression of jovial empathy. In a perfectly open manner, the two friends show that they are not at all grieved by the death of their friend. Their mourning song is just as much a provocation addressed to the embarrassed witness of their performance as a way of responding *in situ* to the original question of whether it is possible to frolic freely in the infinite without worrying about social obligations and duties towards others. They intend to show in a wittingly controversial way how death can be perceived otherwise than as loss and rupture. However, Confucius' words in reaction to this dramatic moment shine a clearer light; they are more reflective in tone than the facetious exhibition of the two companion singers.

Zigong went off to report to Confucius what he had seen and asked him: "Who on earth do they think they are? No manners and no education, they don't know how to behave and they sing away in presence of the deceased without a care, it's unthinkable! Who are these people?"

Zigong is completely nonplussed; he feels desecrated, sullied in the same way as the deceased is being defiled by this funeral masquerade. He hastens back to Confucius' reassuring presence, seeking the moral protection of the expert on ritual, the great man who had given ceremonial a quasi-magical value by revealing a perfect model for social cohesion behind the opulent pomp and decorum of such occasions. For Confucius, rites, appropriate behavior and the science of rank and precedence all come to the assistance of the mind in the practice of virtue. Confucius insists many a time on the importance of showing respect for rites and of feeling grief when required by circumstances: "The Master said: I cannot bear to see the person who in holding a high position is not tolerant, who, when performing rites, is not respectful, and who does not grieve in the mourning ceremonies."[8] How is it possible then to defend the jeering arrogance of the two masters performing a musical display in front of the corpse of their friend? Strangely, in this moment of moral crisis for Zigong, Confucius himself is going to plead their cause. As if Zhuangzi—or the anonymous author behind this funerary parody— was using the first clause of Confucius' statement only to turn it against his confuted disciple: "I cannot bear to see the person who in holding a high position is not tolerant." Historical sources[9] indicate that the intolerant Zigong portrayed here held important political office in the states of Lu and Wei and acted as an ambassador. It is not the least bit coincidental here that a man with great political and financial clout is depicted as an *intolerant ambassador* of Confucius at Sang Hu's wake. Confucius appears at this point about to display the esoteric facet of his teaching, by accepting to talk about things he had not allowed himself to mention in the *Analects*.

Confucius, pariah of Heaven. An implicit dialogue with the *Analects*

Although Confucius had elevated ritual conduct to the highest level of moral practice, here, in this fictional dialogue, he is widening his disciple's outlook by demonstrating that such attitudes, guided by the concern of correct behavior and constantly restrained by rules, can only serve as a model for the common man. He even goes further: he bemoans his own and Zi Gong's blundering blind-certainty and laments at the imprisonment they entail, so absolute that his closed-minded disciple does not even realize his personal condition "within the rules" (*fang zhi nei*).

On the contrary, when construing for Zigong the conduct of the two raffish fellows, Confucius seems to be speaking under a sudden flash of enthusiasm, giving an enchanting description of a vital force that had in fact always escaped him, he, who, according to his own words, had always been enmeshed by worldly customs and social considerations. The pariahs, the accursed, are himself and his disciple, and not the two companions rashly reproved by Zigong for going *beyond the pale* (*fang zhi wai*). In the *Analects*, Zigong mentions (perhaps in a tone of veiled complaint) that he was allowed to hear the master expound on matters concerning culture (*wen*) and its outward emblems and ornaments (*zhang*), but never on human nature or on the "ways of Heaven" (*tian dao*).[10] Now he is about to find himself the target of a startling sermon.

> Confucius replied: "Those men move beyond the rules of this world, while we move within the rules. Outside and inside cannot meet, but I was still silly enough to send you to present my condolences!

Then Confucius continues:

> ". . . Indefinite and undecided, they wander beyond the filth and the dust of this world, free to frolic in the workings of non-action. Why would you want them to dull themselves in vulgar ritual, just to flatter the eyes and ears of the crowd?"
>
> Zigong: "But in that case, Master, why would you respect these rules yourself?"
>
> Confucius: "Because I myself am cursed by Heaven; in the end, you and I have that in common."

We can hear a man well aware of his own limitations, aware of being hemmed in by standard notions of social decency, but delivering a passionate defence of a superior life free of all external rules. Confucius also confided bitterly in his *Analects*: "Labor lost! I will never have met a man able to recognize his own faults nor to be his own prosecutor."[11] Here, the *Zhuangzi* gives Confucius the role of the judge who, having heard about the behavior of the two companions, delivers a harsh verdict on his own misdemeanors. The Ritualists (*Ru*), who appear repeatedly in the *Zhuangzi,* are the favorite scapegoats. Alongside the narrow-mindedness of Confucius' disciples who are haunted by the necessity for meticulous respect of etiquette, the *Zhuangzi* here paints the portrait of a touching, sincere master, secretly gnawed by remorse, pessimistic about himself and his school, repentant of his limitations and fatalistic with regard to his destiny.

For Zigong, the response given by Confucius must come across as another hard blow. Having reported the egregious behavior of the two fellows, he is expecting Confucius to condemn it. But Confucius, showing a profile of himself so far unsuspected, gives his own spin on these two men whom he holds superior to himself. As if a repressed part of the master that had been seething for long finally rang out loud, resonating to that extravagance.

But perhaps even more humiliating for Zigong is to hear Confucius acknowledge that it was a stupid mistake to deputize someone of his ilk to attend the funeral. Indeed, Confucius' reaction can be construed not only as repentance for the intention to present condolences to people with no clue about the purpose of such a custom, but also for having had the idea of sending someone as unqualified and unprepared as Zigong.[12]

> Those men are already mingling with the creator of things, moving within the unique breath of Heaven and Earth; they consider life an excrescence, a protruding wart, and they think death is like the lancing of an abscess, the piercing of a pustule.

Confucius' choice of sordid words and sickly similes—clearly not in keeping with the decorum of Ritualists—convey an unhappy awareness of his own attachment to standards and rules that hold him captive in this nether world, in stark contrast to the elated loftiness of the dead man's singing and laughing companions.

> How could they possibly know a right order for placing life and death? They lend themselves to the diversity of things and at the

same time they are entrusting themselves through those things to the same common source; they forget their entrails, ignore hearing and sight, circulate endlessly from finish to start, unaware of either thresholds or frontiers. Indefinite and undecided, they wander beyond the filth and the dust of this world, free to frolic in the workings of non-action.

Confucius gives way to a poetic flight when evoking the fabulous life of the two heretics and he unspools cosmic images intimating a blissful state of abandon to the vital impetus, in oblivion of all morals. Such expressions have no need for didactic paraphrasing or conceptual elucidation. They are meant to dazzle and fire the inspiration of the reader—just like Zigong—and make them feel for an instant what a life devoid of mundane worries and existential anxiety would mean.

This eulogy on the powers deployed by the two "cosmic characters" can also be read as echoing their fabulous flights of imagination at the beginning of the tale as they solicit a new form of friendship via their provocative enquiries. Indeed, in the *Zhuangzi* Confucius is the tragic figure of impotency. He knows his shortcomings and he is also aware that he cannot get past them and enjoy the full dynamic of personal liberation. He accepts to remain in a world that is for him disenchanted by the awareness of a higher order he feels unable to reach but which he wistfully glimpses from afar. In this tale of a spoiled funeral, his confession is the one true threnody.

"Only Heaven understands me!" Confucius exclaims in the *Analects* (XIV.35). In the present dialogue, the master appears as damned, cursed, excluded, a pariah of Heaven. Confucius remains to the end on the human side, unable to alternate between the dual perspectives of Heaven and Man. Severed from the nourishing roots of life, he is the one who knows but cannot do. Has he always known this to be so? Has he suddenly become aware of it on hearing Zigong's report and taking stock of his situation? Is he now going to bring himself to change? This fictional episode in the life of Confucius does not provide the answer, but the master reappears in another imaginary conversation in the same chapter, praying his own disciple Yan Hui to instruct him, in order to learn how to gradually forget the world and "sit down in oblivion" (*zuo wang*).

The chasm between the order of Heaven and the order of men

> Confucius: "The irregular man is so for men, he moves with Heaven. Which is why we say:
> Lowly for Heaven, princely for men
> Princely for Heaven, lowly for men."

Confucius' conclusion uses the trick of a gnomic formula, a wise maxim constructed around a play of repetitions in inverted symmetry that reveals the irreconcilability of his view—which is also Zigong's—with that of the two iconoclasts. The whole tale is organized around a series of oppositions. Confucius and his disciple Zigong form a constrastive pair with the two men who maintain their friendship without hierarchical roles. Having been apprised of the shameful discrepancy between the rule of silence during funeral rites and the musical improvisation by the two companions, Confucius suggests that there are two ways of leading one's life, one remaining within worldly rules and one that blithely transcends these rules. The Chinese terms for the two types of men in Confucius' couplet, the noble or princely man and the vulgar or petty man, had already been colored with the moral slant imprinted by Confucius on the vocabulary of the nobility. The term lord (or literally "son of a lord," *junzi*) had become, in the Confucian school, the moral man, the gentleman who cultivates a sense of goodness, justice and ritual propriety. The *Zhuangzi* is probably catching both senses, political and moral, in his net, because Confucius' philosophy is in many ways an aristocratic moral code and, partly at least, a moralizing legitimization of the hierarchical structures of society. The *Zhuangzi* affirms a complete break between the world of men and the natural world, between the rules that frame a human community and the principles of conformity to the order of things. The laws, rituals and dispositions that regulate human society are not, as some Confucians would have it, a positive transposition of the patterns of nature, but a perversion of the order of things. The lowly man or, worse, an outcast disgraced by nature like Confucius, will never know what it is to live free of negative feelings and moral pressure; Confucius is aware he is on the side of the lowly men, who linger over pettiness and quibble about peccadillos; he is himself, as shown in other anecdotes in Chapter 20, nature's runt, the laggard lost in argument, the hunched scribe.

For the *Zhuangzi*, the problem of imposing norms is not that the formal setting implied by ritual warps feelings or displays a stifling pretense that the Ritualists tried to deny and Confucius so feared. The snag is that the forms and the norms of propriety are party to the pathological feelings that distort life, imprisoning within it the frontiers of the common world, stunting individual élan. The without and the within never meet. There are two distinct spheres of existence. At one point, Confucius had believed that a juncture between the two was possible, but he is now realizing the incommensurability of the two perspectives. The paradox is seeing Confucius viewing himself and his disciple as the accursed and the exiled from Heaven whereas Heaven was for them the supreme entity organizing the architecture of rituals and the moral disposition they require.

In contrast to the three men who get together at the beginning of the tale and are cultivating a sort of "cosmic camaraderie," to use Peter Sloterdijk's[13] expression, Confucius has disciples but feels isolated. He appears as a powerless and disabused master.

The gist of this story is yet to come. Before reaching a conclusive interpretation, a further tale of bereavement should be examined, and it should be read in tandem with the tale above. Confucius is engaged in discussion with a confused disciple over another case of infringement of rules, a subtler case this time, concerning the intimate prescriptions of funerary ritual. The *Zhuangzi*'s reflection on the value of funeral etiquette and the question of emotions aroused by death is amplified to the point where it resonates within all the main themes of the book.

In a prig's eye

Yan Hui came to question Confucius: "When his mother died, Mengsun Cai uttered the required lamentations but did not shed tears: he was not even saddened in his heart; and during the funeral, he did not appear to be grieved. In spite of these three things, he gained an excellent reputation all over the country of Lu for the way he wore his mourning. Can one really achieve notoriety when it is based on nothing? Personally, I find it disconcerting!"

Confucius replied, 'Well, you see, Mengsun Cai has carried things through to a conclusion. He has gone beyond the stage of knowledge, and returned things to their original simplicity, but you didn't notice. And yet, there are many things that he has already returned to simplicity in a similar manner: he does not know now what constitutes life and death, and which one comes before the other. Destined like everything else to change, he is awaiting the next transformation, without knowing what it will do to him. When one is affected by change, can one know what escapes change? And when nothing changes, can one know what has already been changed? In the end, you and me, we have not even started to awake from the dream of ourselves. Mengsun Cai, on the other hand, can see his body suddenly become affected and can still retain his consciousness. For him, the body is a dwelling place occupied just for one day, without ever feeling a sense of death; he alone is awake and aware. That is why if the others are weeping, he will weep with them, that is his spontaneous way of being, because, like everyone, in the presence of others, he refers to a "self": but in the end, can I really know whether what I consider as being me ultimately is not really me? One night you dream you are a bird soaring in the sky, another night you are a fish swimming in the deep, but when you tell me about it, do you really know whether the person speaking is having a dream or has already awoken?"

This tale presents another type of authentic man, quite distinct from the two rambunctious lads in the previous episode. Even so the dramaturgy is comparable, although simplified in the extreme. Here, Yan Hui, the historical disciple of Confucius appears again, reporting in a disapproving tone on the conduct of a certain Mengsun Cai. As a bereaved son, Mengsun Cai is not displaying heartfelt mourning for his mother. Yet in spite of disregarding the proper funeral ethos, he is held in great consideration by the inhabitants of the state of Lu, the stronghold of the Ritualists and birthplace of Confucius. Once again Confucius is shown coming to the defense of a type of man reviled by the Ritualists. Beneath the indifference and the apparent lack of filial piety of Mengsun Cai, Confucius, in line with his historical reputation as a subtle interpreter of human behavior, can detect the exemplary conduct of an accomplished man. Confucius is excluding himself from this logic, but without the tone of tragic disillusion he used with his other disciple, Zigong, in the previous dialogue.

Insofar as the initial theme of this dialogue is mourning for a parent and the rationale of procedures with death, the controversy raised by Mengsun Cai's behavior should be construed in the light of the basic tenets of funerary ethics in early China. These observations may bear out the claim that this story was written in reaction to the discussions between Confucius and his disciples preserved in the *Book of Rites* (*Liji*), whose exchanges are just as imaginary but which purport to be historically true, as in the chapter "Questions from Master Zeng" where a freely recreated Confucius expatiates on the funeral casuistry that his disciple, quibbling about minutiae in decorum, puts before him.[14]

Mourning for parents in early China

Funeral rites played a central role in early Chinese religion and were one of the main subjects of debate. The mourning period for parents was a serious test of one of the fundamental virtues of the social and political order: filial piety (*xiao*). To get a sense of what this ethical disposition could mean in early Chinese society, we could compare its authority to that enjoyed by the observance of devotion to God and liturgical duties in European early medieval societies.

The mourning of one's parents is, together with public conduct in general, one of the privileged avenues to official merit, general recognition and even, starting from the Han dynasty, material gratification. The gestures, clothes, behavior, and bodily expressions displayed during a funeral were meant to show in a proper and publicly acknowledged manner the affliction of the descendants and their virtuous love for the deceased parent. In the *Analects*, Master Zeng notes: "I learned this from Confucius: if a man has never so forth fully revealed what he is made of, he will necessary do so when mourning for his parents."[15]

Several chapters in the *Book of Rites* concern rules to be observed and the behavior required according to the type of funeral, providing a unique fund of information on early Chinese customs. The behavior observed during mourning was regulated by a liturgical code that sets out a long list of prescriptions that vary according to circumstances and form a detailed manual of mortuary case law. Coming together at some point during the third century BCE in

Confucian circles, several chapters of the *Book of Rites* explain in minute detail the required gestures and demeanor to be adopted. Those unfamiliar with the prescriptions in these texts might be either bored stiff or gently amused by the richly elaborate funeral etiquette. It stipulates, for instance, on what occasion the bereaved relatives should walk barefoot, beat their chests or roll up a sleeve, or how they should greet and receive expressions of condolences; it specifies where to stand or to sit in the death chamber, in which direction to turn one's head, and specifies how many gestures of despair must be executed before the deceased. After dividing mourning into five categories, the Ritualists number within that frame each funeral procedure including the ceremony to bring back the soul of the deceased. Instructions are given for dressing the corpse, for the type of garments to be chosen, the colors and fabrics, the hairpin size for a woman in mourning, the length of her hair, the number of people employed for the presentation of the corpse to the relatives, when to stamp on the ground, and so on.

Very specific rules and details of etiquette correspond to each singular situation, which varies according to the degree of consanguinity between the deceased and the bereaved, the hierarchical relationship with the deceased, the rank and status of the deceased, or the circumstances of death. As one could reasonably expect, this plethora of prescriptions led to endless casuistry and chicanery, and it inspired a number of anecdotes in the *Book of Rites* showing both the fussiness and perhaps, for many a modern reader, the absurdity of the Ritualists' funerary etiquette. The "Tan Gong" chapter of the *Book of Rites* show how Confucius and his followers evaluated and expatiated on who did well and who did not during funerals, and discussed the merits of various people when observing mourning. This chapter also describes many situations of illness, agony and death, and reports the moribund person's last words, along with the reactions of the people present at their deathbed. It is clearly against the backdrop of such debates raised in the Confucian school that these funerary episodes in the *Zhuangzi* should be read and construed.

In contrast to Zigong's indignation in the previous episode, Yan Hui's critique is aimed at the absence of sincere emotions behind Mengsun Cai's funerary performance. Yan Hui perceives in the latter something he ascribes to the hypocrisy of ritual behavior when not supported by genuine feeling, when it becomes mere outward show. Indeed, in the *Analects*, Confucius mentions several times that the affliction of the heart should take precedence over ostentation and opulence during the funeral. Notably: "How could I bear to watch a funeral carried out without sadness?" (III.26); and in III.4, when he is asked about the tenets of ritual, he prescribes the greatest sobriety and reaffirms the importance of sorrow over display. In the chapter "Tan Gong, 1" of the *Book of Rites*, Confucius is reported to have made repeated remarks about the possible conflict between the inner disposition and its external manifestation: "Zilu said, 'I have heard from our master that when it comes to rites of mourning, it is much better to be overwhelmed with grief and deficient in rites, than the opposite.'"

The Confucius portrayed here is at cross purposes with the master in the *Analects*. He considers the displays of affliction and sorrow during funeral processions to be just conventional displays. He makes light of the emotive norms of bereavement (despair and sorrow as guarantees of authenticity and personal virtue, as justifications for the social recognition they earn), suggesting, as a substitute, an interior sentiment of fundamental indifference, constantly set toward what is bound to become. Mengsun Cai respects the etiquette of mourning, even if he has no feelings; nevertheless, "he gets to the gist of things." He weeps and laments as others do, but Confucius discerns in him the perfect model of an authentic life. This is a lesser-known aspect of the critique of the Ritualists in the *Zhuangzi*, because classical commentaries take a different view, setting Zhuangzi and Confucius against each other on the question of rules and rites. The former supposedly defending a set of public forms of expressivity and exalting the spirit of hierarchical divisions; the latter accepting the impulsiveness of nature and transcending social norms. The person described here, Mengsun Cai, carries out his duty according to the rules but without alienating himself. The natural propensity toward affliction or distress when faced with death, which constitutes the psychological framework of ritual manners, is construed here as an un-natural reaction. Tears, lamentations and penitence are further removed from natural life than funeral robes and unhemmed sackcloth. Paradoxically here, it is Confucius who praises the conduct that respects rituals without assenting to their raison d'être.

At the beginning of this story, Yan Hui takes note of what he has seen and goes to consult Confucius. Yan Hui is the master's favorite and is often praised by him in the *Analects*; he is the only one of

Confucius' disciples that the *Zhuangzi* appears to consider as a kindred spirit. So, when featuring Zigong and Yan Hui in stories about funerary ethics, the *Zhuangzi* introduces two very dissimilar Confucian disciples. The former is restricted by his rigid attitudes to rites which go by the book, while the latter is endowed with real intelligence but is still suffering from certain blind spots. In the *Analects*, when Confucius is appraising him, Zigong admits humbly that he would never compare himself to Yan Hui. Confucius takes this further, saying that he also has been surpassed (V.9).[16] Yan Hui's exceptional intelligence, his serenely accepted poverty, his guileless modesty, his privileged closeness to the master, all seem to predispose him in the *Zhuangzi* dialogues to the role of the young man in progress who never ceases to learn and gain from discussion with Confucius until, in a brief and striking dialogue at the end of the same chapter, when finally able to "sit in oblivion," he surpasses his master, transcending his aesthetic and moral teaching.

The reader will have noted that for the Ritualists, exemplary conduct during mourning is not unrelated to the effect it can have on others and to the beneficial reputation it can establish[17]. Yan Hui's view attempts to surpass this formalized attitude; his enquiry is more profound than Zigong's, because he examines an area beyond the strict observation of prescribed behavior, which concerns the inner feelings of the mourner. Yan Hui believes he has exposed a discrepancy between the private sentiments and the public attitude of Mengsun Cai. Undeniably, Mengsun's attitude is very different from that of the two friends singing to the corpse, ignoring and scorning appropriate conduct: he behaves according to etiquette, weeping when it is required, respecting the mourning period and leading the funeral. To Yan Hui this can only mean some kind of morally suspect masquerade. In fact, *pace* Yan Hui, it seems that Mengsun Cai is well aware that "most of our occupations are farcical. (*Mundus universus exercet histrionem*: everybody in the entire world is acting a part.) We should play our role properly, but as the role of a character we have adopted."[18] For the *Zhuangzi*, formal behavior and public persona have no truck with one's authentic nature; they should only be accepted as part of the general order of things in a given society. The social duties that fall on us cannot be in keeping with what lies in one's heart, as Yan Hui would like to believe, but stand on the outside under the same heading as ceremonial vestments and vessels. In social interactions, by a sense of necessity, we can adopt in our words and body this "public language," but still remain internally totally unaffected by it.

Confucius' discourse does not end there. His critique of funeral protocol is developed, with a few highly condensed phrases, and plays out on a wide scale, touching on the conceptions that underlie social behavior, on the delusion of the existence of such a thing as the individual self, and on the impossibility of distinguishing what we ultimately are when we are dreaming and when we are awake. The self appears as a fiction, a set of narrative forms evolving alongside actual experience. Since there is no true, solid, stable self, there can be neither fake nor fallacy in a pure social performance like that of Mengsun Cai. On the contrary, authenticity implies not overidentifying with one's social persona and public role. [19]

What is particularly confusing in these words is the way all the major themes of the *Zhuangzi* meet in one sequence condensed almost to the saturation point, in a stream of sayings and allusions referring to other memorable tales. The dream attributed to Yan Hui where he finds himself being a fish and then a bird, echoes the opening passage of the *Zhuangzi* on the metamorphosis of a fish of Brobdingnagian proportions into a no less gigantic bird traveling to the confines of the universe. The idea that it is in fact impossible to unravel dreaming from awakening, or to know whether one is oneself or other, recalls the memorable anecdote at the end of Chapter 2, where Zhuang Zhou has dozed off and is having a dream about a butterfly who knows nothing of Zhou. When Zhou wakes, he doesn't know whether he is Zhou who has been dreaming of being a butterfly or whether he is the butterfly now dreaming of being Zhou.

In the end, the vindication of Mengsun Cai's conduct leads on not to considerations of him personally but to the kaleidoscopic stuff we are made of. Is there any reason, other than social convenience, to refer to a permanent self? The *Zhuangzi* seems to be saying that there is indeed a legitimate use of the idea of self, but only on the basis of a linguistic convention existing in the context of our relationships with others. However, if our view of the self were to imply that an individual's substantial and permanent identity through change, then we only entertain delusional ideas. This argument is an old and familiar one: the person I was as a child is long dead, and the man I was this morning, if he is the person I resemble the most closely, already differs from me in an infinite number of unknowable ways. I cannot know what of me is changing and what is remaining at any given time, carried forward as I am into becoming, and subject to different types of metamorphosis. In the universal process of transformation, each thing has its own changing way of undergoing change.

The principle of dissimilarity, explaining that at any given moment I differ from what I was a moment ago, is part of the principle of the universal linkage of beings to one another. What is called a person, a self, is understood as being so between birth and death, but in this in between there is endless dying and rebirth in different forms. The shape, content and properties of what we call "me" are completely dissolved and remoulded during these changes. The self refers in fact to a variegated thing, and, as it adheres completely to the present, it can be a bird during a siesta, a child yesterday, an old man today, that fish during a dream last night. The self only exists as multiplicity. The person who is aware that he is no longer the same is already different from the person who has just changed. If identity of the self persists as an illusion, it is because change affects me without my knowing—slowly, stealthily, silently—and because to communicate with others it is necessary to have solid anchors, permanent names and common references. We think of ourselves as subjects, as individuals with a conscious identity, not so much because we actually and personally experience this identity, but, on the contrary, because our thinking submits to a system of forms and meanings in a most unreflecting and reductive way that ingrains in us the belief that, fundamentally, identity prevails over change. And yet, there is no self that is immutable in its substance, but only a multiplicity of beings ascribed and reduced to "me" when I speak. The inherent multiplicity of each being is such that the difference between the being that I was, the one I am and the one I am becoming is no less than the difference that separates me from others.

In his final discourse might Confucius be trying to confuse Yan Hui, or to flummox him completely, or is he just playing with words and fantasizing? What is the point of the argument about dreaming if not to show the substitutability of all our roles, and to demonstrate a fundamental uncertainty about what and where we are? Here, Confucius is enjoying the practice of a hyperbolic form of doubt, offering his disciple a hugely amplified perspective to contemplate the necessary distortions imprinted by social interaction on self-perception. If there is incessant transformation, a continuous passing from one state to another, then we have no reason to observe mourning at any one particular moment. Confucius intensifies the feelings of transformation in order to emphasize the sedulous care Yan Hui takes as regards the carrying out of appropriate rituals, and to expose the biased essentialism that underlies his moral concern. From this angle, it is easier to understand why the *Zhuangzi* associates reflection on the self with the question of manners and norms. If the laws of time, necessity and change turn us constantly into another, not even sparing our faculty of knowing, then opinions and values will suffer the same fate as natural phenomena; caught up in the universal flux, they have the same instability, the same mobility and the same transience. There are only temporary roles. A thing divides into several others, so that having seen it as a bereaved son, one can also see it simultaneously in another light, for instance as "a fish happy to lie on the seabed."

What disappears as a result of this defense of vital dynamism to the detriment of personal identity is the possibility of defining the self. If different voices and styles take their place as "me" according to time, to cycles of existence or to systems of perception, then generation and dissolution are continuously entwined. The consequences of all this are considerable: strict social conformity to norms or fastidious observation of manners can no longer be considered as reprehensible, whereas the strong involvement of the heart in funeral ceremonies represents an inauthentic apprehension of life. Attachment to the self, which is logically implied in ritual ethics, is only a mistaken belief and a source of faulty reasoning. Now this fallacy is maintained by the moral imperative to mourn the loss of certain others at certain definite moments, while we remain unaware that bodily form is really nothing more than an ephemeral abode for the many beings that keep living and dying behind the same name-bearer.[20]

Final words on death in the *Zhuangzi*

The *Zhuangzi* makes a close study of agony, death throes, bereavement, and mourning, all situations where the negative feelings and emotions normally stirred by the thought of loss would rise to the point of horror and fright. In the stories above, we have encountered colorful characters who brazenly scorn the expected emotional reaction, such as the fear of becoming deformed, the terrifying prospect of departure, or sorrow and despair for another's loss. Might this be a cynical way of taming death by pulling oneself loose from conventional pathos? A haughty, stoical attitude detached from "human, all too human" behavior? This thesis has already been raised by many scholars and commentators. It is not an erroneous view, but a seriously reductive one that distorts the literary value of the *Zhuangzi* tales on the subject of death and mourning. In fact, it is one of the weak versions of a thesis on death that sheds, at little cost, the *Zhuangzi*'s core concern with feelings and emotions. Death is indeed problematic for human beings, and must have been so for the authors of the *Zhuangzi*, to judge by the wealth of stories featuring people dying, deceased or bereaved. The tale portraying the four masters paints a terrifying picture of the progression of necrosis and dying, which is hardly reassuring for the reader. The overall dramaturgy of the story suggests that one cannot replace emotions with arguments and that if one really wants to remain immune from the torments inspired by the prospect of death, then one must set out to counter the powerful affects it stokes with equally powerful leverage on one's feelings. And the *Zhuangzi* does not find these levers in reasoning and its deliberations, but in a humorous disposition, as well as in the suggestive force of certain wonderfully malleable images which are created each time for a particular occasion. Such images along with their witty reasonings are free from any metaphysical creed or religious tenet; they are just inventive, and, in a literal sense, *elating*, as they thrust the protagonists forward into drastic change.

There is no doctrinal framework according to which one could outline a specific "conception of life and death according to the *Zhuangzi*." As readers, we are rather facing a perpetual reinvention of discourse confronting a particular situation, or confrontiing specific individuals facing death. In this, the authors of the *Zhuangzi* are, as much as the Ritualists, attached to the prevailing circumstance, and what the characters may say about disease, agony or dying, far from being a universal message, only has a contextual meaning. Evidence of this is supplied by the abundance of eccentric reasoning, dialogues blooming into riffs, farcical sophisms, conceptual try-outs, antic descriptions of animals, playful materialism, or even arguments parodying a Confucian position, which, when considered all together, never form a doctrine, let alone a system. The *Zhuangzi*'s supposed "theoretical framework," the transformation of all things, the constant alternation of life and death, the unity of all things, is only a bag of bare-bones truths, affording an opportunity for all kinds of enigmatic variations. Extracted from their contexts, such declarations read like mystic mottoes on inspirational quote-a-day Chinese calendars. It is hardly surprising then that those wearisome formulae have become the cherry-picked lines by which we adumbrate the *Zhuangzi*, and reduce its stances to a simplistic message, devoid of mirth and humor, urging us to revert to a life of harmony with nature, while leaving out of consideration many an ambiguity, eschewing a political vision that is deeply unsettling, or crowding out questions on stories so doctrinally inconsistent as to defy all attempts at theoretical reconciliation. These moral inventions are restored to poetic virtue and vigor when we discover in which narrative context they arose.

What makes these stories so singular is the positive value assigned to voluntary illusion, just as salutary as the clear understanding of the workings of life and death. The impassioned discourse of Master Yu, as he becomes a dying monster, and Master Lai's words as he jovially breathes his last, are very dissimilar, and confirm that the right approach to death is always singular, a thing of mood and moment. The *Zhuangzi* does not issue any recommendations, considering that each us is free to flesh out the idea of transformation in our own way, whether in folly or with reason. No specific idea or attitude must be brought to the fore when faced with death, only baroque images which by their energizing virtue can heighten and carry feelings far from the suffering of the present moment. The question that appears to guide the *Zhuangzi*'s approach is how to dispose oneself, how to organize one's own sensitivity, *by all possible means*, to ward off the negative effects of aversion, hostility, and fear.

Usually, the very thought of being on the cusp of death is enough to cripple the imagination or weaken the will. For the authors of the *Zhuangzi*, putting dynamic imagination to work is what enables characters to rise above their personal fate. The words they utter propel them towards participation in a wider dimension, at the cost of their personal form of existence. In the dying Master Yu's words, we read a speech of autosuggestion: his delirious words are the perfect way *for him* to resist the initial shock of hideous deformity. The stirring speculations and striking images taken in the *tours de force* of the dying characters have only a veneer of rationality: Master Yu can rejoice in advance that he will "announce daybreak" if his arm is transmogrified into a cockerel. The exuberance of this imagery is a prelude to happy daydreaming on what is to become. In the story of Zigong and the profanation of the funeral, the two iconoclasts are lamenting and pitying themselves, condemned as they are to staying alive: "Ah Sang Hu! You have now returned to the Authentic, whereas we, still human, must remain!" This use of black comedy is another way to dilute the affect that might overwhelm them as they pay their respects before the corpse of their friend. Far from really being in despair at the idea of having to outlive their companion and feeling genuine envy for the dead, here, as one might well guess, is another joyous masquerade, a subversive joke that, by its impetus, carries the friends towards to a complete reversal of the natural inclination to cherish life and to hate death. Their attitude directly conflicts with the pathological sensitivity underlying funerary etiquette, in order to remain faithful to their vow of free and open friendship. The reaction of Zhuang Zhou himself at the death of his wife, related in Chapter 18, "Supreme Joy," is a perfect example of the creative resources of language in the event of death. The brilliant Sophist Hui Shi discovers his friend Zhuangzi, all disheveled, crouching beside the corpse of his wife, tapping on the jar he is holding between his knees, his legs splayed, and humming a little tune. Shocked by this unseemly posture and lack of proper response before the body of a woman with whom he shared his life, Hui Shi is told by his friend that although he had indeed been momentarily overcome by grief, he soon realized that whatever he may have felt is irrelevant in light of the cosmic process by which life emerges, flourishes, and wilts away. Understanding the absurdity of his misunderstanding of the way things work in the universe, the irrelevance of his wailing, brought him up short.

"At first, when she had just passed away, how could I not give in to sorrow? But when I started considering what she had been at the very beginning, and the original phase when she still was not born. Not only was she not even born, but she had no physical shape at all, and, what is more, no breath of life at that inchoative stage. And suddenly, amidst the haze and the dark something began to sprout and change, and there she was, endowed with a breath of life, and as this breath began to change, she took on a shape and this shape began to wake to life. Now, by dint of another transformation, she has departed towards death, caught in a cycle similar to the changing seasons. While she was already resting in peace in the vast hall of the universe, I was still stuck there, weeping and wailing: really, that was a complete misunderstanding of destiny. So I just stopped!"[21]

The words used to justify himself to his friend must have been precisely those that gradually brought him out of his mumbling stupor. It is by reacting to an unexpected arrival and by being goaded into a coherent reply by a friend in a conversation that he can overcome the pathos of the situation, and that he can talk his way out of grief. Before the arrival of Hui Shi, we can imagine Zhuang Zhou squatting by the deathbed of his wife, slouched against the wall, his head lolling forward, humming and drumming incoherently. He "finds" reason through being called upon to justify his conduct, but this reason is a retrospective construction.

The singular power of these stories springs from the deft use of those imaginative resources that exalt language and aim to completely renew the traditional discourse on death. The wise discourse of the sage, peppered with sound didactic arguments, is only an appearance; the *Zhuangzi* always uses it ambiguously, assuming its plain message while often giving it a parodic twist or playing it out in a burlesque way according to the characters he features. There is no definite and unequivocal message concerning the art of living or a recipe for existential issues in the *Zhuangzi*, but a choice illustration of critical moments, with variegated duos, trios or quartets of characters facing sickness or death, who parry the unknown with superb poetic sallies and whose words and responses cannot be taken at face value. Indeed, the *Zhuangzi*'s last word, if one really wants to make a distinction of that sort, is that of a poet rather than a philosopher: a man braced up or buoyed up in a near-death situation by relying on his own inspiration and on his capacity to spin a story and string words together. The point is not to reason in the face of death, but to stimulate one's sensitivity, opening it to a glimpse of a depersonalized life. In doing so, it reduces to nothing the lamentations of the nearest and dearest, as well as the old habitual words of comfort. The reader will not consider himself as now having a stock of rational arguments against death and all catastrophes in this life. But (s)he may freely follow the *Zhuangzi* 's wanderings, and remember, when the time comes, these brief mythologies full of jest, these tiny yet boundless myths that are, so to speak, the very pith and gist of literature.

PART THREE

Human versus Heaven

5

Ascesis and Ecstasy

The philosophical tale presented here, drawn from Chapter 6 of the *Zhuangzi*, "The Primordial Master" (*Da zong shi*) takes the reader into a strange game of patience, a treasure hunt. It is one of the rare examples in early Chinese literature where the authentic experience of ecstasy is directly approached and described. Rather than being used as a sort of occult and conjectural background to provide meaning for a text rashly classified as mystical literature, the spiritual experience is explicitly presented as the core theme of the dialogue between two characters, an old witch-like woman and an ambitious but ignorant disciple. At the same time, this tale is a fine example of the universality of certain intuitions of nature that can also be found in strikingly similar forms in Western literature. From this perspective, it is clear that certain quintessentially Chinese notions such as "Tao," the mention of which usually results in a general abdication of all critical intelligence, can suddenly become accessible and illumine a major portion of our experience that is normally left in the shadows.

Zi Kui of the Southern Walls questions Dame-Twist:
"You have reached an advanced age, and yet you have the air of a young child, how can this be?"
"I have heard word of the Way."
"And this Way . . . can it be learned . . .?"
"Aha! No, that . . . Impossible! Anyway, you are not such a man as that! Buliang Yi—now he had the gifts required to become a sage, even though he did not have the way of the sages; whereas I had this way of the sages, even if I do not have their gifts. And so, I wished to teach it to him: who knows, perhaps I might have

made a sage of him? Even if I did not succeed, it was always easier, don't you see, to transmit this way to someone gifted in wisdom. Therefore, I kept him with me to teach him, and three days later he could put the world outside himself; when he managed that, I still kept him with me: after seven days, he could put all beings outside himself; at that stage still, I kept him with me, and on the ninth day, he succeeded in putting life outside him; he became as diaphanous as daybreak. Being diaphanous, he could open himself to *the One and Only*, and from then on, for him, there was neither past nor present; when he had removed past and present, he managed to go where there is neither life nor death, because that which makes life die is not subject to death, that which engenders life cannot be engendered. *That thing*, there is nothing that it does not entertain, there is nothing that it does not return, nothing that it does not destroy and nothing that it does not accomplish. It is named 'Calm in the tumult,' Calm in the tumult, because it is only through tumult that things are accomplished."

"But you yourself, from whom did you learn these things?"

"I learned from the son of Auxiliary-Inks, who himself learned from the grandson of Chain-of-Recitations, and who learned from Clear-Vision, and Clear-Vision from Whispered-Agreement, Whispered-Agreement from Service-Required, and Service-Required from Humming-Tunes, Humming-Tunes from Abyssal-Indistinct, Abyssal-Indistinct from Infinite-Reaches, Infinite-Reaches from Uncertain-Beginning."[1]

Misunderstanding on the Way

The narrative of this strange encounter between Dame-Twist and Zi Kui plays on the different meanings of the word *dao* (translated here "way" or "Way" according to the context). The first meaning of *dao* is a road, a path, from which derive the notion of a way of proceeding, the "path" that a person takes, a way of thinking or behaving, a *method* (as the Greek reminds us: *meta hodou*: according to the way, along the path). The word *dao* may mean, more specifically for a master, his doctrine, his art or his sayings (in addition to meaning "to guide," as a verb *dao* also means "to say" or "to speak"). It is used by Laozi to refer, by default, to the dynamic principle that presides over the workings of all things in the universe.

The dramaturgy of this tale starts with the semantic friction between the *dao* as a personal art and the *dao* as the Way, the supreme force generating and guiding the universe. To what extent can intimate knowledge of the Tao be realized and transmitted? In other words, what *dao*, what art or what method can take charge of the transmission of the Way? And if the Way can indeed be studied, or approached, does it take someone special, an exceptionally gifted nature? The way in which the meeting between the two protagonists begins is decisive in this matter.

Zi Kui is greeting a woman[2] whose physical appearance he finds intriguing. She is old but with the skin complexion of a baby; he is curious and questions her, because she obviously has a miraculous aptitude for preservation and longevity; her youthful features and the complete freshness of her face suggest that at her age she possesses an art or secret method for nourishing the vital essences within her. Zi Kui jumps on the occasion to ask her to impart her method. The old woman vigorously rejects his demand, because she can guess that Zi Kui is immature and riveted to the sole intention of personal benefit; from the outset, self-interest undermines any possibility of an authentic relationship, and thus precludes any access to the Way.

Dame-Twist first says that she has "heard of the Way." The misunderstanding persists for Zi Kui who seems to see the Tao as an art to be verbally transmitted and asks if this knowledge can be imparted to him. However, in literal terms, Zi Kui's formulation is rather more ambiguous. He is asking to be instructed in this art, but his question has an impersonal tone. It is a common instance in classical Chinese where sentences can function without an explicit subject. So, the question asked here can mean "Can I (me Zi Kui) study the Tao?" but also "Can the Tao be an object of study?" With the question formulated in this way, Dame-Twist can reply with similar *double entendre*, and maintain the fundamental ambiguity of the *Zhuangzi*'s position as regards the Tao. Her repartee is sharp and wounding, unsettling Zi Kui's pretentions and rebuffing his aspiration for study:

"And this Way . . . can it be learned . . .?"

"Aha! No, that . . . Impossible! Anyway, you are not such a man as that! Buliang Yi, now he had the gifts required to become a sage, even though he did not have the way of the sages; whereas I had this way of the sages, even if I do not have their gifts. That is why I wished to teach it to him: who knows, perhaps I might have made a sage of him? Even if I did not succeed, it was always easier, don't you see, to transmit this way to someone gifted in wisdom."

With this provocative outburst claiming the impossibility of teaching the Way, Dame-Twist is undermining a common expectation regarding the role of masters, and she is also questioning the meaning of teaching through speech and imitation; in fact, she is rejecting a potential disciple who is very keen to learn and to study with her, by implying that he is not good enough, neither is he the type of man required (Confucius prided himself on teaching anyone, whatever their rank or background, so long as they ached to learn and were fully dedicated to their studies).

Dame-Twist's remarks are colored by a series of tensions and paradoxes that are probably very confusing for the poor aspiring disciple. She is simultaneously instilling in him the idea that it is absolutely impossible to learn the Tao and that, even if it were possible in some way or another, he is so lacking in potential as to make study futile. She also tells him that she herself possesses the Tao, but that just like him she lacks the gifts required to become a sage; finally, she says that she did once teach someone who had an evident gift for wisdom, although, as it happened, unlike her, he was unable to find the way of the sages on his own.

If someone like Dame-Twist who is not gifted as a sage can still possess the art or way of the sages, and even instruct a person like this Buliang Yi character, why would she reply that wisdom requires a particular personality, a certain natural aptitude? This is probably in order to disarm the newcomer and to dash his hopes of *possessing* the Way. In fact, Zi Kui's application to Dame-Twist is refused because he wants to establish an instrumental relationship that is subordinated to and directed by his desire for personal gain. From the start, Dame-Twist is aware that Zi Kui believes that her miraculous youthfulness is the result of a personal practice, a desirable accomplishment purposefully acquired through a series of intentional actions. He cannot understand that it is a secondary, derivative effect, a by-product, in sum, of an inner transformation that is greater than anything he can possibly imagine, something that cannot be "willed." The divergence between Zi Kui's request and the nature of the object he desires marks the distance between the Tao as the art of a master and the Tao as the universal workings which underlie reality.

Dame-Twist is intending to annihilate Zikui's forceful intention to *get* the Way. First by frustrating him, by bringing him up short, she is trying to imprint a certain disposition that will allow him to become attuned and to listen with no ulterior motive.

If Dame-Twist seems so young, it is because she knows how to retreat from life, or to "put life outside" (*wai sheng*) to use her own expression describing the ecstatic meditation of her pupil Buliang Yi. The comparison with a baby's complexion is not gratuitous either; Dame-Twist knows to return to the source of life. What is more, the fact that the character who incarnates mastery of life is a woman can be taken as provocation aimed at the category of male masters representing informed and moral authority.[3] Her sex associates her with the Yin, and this is underlined by her name.[4] Her bent profile shows that extreme youth and great age are both present in her. She is crouched, like a baby who has not yet learned to stand upright, or like a fetus curled up in the amniotic pouch (the Yang, the male principle, being associated with expansion, radiant unfolding, occupation of space).

"Dismissing life"

Although, in the first instance, Dame-Twist belittles Zi Kui and refuses his request, she does not cut the meeting short. Without any apparent reason, she starts telling him about the experience of a man she trained, a man endowed with an authentic aptitude for wisdom, Buliang Yi. This is the decisive element of Dame-Twist's lesson. She is involving a third person to defuse the frontal opposition between herself and Zi Kui, and to divert the latter's attention in the direction of an imaginary scene, which will open his mind while allowing him to preserve a passive and neutral attitude, because he must now think that he has nothing to gain from her words, delivered as they are, in the manner of a lengthy aside. So, what exactly did happen to Buliang Yi?

> "So I kept him with me to teach him, and three days later he could put the world outside himself; when he managed that, I still kept him with me: after seven days, he could put all beings outside himself; at that stage still, I kept him with me, and on the ninth day, he succeeded in putting life outside him; he became as

diaphanous as daybreak. Being diaphanous, he could open himself to *the One and Only*."

Dame-Twist has accompanied Buliang Yi on his meditative journey, following his case like a doctor caring for a patient. Doing what exactly? The word that she uses repeatedly, *shou* (meaning to watch over, preserve, shield, protect, keep) refers to behavior that is close to non-action, but that shows the constant care, attention and influence of Dame-Twist over Buliang Yi, and it marks his progress until he reaches the vision of "the one and only" (*du*). During this phase, Dame-Twist does no more than support his efforts to concentrate and maintain a tension that is just enough to prevent him from abandoning the process or from being distracted.

Dame-Twist claims to have enabled her disciple to develop the aptitude to withdraw from the world and, later on, from beings and things. In the final stage, when she *lets go* of him, he manages to put "life outside." One can imagine contemporaries of the *Zhuangzi* being just as intrigued or confused as readers are today by such expressions. Some of the translations and commentaries on the *Zhuangzi* choose not to translate the term Tao and explain that gaining access to the Way means immersing oneself in the great All, or that the Tao is the reabsorbing of oppositions, or a spiritual illumination. These glosses do little more than paste on a thin veneer of keywords to explain away the story. Although the reader can see that Buliang Yi is progressing from one state to another during these three stages, and that he is gradually acquiring a more radical power of introspection, the experiential content still needs to be clarified.

The description of the gradual honing of the powers of concentration proceeds first with a series of negations and dismissals. How should we understand "putting the world outside"? Dame-Twist's program of inward training consists in a process of liberation from the mental conditioning whereby we create a comparatively stable picture of the complete network of links connecting the self to the world. "Emptiness and unconsciousness mean only the state of relating directly to the world, *without relating also to the relating*" writes the philosopher Jon Elster in his analysis of the traps and fallacies awaiting anyone who wishes to lay hold of the state of non-thought by resorting, paradoxically, to instrumental rationality.[5] Buliang Yi starts by ceasing to "bring the world into him" in his usual fashion via intentional consciousness, which ties him to the world through representations, desires or will. The world as a construct of his consciousness, which becomes a preoccupation when he is awake and the subject of dreams when he is sleeping, ceases to impose itself upon him at all times; he learns, maybe when exhaling during breathing exercises, to empty himself of all the thoughts that preserve within him, in the form of harassing desire or worried agitation, the presence of the outside world. In psychological terms, this corresponds to a way of disengaging oneself from the continuous influx of representations and perceptions that block and saturate the mind. This experience is familiar to anyone who is used to mental preparation for high-level performance, such as acting, competition sport or a musical recital. It is the sort of experience that is denoted by the common expression "emptying one's mind", that anyone can undergo when a state of deep calm and an unwavering concentration are combined (though the very fact of *trying* to trigger this state of mind more often than not proves counterproductive).

Buliang Yi "un-busies" himself, he offloads the weight of the presence of the world, stops the constant inner monologue which prevents him from gathering himself together and from concentrating on the inner flow of energies that nurture his physiological processes such as breathing. Like the *Zhuangzi*, Henri Michaux explores this particular type of analysis of the self, when after some "happy ingesting" of a certain brown substance, he divests himself of the external and takes note of the transformations that he then feels happening within; he describes this in *Passages*: "This detachment, above all perhaps the concomitant fading away of all ambition, all will and all design regarding everything in the outer world, makes one feel aerated, disintegrated."[6]

Three days later, in spite of his progression in the exercise of detachment, Buliang Yi is still intermittently perceiving things existing outside. He is still conscious of other beings, which bars the way to fully seizing the hidden principle animating all things. At a further stage (on the fifth day) he can stop regarding the world as an outside space where things are posited and where events take place; he can finally cease to perceive himself as a living thing among others (*wu*), with a shape, a volume and a specific nature. He frees himself from the perception of beings as productions to return towards the producing principle itself. He passes from the usual perception of *natura naturata* to the level of *natura naturans*, for which there are no things any longer, but a dynamic continuum of energy (*qi*) in a never-ending cycle of production and disintegration.

In Chapter 2, "All things on a par," the *Zhuangzi* describes this intuition in a different form, shining light on Dame-Twist's words:

> Among the Ancients, knowledge had reached peaks. What peaks? For them, there had never existed "things": What a peak! What an outcome! Really, nothing to add! Then, at a lesser level, some considered that there were in fact things, but that there were no limits or boundaries between them.

External things, far from existing as such outside us, result from a specific use of perception and language, which delimits, separates and entrenches. Our language and logical categories force us to fragment the world into an indefinite number of things and to see them as distinct from each other. Later in Chapter 2, the author asserts, "By being named, things become what they are." The progression achieved by Buliang Yi during his meditation is a brake against the current of devolution of human perception in a world subject to imperatives of gain, to the logic of usefulness and of self-interest. At the stage furthest from the Way, it is not possible to perceive anything more than the world as the totality of outer things, reduced to an ensemble of artificially stabilized representations, of ready-made oppositions and binary sets of values. Buliang Yi is experiencing a gradual deconstruction of this type of perception.

Naturally, when knowledge is subordinated to the imperatives of action or usefulness, we can admit that things do exist; it is even a necessity in the practical world to do so. But using this convenient trick to explain how the world is ultimately structured and "furnished" is unacceptable. "Putting life outside" is the final stage of this mental fasting, which consists in freeing oneself from the world built by reductive perception. Again, in Chapter 2, the Master Nanguo Ziqi,[7] as he comes out of a trance, admits to "having lost his self."[8] The disciple who observes him is terrified at seeing him "physically identical to dead wood and internally like cold ashes," having removed himself from his own external existence, in order to start listening within him to the resonance of the Way, symbolized by the "pipes of heaven" (*tian xiao*). Buliang Yi also completely de-individualizes himself in order to become nothing more than a pure stream of life connected to the dynamic principle of reality. He experiences what happens when his self shrinks to pure listening to his inner workings. At this stage, there is no longer anything stable, fixed, nameable, differentiated, there is only the unique current of life that he can perceive flowing and unfurling within and that seems to coincide with the principle that moves the world, the Tao. Thus, Buliang Yi leaves his personal life, to grasp the dynamic flow that is the foundation of his own existence. He rests in the heart of nature, "in the primordial basis of creation where the key to all things lies concealed" to quote Paul Klee's evocative expression in his essay "On Modern Art." Once Buliang Yi has extinguished his awareness of the outside world, he is in union with the dynamics of his inner processes. The optimal experience of reality demands not only abstraction from the world of things and the abandonment of one's own life, but more radically, as the next part of Dame-Twist's narrative indicates, departure from the outside world with its appearance of massiveness and stability.

After nine days, Buliang Yi is ready to experience the welling up of creative and chaotic forces that "fabricate" life and death, where the grand furnace moulds all things forged by the master of transformations:

> "At that stage still, I kept him with me, and on the ninth day, he succeeded in putting life outside him; he became as diaphanous as daybreak. Being diaphanous, he could open himself to *the One and Only*, and from then on, for him, there were neither past nor present; when he had removed past and present, he managed to go where there is neither life nor death, because that which makes life die is not subject to death, that which engenders life cannot be engendered. *That thing*, there is nothing that it does not receive, there is nothing that it does not return, nothing that it does not destroy and nothing that it does not accomplish. It is named 'Calm in the tumult': calm in the tumult, because it is only through the tumult that things are accomplished."

The expression "diaphanous as daybreak" (or literally "he was capable of the transparency of daybreak") is one of the *ad hoc* expressions coined in the *Zhuangzi* to evoke the state of mind that declares itself in the novice Buliang Yi, who is suddenly plunged into a dimension similar to dawn in its pristine purity. Dame-Twist revives the feeling of wonder that her pupil must have experienced when engrossed in the meditative experience under her guidance: what he perceives is nothing other than the powers through which he perceives, he sees the source of light itself and not what it sheds light upon. At this moment, his inner workings and the workings of the universe are one and the same thing: *du*, the "only," the "single," the "that alone." Here Dame-Twist takes care not to name the Tao explicitly, in order to avoid a discourse that might be construed as didactic (remembering that from the start she has refused to teach the Tao or to make Zi Kui her disciple). Buliang Yi no longer sees things via actions that objectify things in the world of "taking and giving," the world of usefulness, preoccupation, consumption or exchange; he has also ceased to see things as things, as a collection of individual realities in space. He realizes that the forms we perceive are not stable configurations but formations, or processes of coming-to-be and passing-away. He passes from an awareness of multiple forms to an awareness of the forces that underpin them; he becomes able to grasp the *working* inside all things, regardless of things themselves. He sees it in an *absolute* manner, liberated from the discursive representations we use to bring ourselves towards the idea of the Tao. Buliang Yi now sees *only this*. He is in a state of ecstasy, outside his usual self, beyond the customary referential frames of time and space, with no adequate words to qualify what he now is in presence of.

Here Buliang Yi's singular experience is marked by a discontinuity. In the first phase, he finds himself in a condition of continuous tension and increasing ability, as indicated by the notable repetition of the terms *shou* (maintain, watch over, guard) and *neng* (can, be capable of) that set the pace of his progression. His attainment of successive levels of the comprehension of life is marked by time (three days, seven days, nine days). Then suddenly, everything becomes diaphanous and the notion of time disappears from his perception. Arriving at the stage of "translucence of dawn" is the crowning moment for his inward training and marks the optimal development of his capacities. The continuous progression then gives way to a condition of unknowingness in which notions of time disappear. At this final stage, he contemplates the universal dynamic that forms and dissolves living beings, "receiving" them (*ying*) and "accompanying their return" (*song*), aware of them as nothing more than temporary formations of the vital breath.

In contrast to other contemporary texts, the *Zhuangzi* does not envision the Way solely as something positive. In the four treatises of the "Mental Techniques" collected in the *Guanzi*, written roughly in the same period,[9] phenomena such as death, sickness, and confusion are explained by the absence or the loss of the Tao. The vision of the Way revealed here is far more radical because it appears as the unique principle of opposing activities, the free play of which produces the whole range of transformations. The Tao is not only the power to make things grow; it also engages the opposing forces of destruction in its cosmic activity. The meditating Buliang Yi becomes aware of the dual process of forces operating from "the one and only." "That thing, there is nothing that it does not receive, nothing that it does not return, nothing that it does not destroy and nothing that it does not accomplish." The universe understood in this way is intimately connected to a certain mode of perception: Buliang Yi has jettisoned the world as a collection of things and belongings, he has broken off from the false familiarity that he maintained within himself, he has *dehumanized* the world by blocking out all considerations of time that organize his daily experiences.

Dame-Twist likes to call the experience of these forces that make up reality "calm in the tumult." This expression precludes any personification of the Tao. There is no trace here of a theology, even a rhetorical one. "Calm in the tumult" is more a description of Buliang Yi's mental state than anything else. While this state of calm evokes the "diaphanous" understanding and the luminous awareness of "that One and Only," next to it, the tumult, or the *intrusion*,[10] is due to the profuse activity of the Way in all directions and in all places. At the end of Dame-Twist's instruction and guardianship, Buliang Yi has become fully aware of the simultaneous movements of growth and destruction by which things appear, develop, and then decline and pass away, and he feels transported by the flow of these forces. He is conscious of himself as an integral part of the dynamic that is surrounding him and "kneading" him.

The Tao is not an objective reality but the dynamics at the heart of reality. It cannot be grasped as a substance, it is pure process, whose images are used repeatedly in Dame-Twist's narrative:

accompanying, escorting, going and coming, like entering life at birth and leaving life at death. The journey of all individuals and the march of the world coincide in these verbs describing opposite and complementary motions.

The untraceable origin

The description of Buliang Yi's ecstasy, which, one imagines, must leave Zi Kui quite baffled, continues with the mind-boggling enumeration of the lineage of masters who have transmitted their art through time and space. Here, once again, Dame-Twist mocks Zi Kui's ambitions to knowledge.

> "But you yourself, from whom did you learn these things?"
> "I learned from the son of Auxiliary-Inks, who himself learned from the grandson of Chain-of-Recitation, who learned from Clear-Vision, and Clear-Vision from Whispered-Agreement, Whispered-Agreement from Service-Required, and Service-Required from Humming-Tunes, Humming-Tunes from Abyssal-Indistinct, Abyssal-Indistinct from Infinite-Reaches, Infinite-Reaches from Uncertain-Beginning."

Rather than a response, this is a solution resulting from the simple description of the learning process of Buliang Yi. Dame-Twist concludes the dialogue with a parody of genealogy. The allegorical names in the chain embody various acts of perception, understanding, and communication, which are as many ways to learn about the creative activity that underlies the flow of things. It should be noted that Buliang Yi's nine days of training correspond to this cast of nine characters.

Dame-Twist's dazzling restitution of the filiation of knowledge of the Way reflects the formal procedure used by members of the various sects and schools during the Warring States period, who prided themselves on their training received from such-and-such a master, thus pretending to be in possession of a privileged repository of teaching in direct line from a founding figure and earliest ancestor of a textual tradition. As is evinced by his name, the earliest on the list of masters of the Way, instead of being the uncontested rallying point of the various masters in question, is himself imperceptible and irresolute, *Uncertain-Beginning (yi shi)*. But for the moment let us go back to the latest in the list.

The "son of Auxiliary-Inks" represents the written legacy transferred from master to disciple, recording the words of former masters or sages of the past, but these records are only considered to have a derivative or secondary status: writings are the orphan offspring of the words of the dead. In another memorable tale from the *Zhuangzi*,[11] Bian the wheelwright taunts Duke Huan of Qi, who is absorbed in reading the works of the wise rulers of the past: these sages' remarks are nothing more than the dross and dregs of the deceased, rubbish that is as good as useless for the present generation. Might there be a way to use speech in order to preserve it and ensure its place in the transmission of the Way? If writings as such teach next to nothing, ingesting them gradually by repeated chanting can reanimate them, and "warm them up" as Confucius says when he talks about the past *(wen gu)*. Writings are situated at the far end of a chain of transmission that, taken backwards, eventually returns to the authentic principle of knowledge, speech, and teaching. "Auxiliary-Inks" received his training from "Chain-of-Recitations" who, as disciple to "Clear-Vision," acquired a true perception of the way in which things take shape. But understanding the recitations requires, beyond the vision, careful listening to phenomena and being so attentive that it becomes possible to apprehend something that remains only as a murmur, deep down in the silent fund of natural processes: and so we return toward "Whispered-Agreement." This finely tuned hearing is itself the result of a practice of concentration and internal training, represented by "Service-Required." Such a practice demands the return step-by-step to an intimacy with the invisible and immaterial Principle, that encompasses everything, from interior activity to the "Infinite-Reaches"; we are then brought back to the start, back to the inchoate phase of the world, to the uncertain, doubtful figure of a primeval Master, "Uncertain-Beginning." With her checklist of sorts, Dame-Twist returns towards the indistinct, she regresses toward the indeterminate rather than toward a firm foundation. This may well also be Zhuangzi discreetly taking a metaphysical stance, saying in passing that nothing can define or situate the moment when things began. The Way is the animating power of the universe that escapes our intellective and perceptive understanding because of its omnipresence and because of its absoluteness that transcends all categories of language and all qualities of the senses (hence the appellation "the Unique" or the "Only"), even though the Way is the origin of all perceptible forms, which hide it while also proving it by their visible emergence and incessant transformation. The Way has nothing of the static and massive character of Being, one cannot make it a *causa prima*.[12] As is explained by Confucius to his disciple Yan Hui, when they find themselves famished and surrounded by enemies:

> "Something transforms all living beings, and yet we do not know how these changes are worked out. How could we know what brings them to an end? How could we know what makes them start again? We can only behave rightly, then 'wait and see', that's all !"[13]

But this "Uncertain-Beginning" can also be understood as a judgment on the delusion that knowledge can pass from mouth to mouth. Zi Kui lives by the myth of pedagogy. He thinks that true knowledge can be conveyed from master to disciple and that the world is divided into two parts: the ignorant and the wise, those who know and those who must learn, those who have got the Way and those who are in search of it. No wonder he yearns to appropriate Dame-Twist's methods and join the other side. He then asks her for the name of the master who authorizes her to speak as she does. However, if true knowledge proceeds backwards as this parable suggests, then the myth of a firm and definite source of knowledge disintegrates. Because knowledge cannot start with the inaugural words of the master or with the possession of texts, the "beginning" can only be "uncertain." Knowledge starts and culminates in an act of inner perception, which propels us into a dimension where language barely exists.

This gradual elevation toward the Tao—the only authentic master—runs counter to the process that downgrades from the great Tao to a particular tao, from the Way to a method, from natural processes to human procedures. The acts of writing, reciting, seeing, murmuring, and listening represented by the fictional masters are associated with the different phases to be experienced by anyone who aims at unity between his own vital activity and the dynamic principle of reality.[14] In other words, the amusing names used for the imaginary masters represent the various stages completed as the person meditating returns toward the Way. Apparently, the ear can hear further than the eye can see. Hearing over distance is more acute at night, in depth and in the abyss evoked in the allegory. Of the senses, the one that is privileged at night is hearing.[15] The reader may wonder whether Dame-Twist is imparting universal truths or whether this is all facetiousness on the *Zhuangzi*'s part. This apparent dilemma evaporates when one realizes that the author never expresses anything profound without a touch of humor, parody or playfulness. Indeed, the very name Buliang Yi is probably a pun of sorts: written with different characters but with a similar pronunciation, it means "Non-duality (*bu liang*) and Unity (*yi*)." This play on words concerning the mysterious central character would suggest that behind Dame-Twist's narrative there is another truth that has been latent from the start: Dame-Twist and Buliang Yi are not a master-disciple pair, they are one and the same being. Dame Twist, like a midwife, watches over (*shou*) Buliang Yi who is the being she will become once she enters a state of ecstasy and has overcome all duality (life and death, past and present). She is thus speaking of herself, but from a distance, under the cover of this almost too-transparent name, in order to defuse any potential conflict with Zi Kui, and *neutralize* his attention.

The description of Buliang Yi's meditation and the enumeration of the masters appear to have contrasting objects: one deals with inner training, the other with outer transmission. But as we saw above, the genealogy of sages echoes the stages reached during the nine days. Apprenticeship, which starts with texts, is exterior to begin with, then it concentrates on recitation, the first type of appropriation of knowledge; at last the apprentice begins to listen to the barely perceptible activity of natural processes, hearing from afar; finally, the process concludes with an indeterminate beginning, and is left hanging in the balance. This is just what happens to Buliang Yi: on the ninth day, in a state of rapture and revelation, he attains the dawn of the universe, the inchoative dimension of the world.

A lesson on all lessons

The indirect teaching delivered by Dame-Twist to Zi Kui says much about how the author conceives of an authentic human relationship. Dame-Twist pretends to stall on Zi Kui's request because, were she to consent openly to instructing him and to accept him as a disciple, something in their exchange would be immediately lost or distorted. A conventionally-established relationship, submitted to hierarchical roles of master and disciple and subservient to the logic of appropriation, would inevitably hobble the strength and scope of her action. Zi Kui must remain in a state of shock, be troubled, dismayed, and confused, so that he can absorb the full impact of her words. Accomplishment only comes after the completion of tumult, just as Zi Kui himself needs to be overcome by the ardent confusion of Dame-Twist's language to begin to see clearly. The pure perception of life, which Buliang Yi, fashioned by Dame-Twist's silent treatment, can experience, requires a radical extraversion of consciousness. This can only be developed by muddling the usual boundaries, parameters, and criteria by which ordinary perceptions and actions are organized. It brings in the pupil a sort of ecstasy, where the distinction between inner and outer is abolished, as well as any sense and direction of time.

Dame-Twist's lesson doubles as a reflection on the limits of the transmission of knowledge, and therefore on the possibility of a tradition. Authentic knowledge, although it begins with words, culminates in a personal experience of the animating principle of the world, made up of opposing forces perceived in their functionality and their dynamic; here, the so-called master can at best only play the role of a silent presence in the voyage toward the "distant interior." All Dame-Twist can do is to be there, next to Buliang Yi, to observe and watch over him.

At the end of the story, Dame-Twist eludes Zi Kui's inept question about the transmission of the Way, as we saw above, by recreating in parody a line of descent of the masters, which situates on an allegorical plane the poetic genesis of actions that have to be initiated inwardly before one can reach the Way.

She claims she holds her knowledge from the son of Auxiliary-Inks: is she not herself the creature of ink devised by Zhuangzi who delivers to his readers exactly what Dame-Twist gives Zi Kui to understand: a possible personal re-creation of the Way by the virtues of inventive language? Zhuangzi is manipulating the hidden side of his explicit subject matter, the impossibility of transmitting the Way: the *saying* of Dame-Twist (her Tao) in this tale commands force and fecundity similar to that of the Way (Tao), because she is bringing around Zi Kui, her interlocutor, towards a state of deep calm. He is in a zone of disinterested listening while simultaneously being stimulated by the vertiginous vision of abandoning life, and returning to the fusion of vital activity with the dynamic of nature. This hardly seems a matter of mystical contemplation of a transcendent being, but rather of a personal exploration of the forces of life in the body, as they silently unfurl and unleash themselves. Nietzsche, too, afforded an unprecedented philosophical scope to his intuition of the dynamic root of the real, calling it "boundlessly extravagant, boundlessly indifferent, without purposes or considerations, without pity or justice, at once fruitful, fertile and barren and uncertain: imagine to yourselves *indifference as a power.*"[16] He ascribed all existence to this blind activity of terrifying forces, embodied in Dionysus, that are endlessly creating and destroying. However, the consequences for individual existence that he finds there lead the reader elsewhere: for Nietzsche the inhumane and pitiless workings of nature encourage the cultivation of an aesthetic attitude toward the world, an attitude nourished by ancient myths and dazzling illusions, stimulated by an abundant stream of shapes and sounds, propped up by apparent lightness as a means to keep at bay the terrifying knowledge of the depths that draws us toward death and nothingness, while remaining secretly inspired by it. For the *Zhuangzi*, artistic activity is never considered to be an end; his characters venture happily "into the heart of the volcano," into the hidden foundations of existence, and there they savor a sort of vertiginous peace, far from the metaphysical anguish permeating German Romanticism from Goethe and Schelling to Nietzsche and that is still perceptible in Heidegger.[17] The authors of the *Zhuangzi* have tried to communicate in many literary forms their amazement at the continuous workings of a cosmic power within all things, a power that accounts for the never-ending genesis of reality behind the solid and stable appearances of the world our ordinary perception constructs through language and its inbuilt logical categories. This "metaphysical intuition" which Dame-Twist seems to share with us and with the ignorant disciple Zi Kui appears almost in the same terms in the obsessions of Hölderlin, who enjoins the reader "to be one with all living things, to return, by a radiant self-forgetting, to the All of Nature."[18] Indeed, the meditation experience as described here by Zhuangzi is not irreducibly Chinese. When confronted with the enigma of the visible world and the perception of its hidden source, it seems that the singularity of an author lies not in the set of cultural concepts he brings to bear (Way, Nature, Principle or Being), but primarily in the kind of inspiration he draws from the contemplation of the depths of nature and from the kind of narrative he devises to recount his ecstatic experience.

6

The Way of True Men

Can the notion of an authentic life be entertained without addressing the question of true knowledge? Can the problem of knowledge be discussed with a certain detachment, removed from those areas of our concrete existence where eating, sleeping, feeling, and breathing play a major role? Or is it because practical wisdom shuns the dry theoretical approach to the problem of true knowledge and ignores the problem of conciliating logic and existence, that it risks being reduced to a mundane stir-fry of commonplace remarks served up in stodgy prose? Wisdom, as distinct from philosophy, often proves something of a disappointment when it appears in bare truths and boilerplate remarks, missing the adventurous dimensions of human thought when it sets out for uncharted territories of experience.

From among the many narratives about the various sages who appear in the thirty-three chapters of the *Zhuangzi*, I have chosen an especially continuous and detailed account of those characters the author dubs as "the true men of ancient times." The *Zhuangzi's* Chapter 6, "The Primordial Master," opens with their description, presented below in full.[1] This is one of the passages that shows with utter clarity how Zhuangzi's style allowed him to sidestep the two obstacles of theoretical knowledge and platitudes of wisdom, by discarding the first and subverting the second.

This is not for once, a story or a dialogue, nor is it an infratheoretical discourse, but a *biography*, in the most literal sense, an attentive description of the way a sage uses his vital processes to breathe, feed, sleep, exist, and die. This sort of description, by turns playful, meandering, and obscure, allows Zhuangzi to position himself halfway between proposing universals and offering a set of specific notations.

The portrait of the "true men of old" opens with a discussion of the difference between Heaven and Man. The introductory remarks appear to be leading the reader towards a definition of this distinction. But an unexpected kink in the narration points to discrediting the sort of knowledge that can reveal this distinction, which is then left abandoned on the roadside. Only then can the "conceptual characters" of the true men be presented on the philosophical stage.

Heaven and Human: the two modes of action

Understanding the heavenly workings and the human workings: this is the greatest height.

He who understands the workings of Heaven lives in the mode of Heaven.

He who understands the workings of Humans uses what his knowledge understands to nourish what it does not understand.

To live out the years that Heaven allots, and not die before the natural term, cut down along the path of life: this is taking knowledge to its peak.[2]

The peak that can be attained is the awareness of the working of Heaven within the self when one is able to distinguish this from proper human agency (*ren zhi suo wei*). Heaven is the dynamic principle of all natural activity in the widest sense. It can be taken as a synonym for "nature," but in the strictest sense, not as we understand it in a modern way (from the 17th century onwards with Descartes and followers such as Malebranche) as an ensemble of physical laws, nor as an object of observation, of theoretical research or of practical exploitation. Here, nature is rather the movement of life constantly actualized in innumerable concretions.

The activity of Heaven is characterized by efficiency, fluidity, and spontaneity, though this kind of spontaneity should be understood not as an innate and immediate disposition, but much rather as a conquest, as the gratifying result of a long practice (think of the fluid footwork of a figure skater on ice rather than a toddler's stumble). Now this graceful efficiency, which is illustrated in many stories of the *Zhuangzi*, is disabled by the reactive, conscious or calculated functions upon which our intelligence of things is spuriously constructed, and which are then identified as belonging to the Human mode (*ren*).

Becoming conscious of the workings of Heaven means being attentive to the manner in which one is "worked" from within by an ensemble of forces once one's consciousness has ceased to warp, distort or skew the workings of the internal spring that moves the body. The Heavenly and the Human designate here two kinds of *modus operandi* competing or cooperating in a given individual animated from within by the *qi* (the substantially constituting energy force). This activity includes all the spontaneous workings by means of which the body acts, reacts, adapts, and regulates itself in every instance. The constant flow of this *qi*-based activity enables our motions and our thoughts to proceed with a spontaneous understanding of what surrounds us and interacts with us. It draws on an implicit non-verbal knowledge that far exceeds the powers of consciousness and will. It is from this perspective that the *Zhuangzi* decrypts the true men of old, seen as beings "actioned" or "nurtured"[3] by Heaven.

The Heavenly is a force and the Human mode is also a force; they are in a constant state of tension in the body. Zhuangzi devotes his philosophical acumen to exploring in many tales and more theoretical passages how the two forces play themselves out through our lives. A person's activity is determined essentially by the relationship of Heavenly and Human forces that may cooperate and take over from one another, or, on the contrary, devour each other. A person's activity is determined essentially by the relationship of Heavenly and Human forces that can cooperate and take over from one another, or, on the contrary, that can interfere in each other's workings. Heaven is the active force *par excellence*; the Human is but a lesser mode of interacting with reality often fraught with partiality and error.

One can become aware of the Heavenly workings only via the Human workings, because the former merges with the forces and the springs, which, by their very nature, are not governed by consciousness. "He who understands the workings of Man uses what his knowledge understands to nourish what it does not understand." The workings of Heaven are not fundamentally amenable to mental representations and verbal formulations and we can only get to know them indirectly by means of free-ranging consciousness, advancing from the known to the unknown, towards the *sinews* of the power within that lies buried under layers and layers of verbal knowledge and mental images. The difficulty lies in avoiding disturbance of the dynamic of Heaven by the Human mode of action. The celebrated concept of "non-action" (*wu wei*) in Taoist thought is primarily a call to avert the interference of the Human factor (*ren*) with the natural workings (Heaven or *tian*) in our daily small and big actions, an injunction to avoid the use of the intellect to *deflect* Heaven's input within us. To achieve authentic knowledge, it is necessary to distinguish between what *we* do and what *is done* within us, and to be led through from the Human mode to the Heavenly mode, so that in the end we become one through the seamless passage from one mode to the other.

Ideally then, as Zhuangzi claims, the ability to discern the difference between the workings of Man and the workings of Heaven should be sufficient to access an intuition of life whose effects would have repercussions on one's health and vitality. True knowledge is related to the capacity for an easy and unimpeded use of these two modes, in other words the ability to be sure that awareness of the self will not cloud the principle of natural operativity. But here's the rub. Zhuangzi immediately puts this distinction to the test, because it proves impossible to theoretically define these two modes when fixed referents are applied.

"Now, the only trouble is that to be adequate, knowledge must rest on something; yet this prop is nothing fixed. How am I ever to know whether what I call 'Heaven' is not in fact 'Human,' whether what I call 'Human' is not in fact 'Heaven'? In this respect, there can never be true knowledge without first having a true man. Which comes down to asking: what is a true man?"

Zhuangzi is voluntarily facing the stumbling block of matching between names and things as formulated by the later Mohists, in the early third century BCE. The disciples of Master Mo's sect laboriously drew the outlines of an analytical logic of language and the rudiments of an epistemology.[4] Zhuangzi seems to be responding to them here by saying that if words can only retain the fragmentary, mobile, past or provisional aspects of things, then knowledge must resist the temptation to apprehend reality through language. He is seeking to dispense with the sort of matching that implies a dependence on instability, not via the royal way of metaphysics that postulates the existence of independent and stable contents of knowledge, but inversely by *mobilizing* the figures of true men, by consenting to drift, to ramble towards the Way by "winding roads and wandering pathways" (as the hermit Xu You says in the same chapter). This is a far cry from the classic problem according to which the ontological indocility of phenomena renders them too mobile a target for apposite naming. If the type of knowledge that Zhuangzi is trying to reveal relies upon something that is never fixed, it is precisely because that something is not an object, but a dimension of vital activity. The critical impact of this passage would be lost if the reader were to imagine that Zhuangzi's effort is directed toward the possibility of going beyond the aporia of theoretical knowledge or the possibility of finding an objective guarantee of correspondence with the real. The Heaven and the Human are two distinct modes of activity that are more or less mutually permeable, and they can operate in harmonious continuity just as they can proceed separately in an exclusive manner. But since in both cases dynamics, tendencies and impulses for action are involved, how then can I determine which part of my actions and my perceptions originates from the Heavenly mode and which from the Human mode? Am I in the perspective of the Human or of Heaven when I try to evaluate this distinction? These two expressions "what Heaven does" and "what Man does" do not cover two areas where things done by humans and things done by Nature can be tidily classified, but two ways, or two styles, of establishing a physical or perceptual contact with the outside world.

It is not therefore by overlaying a fixed thing with a name but by adhering to the real that one can conceive of true knowledge, which requires adjustment to change. Zhuangzi turns away from the direct correspondence between the thing and the mind, in order to examine the capacity of the human being to grasp the action of Heaven and to espouse its process. That is why he ignores the problem of theoretical knowledge rather than trying to solve it.

There can be no true knowledge unless it can be shown what the life of the true man looks like. In the way Zhuangzi describes it, the temperament of these "true men of early times," or their way of reacting to what happens to them and their ability to adapt themselves to the order of things, gives a hint of what a perfect active life would be. It is defined by the capacity for detachment and obliviousness necessary to avoid dramatizing the negative phases in existence, by not opposing self to world but, on the contrary, being unreservedly acquiescent and ready for anything that happens. Zhuangzi's description of true men is able to reveal the pulse of beings whose "mode of Heaven" extends unhindered. But curiously, this portrait of the vital force at the height of its fullness is marked by cycles of deprivation, negation, ignorance, and incapacity that indicate the fissure between a life directed by the desires and calculations of consciousness and a life inspired by the dynamic of Heaven. The true man is characterized not by a set of acclaimed values, nor by a high degree of knowledge attained through study or reflection, but by a certain temperament, a certain global physiology that is probed by means of a "diagnosis".

In olden times, true men did not rise up in need, nor did they glorify their exploits. They did not make plans.

They were such that when they overstepped the mark they had no regrets, and when their aim was right they did not make much of it; so they rose up without trembling at heights, plunged into water without getting wet, walked through fire without being burnt; such are those whose knowledge is elevated to joining the flow of things.

In olden times, true men slept dreamless sleep, and, waking, had no worries; they nourished themselves without seeking flavor, and their breathing was profoundly deep! The true man breathes from his heels, the ordinary man from the throat. Those who live bowed in submission appear to spew out the words that obstruct their throats. The greater the extent of their tastes and desires, the lesser the effect of the spring of Heaven within them.

In olden times, true men had no notion of rejoicing in life or hating death. In blossoming, they did not rejoice, in decline, they did not resist. With ease they came and went, and that was that. They did not forget what made them quicken to life, and they did not enquire what would put an end to it; what they received, they enjoyed, but forgot it once they had to give it away: this is what we call not assisting the Way with the mind, or non-assistance of Heaven by the Human. And that is the meaning of 'true man'.

In such men, the mind is absorbed in oblivion, the countenance is quiet, the forehead broadens; desolate like autumn, gentle like spring, their furies and their joys are in tune with the seasons. They adjust to things, and no one knows to what extent.

It would surely be a mistake to consider that Zhuangzi here is trying to provide a faithful and literal description of the men of the past. It is far more likely that he is drawing the reader's attention to distant forms of existence that reveal by contrast our fruitless attempts to order and rationalize a world that is basically resistant to the enterprise of theoretical knowledge and intentional action. In the mode that Zhuangzi calls celestial or "Heavenly," personal existence imposes no finality, it construes no particular meaning and remains "lodged" in necessity. The *Zhuangzi* is not elaborating a fiction of an original condition implicitly prophesying the history of human decay. It is not about defending a thesis on man, or about following a genetic process of the development of consciousness starting from considerations about primeval humans the point is to display spontaneous responses to certain ordinary situations, presenting them in such a way that ethical values arise naturally from simply describing them. These descriptions help us imagine the limitless range of action associated with the vital potency of these "true men." The "true men of old" far from aspiring to a loftier existence detached from all the contingencies of carnal existence, are propped up by the primordial forces of Heaven, unmediated by conscious will or a purposeful mind.

> In olden times, true men did not rise up in need, nor did they glorify their exploits. They did not make plans.
> They were such that when they overstepped the mark they had no regrets, and when their aim was right they did not make much of it; so they rose up without trembling at heights, plunged into water without getting wet, walked through fire without being burnt; such are those whose knowledge is elevated to joining the flow of things.

Zhuangzi's description throws into relief the indifference of true men towards any form of success, failure or need. Zhuangzi's omissions are loaded with meaning: he intentionally lays aside the canonical figures of sages championed by his contemporaries. His authentic men of the past contrast in every way with the legendary Emperors, Yao, Shun, and Yu; with the saintly kings of the past, Wen or his son Wu; with their accomplished ministers, whose names evoke a glorious age when virtue reigned supreme in the world. By quoting Emperor Shun's words or by mentioning King Wen's conduct, a minister at court, a royal advisor or a simple retainer, could impose his own will and his values. The uses and abuses of these illustrious names has been such that as early as the Warring States period they might be adequately compared to wax noses that can be bent to point in any direction one wishes. By choosing anonymity for his true men, Zhuangzi is protecting his descriptions of vital power from any aim of securing moral edification or political credit. At the same time, he blurs the distinction between the descriptive and the prescriptive aspects in the depictions of these true men.

More radically, the "genuine man of old" makes no projects, nor is the focus of his strength and schemes his anticipated interest. His activity is directed solely toward the instantaneousness of living. This description of a true life stands in complete opposition to the dominant strategic discourse of Zhuangzi's time, when reflections on diplomatic and military matters, on alliances and stratagems, take pride of place in the writings of the masters, attracting the attention of the majority of statesmen who were engaged in the fierce and frantic race for political supremacy. At the turn of the fourth and third centuries BCE, a crowd of experts and masters versed in a smorgasbord of different disciplines, from self-cultivation to military strategy to divination to fiscal administration, developed a rich literature around the themes of anticipation, premonition, calculation of probabilities or tactical opportunity. This literature redefines the major and legitimate figures of the political order: the monarch and his reforming minister, the military commander, the diplomat-sophist and the scholar-administrator. Social roles are also strictly determined: the peasant-soldier, the clerk, the small-scale trader, the artisan in the state workshops, all seen as servants of the newly centralized and bureaucratic state. Among those servants whose talents were most appreciated were the specialists in warfare, the generals and the ministers undertaking wily maneuvers to address the balance of power between rival kingdoms. Zhuangzi's portrayal of the authentic man is directed against these types of men, promoted by the intelligentsia of their time; hence the true man is portrayed through a striking series of emphatic negations. At this early stage of its development, Chinese thought already shows in the *Zhuangzi* a constant tension between *premonition* (an anticipatory wisdom still imbued with a magical aura, inherited from the divinatory imagination of ancient times) and the mindfulness of the present that means that one is wholly focused on what is happening now, with no ulterior motive, no emotional traces from the past, no strategy or conjecture regarding the future. Plans, projects, and machinations—the main meanings of the term *mou* used by Zhuangzi in a negative sense—are travesties of the spontaneous efficiency of Heaven transformed into a frenzied quest for profit. Endless predictions and calculations of benefits must be cut short.

Zhuangzi simply describes the optimum mode of functioning of the vital process, when it is not hindered by "human" sensibility. But even so, is it possible to avoid planning without renouncing action? How can one abandon all pretention to control what is to come? Zhuangzi's "true man" is no man of action, because he does not make plans, and the time involved in his activity is not subject to calculation. Activity is the mode by which we respond, adapt, and move, a mode that grows in intensity while self-consciousness is being resorbed. As distinguished from activity, action relates to the daily management of the self. It is linked, and subservient, to intentions, calculations, projections and plans. When an artist promotes his work, (s)he is in the mode of "action." When a musician is in the process of composing a symphony, (s)he is engrossed in "activity." These are two systems of coordinates for functioning: now an individual consciousness facing an exterior world made of things and people, and relating to them by intentional action; at another moment, a partial or total forgetting of the self, when the old oppositions between the ego and the real, between individual action and outside forces, no longer hold. Zhuangzi calls these the Human mode and the Heavenly mode. They alternately take precedence in the self. And for the true man, these two unitary modes are no longer in conflict but nourish each other.

Zhuangzi mentions true men again when "they fail without regret." The moral pitfall is to think that, because success has been achieved in something planned, it has been accomplished by willpower. Ideas of merit and regret, or of success and failure, develop from this. For the true man, the discrepancy between failure and success, between attaining and missing the target, counts for nothing, for he lays claim to no reward or gratification and does not combat anything. He does not think about the possibility of confrontation between word and fact, between plan and result, but only the full adequacy of one's activity, which is missing as soon as it turns into a series of actions based on will and forethought. True men can fail or fall short of their aims without regret because they do not make theirs the logic of capturing the right moment, of seizing an opportunity, of choosing the propitious time. The true man is not pugnacious, he makes no efforts, has no notion of repentance, neither does he have any use for the past. The discordance between Zhuangzi's true man and the righteous man according to Confucius, is obvious. In Book One of the *Analects*, one of Confucius' disciples, Master Zeng, declares that he carries out a moral introspection of his behavior every day, in order to test his sincerity concerning his attitudes towards others. He questions himself in particular on his loyalty when making plans (*mou*, the same term as that employed negatively by Zhuangzi[5]) concerning other people.

Zhuangzi's portrait of the true men of old tells the reader not only about an ideal but also about certain clearly stated denials: the rejection of the heroic route, the philosophical route, and the strategic route all at the same time. The rejection of philosophy has already been located in the redundancy proposed for the problem of the theory of knowledge. The rejection of the heroic conception of wisdom takes shape in Zhuangzi's remarks on the conduct of true men. Unconcerned by plans, indifferent to calculated mastery of their fate, they know nothing of the conspiratorial intelligence of the strategist that makes life a phenomenon of self-interest, subject to the logic of desires and social judgment.

They were such that they rose up without trembling at heights, plunged into water without getting wet, walked through fire without being burnt; such are those whose knowledge is elevated to joining the flow of things.

The evocations of walking through fire, plunging into water or rising above the clouds usher the reader into a world of activity belonging to the substrata of shamanic culture. But these vestiges of magical thinking have been resituated here on a literary plane and show in hyperbolic form that the true man is not limited in his mobility or in his capacity to circulate among heights or in the depths, or in his full communication with the primordial elements. Nothing can change or challenge him, obstruct or harm him; for him, everywhere is home.

Signs of Heaven in the body

... Behind thy thoughts and feelings, my brother, there is a
mighty lord, an unknown sage—it is called Self; it dwelleth
in thy body, it is thy body.
NIETZSCHE, *THUS SPAKE ZARATHUSTRA*, 1 "DESPISERS OF THE
BODY" (TRANS. THOMAS COMMON)

"In olden times, true men slept dreamless sleep, and, waking, had no worries; they nourished themselves without seeking flavor, and their breathing was profoundly deep! The true man breathes from his heels, the ordinary man from the throat. Those who live bowed in submission appear to vomit the words that obstruct their throats. The greater the extent of their tastes and desires, the lesser the effect of the spring of Heaven within them.

In olden times, true men had no notion of rejoicing in life or hating death. In blossoming, they did not rejoice, in decline, they did not resist. With ease they came and went, and that was that. They did not forget what made them quicken to life, and they did not enquire what would put an end to it; what they received, they enjoyed, but forgot it once they had to give it away: this is what we call not assisting the Way with the mind, or non-assistance of Heaven by Man. And that is the meaning of 'true man.'

In such men, the mind is absorbed in oblivion, the countenance is quiet, the forehead broadens; desolate like autumn, gentle like spring, their furies and their joys are in tune with the seasons. They adjust to things, and no one knows to what extent."

True men are now defined by the daily round of actions that nurture life: breathing, sleep and food. Such remarks, however brief, and however fundamental the activities concerned, may well perturb the reader expecting loftier considerations. Why would one tarry here, at so basic a level of existence, with physiological concerns? Indeed, feeding, breathing and sleeping are all specializations of the body that would appear to lead nowhere; but by describing these activities Zhuangzi uncovers the nature of the true man, who fully dissociates his organic functions from his desires and his will. He has a potency that escapes the normal reactions of consciousness and which underpins the manner in which adaptive and preservative functions are carried out. In this sense, these phenomena of the vegetative or animal life are a quasi-therapeutic way to test vital processes that are infinitely superior to habitual ways of feeling and thinking. If Zhuangzi starts from the "lowest" behavior, this is not because natural order makes the development of higher behavior possible; on the contrary it is because the mode of Heaven is already entirely present in the primitive manifestations of vital activity. It is a way to detect an experience stemming from somewhere between instinct and circumstance without the intervention of the consciousness that makes every effort to separate the person from the world in order to constitute a self. True men, as is provocatively intimated, hardly have a notion of self and do not even remember what they just said.

The dream, a nocturnal double of worry

"To sleep, perchance to Dream; ay, there's the rub."
SHAKESPEARE, *HAMLET*, ACT III, SCENE 1.

"To all those belauded sages of the academic chairs, wisdom was sleep without dreams: they knew no higher significance of life."
NIETZSCHE, *THUS SPAKE ZARATHUSTRA*, 2 "THE ACADEMIC CHAIRS OF VIRTUE" (TRANS. THOMAS COMMON)

"In olden times, true men slept without dreaming and their days passed without worrying." As the parallel structure of this sentence would suggest, common men are prone to worry during the day and are troubled at night by their dreams. For Zhuangzi, dreams, seem to express a constant irritation of one's energies, a hoarded anxiety, a nervous residue of the previous day's activity. Dreaming is the fretting and rattling of the mind that burdens the body just when it requires relief. If one could be freed from desire and from the will to plan and implement, then dreaming would have neither point nor purpose: there would be nothing to live through again, nothing to reconstruct or program, no projects and no follow up. Sleeping would be real repose. Dreaming is the nocturnal version of worry, worsening the pollution caused by chronic preoccupation. "If it be an annihilation of our being, 'tis yet a bettering of one's condition to enter into a long, peaceable night; we find nothing more sweet in life than quiet repose and deep dreamless sleep." These were the words that Socrates supposedly used before his judges in order to allay the terrifying prospect of death.[6] Sleep does not constitute an action as such. It is more of an activity for restoring strength to the body by non-action. Maurice Merleau-Ponty offers a compelling description of the state of sleep: "a modality of perceptual progression—or more precisely its temporary involution, the dedifferentiation, the return to the inarticulate, the return to a global or pre-personal relationship with the world that is not really an absence, more like a distancing where the body marks one's position . . ."[7] When he sleeps, the true man does not enter an imaginary world, he does not substitute a fantasy double for the elision of the real world where he can participate and use his energy, thereby upsetting the primary function of sleep, which is to restore strength, just as breathing or eating renew the life-breath. When the true man sleeps without dreaming, he knows how to take leave of the world—in the absence of dreams he is not intentionally joining up with the world—while staying comfortably in it. In dreams, the world is detained in a traumatic form; the sleeper denies it without being able to erase it. "The elimination of dreams from the worldview of the Saint means rejecting the most dramatic duality structuring human consciousness, and it engages the demonstration of the unity of opposites. Indeed, the alternation of dreaming and waking evokes by analogy multiple pairs of apparently antagonistic realities, starting with life and death. The reduction of this alternation to the unit is a prelude to the treatment of other binary systems."[8]

Food, between frugality and feast

When the true man feeds, he does not seek the pleasures of flavor, enjoyment or delight. Tasting involves discriminating; focusing on the finesse of aroma for the enjoyment of the senses is detrimental to the basic restorative needs of the body. The sage does not seek to satisfy his palate, he just fills his stomach and seeks to nourish his bodily form from throat to toe by appropriate breathing. Education, or the *filtering* of immediate life by human concerns, perturbs these sensations. The need to eat is then collated with desires that can only be satisfied at great cost, leaving the palate hard to please, the stomach delicate and soon repelled, using quite considerable resources that only cause pain and strain.

However, it is not really possible to comprehend the full scope of this affirmation until its resonance in the political sphere is taken into account: it should be read in counterpoint to the politico-moral commonplaces on the art of food preparation and the mingling of flavors and aromas, a frequent theme in the philosophical literature of the Warring States period. An exquisitely prepared dish from the king's talented chef is a recurring metaphor for appropriation of the world in its different essences through gustation. Zhuangzi's true man is placed in direct opposition to the archetype of the political man: the true man does not manipulate flavors in a quest for a beneficial or morally nourishing harmony; he is sated with everyday food, not dainty dishes. No meal can titillate him, so in the literal sense he does not *break fast*, he maintains a practice of social fasting in that he seeks nothing more than sustenance. This brief line about the way the true man feeds himself should be read not only as an additional remark on the sage's lifestyle, but also construed as the rejection of a system for establishing social and moral authority through the distribution and consumption among the happy few of rich and flavorsome foods. Moreover, the true man's attitude to food corresponds exactly to the prescribed ritual for periods of mourning. "When he is in mourning for his parents, the gentleman, were he to eat good things, does not take pleasure in them"[9] as Confucius reminds his daring disciple Zai Yu who is hoping to take certain liberties with the observance of the three-year mourning period. But for Zhuangzi such an abstemious disposition has an entirely different significance. If the true man normally behaves as the Confucian gentleman does during mourning, it is only because he is unaware of the moral implication of the prohibition of feasting at funerals. Mourning that requires penitence as part of the ritual moral code constitutes a radical break from the usual regime and is considered to be deprivation by choice.[10] In contrast, as the true man is fundamentally uninterested in the enjoyment of flavor, he places himself beyond the alternatives of consumption and abstinence, of feasting and fasting. He neither deprives nor restrains himself, and therefore escapes from the narrow ascetic path of funeral ethics that banish pleasures of the palate, handsome apparel and courtly music for the duration of the mourning period.

Defined in opposition to the harmful interventions of the worried, desirous, gluttonous, and agitated self, the flourishing life of these true men does not come about as a result of the assertive cultivation of virtues, or the possession of a special knowledge, or a spiritual conversion. It is much rather defined by what is "removed," by what it is deprived of (*wu*): plans, regrets, pride, worries, dreams, and flavors.

Respiration vs. perception

Their breathing was profoundly deep! The true man breathes from his heels, the ordinary man from the throat. Those who live bowed in submission appear to spew out the words that obstruct their throats. The greater the extent of their tastes and desires, the lesser the effect of the spring of Heaven within them.

What better than breathing to express the continuous exchange between the self and the world, between inside and outside? The way an exchange of air takes place necessarily affects the pulse of our vital rhythm, of our inner tempo. Breathing is the barometer of living beings: yawning signals energy level at a low ebb and the onset of sleepiness; sighing indicates fatigue and reduced moral energy; panting is an extenuating staccato expressing anxiety or fear; dilating the nostrils allows exhilarating fresh air to revive the body from the inside and to absorb ambient scents and smells.

In this brief passage, the many who only breathe from their throats are suffocating, their breath is constricted and they seem to spit out their words: this short but striking evocation uses harsh metaphors of chronic disease, fatigue and sickly weakness, psychological asthma, and incurable logorrhoea, to describe the common condition of humans when, laden with age and worries, they can no longer enjoy the benefits of absorbing the vital breath. This is echoed in Montaigne who also remarks that ordinarily we are "all cramped and confined inside ourselves."[11] "Our mind as it ages becomes constipated and squat" using terms that debase the mind by describing it as if it were part of the bowels.[12] Zhuangzi is saying here that in their own way, words are also obstructions that curtail the refreshment of attitudes to tune in with the present moment.

The image of breathing from the heels, an unexpected comparison, refers to the actual experience of learning to breathe with the whole body, a technique that is familiar to adepts of the art of controlled breathing.[13] It means understanding that breathing is more than just the inhalation and then exhalation of air through the nostrils and the mouth. It is a way to ingest, to nurture oneself from the outside, and to *give back* what is inside with every breath in a two-way process tuned to the workings of the world. In a way, one expresses oneself in the same manner as when one exhales: when one breathes from the heels, the whole body is involved, mobilized, and benefits from the continuous renewal of energy breath that both builds and animates all beings.

This description of breathing from the heels finds its literary meaning primarily in the dynamic effect created in the reader's mind: the image of the sage breathing deeply and amply from his heels weaves a tensile web arising from the dialectics of motion; he appears to take root in the earth by the base of his feet and makes inside air flow upwards in a rising movement, increasing internal fluidity by drawing potency from the deepest recesses of the body. A later Taoist interpretation of this phrase has it that the man who possesses true knowledge of natural processes captures the Yin energies of the earth through the soles of his feet and makes them rise and flow through him. This is a plausible interpretation, but most likely, since the *Zhuangzi* every so often mocks the technical and overly assertive forms of self-cultivation, this phrase is probably not referring to an actual practice; in the context of this long passage about the authentic men of olden times, the author is freely unspooling a stream of striking images that give an idea of what living looks like when one is not stunted by a cramped and worried mind, when one's energies are fully adduced and flow freely throughout the whole body.

Awake without worries, asleep without dreams, eating without flavors, letting the body breathe at ease without blocking the throat with the constraint of appetites, all this shows how Heaven moves in the true man as he revives himself far away from the interference of human society. The true man is entirely in rhythm with his activity: "When I dance, I dance. When I sleep, I sleep."[14] Behind this apparent truism, whose rhetoric is also knowingly exploited by Chinese authors, Montaigne, in a distant echo to Zhuangzi's expressions, illustrates the perfect coincidence of what one is and what one does, this art of "living in relevance."[15] The free flow of one's internal natural resources is not to be confused with the superficial stimulation provoked by the connection between the senses and external things. Heaven nourishes the bodily form while the energy aroused by desires is a wasteful compromising of vital potency.

> In olden times, true men had no notion of rejoicing in life or hating death. In blossoming, they did not rejoice, in decline, they did not resist. With ease they came and went, and that was that. They did not forget what made them quicken to life, and they did not enquire what would put an end to it; what they received, they enjoyed, but forgot it once they had to give it away: this is what we call not assisting the Way with the mind, or non-assistance of Heaven by Man. And that is the meaning of "true man."

Again, the description of the sage's naturalness evokes vital strength hidden beneath a veneer of incapacity or inability: he does not know how to enjoy life and is not saddened by death. Whether positive or negative, his life is untouched by feelings, as though he were entirely taken up by being alive, having no awareness of the representation of the self that undergoes whatever befalls him. This is not a cognitive type of ignorance, but a basic state of non-concern that displays a capacity to remain open to all developments. Because he does not situate his existence in an individual perspective, his days and nights are not troubled by concerns about death. In a way, the sage is like the animal, which envisions death as something external; it is not carried within him, with tragic awareness of finitude, because he has not internalized it. The words used by Zhuangzi which I have translated by "blossoming" and "decline" also mean to exit, to emerge (*chu*) and to enter, to resorb (*ru*), in other words, the hatching of a living form that becomes visible and then returns to the void. These two words, which function in Chinese as a pair of opposites, also express the dual and alternating movement of breathing: inhaling when air is concentrated in the lungs, and exhaling when the air leaves the lungs and is diffused throughout the body. This passage prompts the reader to consider one's life like the act of breathing, which the true man follows to the full and with equal ease in its two opposite phases. These natural movements should cause neither joy nor sorrow. To fight against decline, to stiffen against resorbing, would be like blocking one's windpipe by holding one's breath to retain all the inhaled air. As Zhuangzi would say, this is *assisting* the Way with the mind by intending to intervene in the natural order of things.

> "In such men, the mind is absorbed in oblivion, the countenance is quiet, the forehead broadens; dull and desolate like autumn, gently warm like spring, their furies and their joys are in tune with the seasons. They adjust to things, and no one knows to what extent."

In this portrait, the true man offers a cold, mirthless and inert autumnal exterior and then exudes the revived heat of spring. Zhuangzi is emphasizing a way of adhering so intimately to the process of the seasons that internal dispositions evolve according to the humors and influxes wafting out from heaven and earth. This portrayal of true men, with its brief evocation of their physiognomy and physiology, stands clearly apart from the edifying descriptions of the outward signs of virtue found in the texts concerning practices for perfecting the self, which were beginning to circulate widely over the course of the fourth and third centuries BCE. In some of these self-cultivation texts, such as the treatises. "Mental Techniques" in the *Guanzi*, the sage is portrayed as a sort of superman, with robust bone structure, vigorous muscles, and taut skin, whose aura commands immediate acquiescence. Instead of the athletic physique of this sage, who gradually transforms into a conventional rhetorical figure denoting the sovereign who can steer and sway the whole world, Zhuangzi presents an apathetic figure who seems to fade into the background.

Their moods develop in tune with the weather. The internal humors of the genuine men, who does not obstruct the way of Heaven with the Human element, respond to the vapors emanating from the sky (the term "desolate," which is pronounced *qi*, signifies a cloud forming, a state of extreme cold produced by condensation of the breaths). Emotions are simply considered to be internal modulations of a global climate affecting the world in the form of seasons.

> In this way[16] they were one with what pleased them, and one with what they disliked: that they were one and the same or not so, in both cases, it amounted to the same.
> Making everything one, is being companion to Heaven; not making everything one, is being companion to Humans. When the Heavenly mode and the Human mode do not take precedence over one another, there is the true man."[17]

In his typical jocose vein, Zhuangzi uses parallel sentence structures, wittingly taut and abstruse, which, in a play of cross-braced symmetries, endlessly divide and combine. It sets itself against the disjunctive and determining logic that language imposes on the perception of things, as if Zhuangzi wished to make language work against its own nature for it to attain a higher form of cohesion. Now he no longer questions the reality of the terms Heaven and Human, but their duality. He concludes with the affirmation of the genuine man's alternate unity, his double "companionship," while duality in its essence is maintained, because the double foundation of human existence is not resorbed into a unity to the benefit of Heaven. This passage is extremely intense; it is the moment where Zhuangzi maintains the double affiliation of the human being and the contrast between two forms of harmony with the world, without attributing a hierarchy, without letting one prevail. During the variation in his moods, the true man meets things, people, and situations with which he becomes one and to which he belongs; he meets others that he resists or refuses. So, he is either being "one" or "non-one." But in both these ways of reacting or of positioning himself he remains fundamentally "one" and is never altered. In the world of things, the true man can love, detest, judge, discriminate, evaluate, differentiate, and in doing so he is living his life in the Human mode. But that does not prevent him from making a timely relocation in the perspective of Heaven. Things can please or displease the true man, but in both cases, whichever way he is affected, he remains whole and unified in his activity.

Zhuangzi is not satisfied with maintaining the simple stance that relates Heaven to unity and the Human mode to multiplicity. He is trying to build a unity through the continuous alternation of these two modes of perception and action. Unity is not on the side of Heaven: it is to be found in the maintenance of continuous tension between these two forces that nurture our activity. His capacity of integration is the condition of his integrity.

This is how Zhuangzi situates the capacity of the true man to be one and whole (the two meanings of *yi*) on two levels: he remains one through the alternation of his tastes and dislikes, of what he adores and abhors. His vital rhythm is always in tune with what he encounters: ardent in anger, calm in friendly encounter, adapting the movement of his humors accordingly, allowing himself to be relevantly affected without losing unity. What makes a man "genuine" or "true" (*zhen*) is his capacity to act, sometimes by what Heaven does, sometimes by what the Human mode does. He can be sometimes one and sometimes not-one, and in either case it is all one for him.

The distinction Zhuangzi makes between Heaven and Human constitutes the structure of human life considered as a "practice." How are we to understand the duality and the unity that he suggests? The distinction between Heaven and Human raises two problems: the first is the question of the nature of the gap between the two principles; the second is to understand the meaning of this gap. Can this duality be carried through to a conclusion? Does it not have to be integrated into a higher unity? Unity is maintained in the form of a *practice* and requires the capacity to remain intact even when one is overcome by certain emotions. The Human mode fulfils a practical function: organizing the relationships between objects and language, setting up relationships between consciousness and environment based on projects and planning. Zhuangzi suggests that this is the best we can do in everyday human society. But at the same time, this practical function creates something of an obstacle calling for self-control in order to counter the temptation to submit to the logic of desires and things. The intuition of the Heavenly mode enables us to relate to the vital force smothered by all our everyday efforts, and learn to channel it without the filter of a human lens. This is what we do without realizing it when we are in a state of unconscious mastery, when, improvising on the piano for example, we let ourselves be guided by the spontaneous forces of the body without exerting control over it. At this point all that remains is a pure unreflecting activity relieved of will and self. Zhuangzi is referring here to two ways of establishing a relationship between the self and the outside world, two contrasting perspectives, but which, in an individual's life, mingle, interact or cooperate. The original intuition of the fundamental distinction between Heaven and Human, and the very problem posed by this duality, is at the source of all the obstacles that people encounter in daily life and that Zhuangzi considers throughout the work: the pitfalls of language losing itself in its own profligacy, the tyranny of will and the indulging servitude to desire, the exhaustion of energy in the pursuit of name and fame, personal conduct inevitably involved in power-game strategies, and, finally, issues of bereavement, mourning, and one's own death. Zhuangzi does not attempt to use arguments or reasoning to square difficulties but he continuously suggests, or illustrates, how some people with a natural propensity can sometimes manage to find their way along these shifting tracks.

Conclusion

There is doubtless a great mystery as to why any such thing as being conscious should exist at all.

HUMAN NATURE AND CONDUCT, JOHN DEWEY

In the six chapters of this book, the reader has been introduced to stories and dialogues where the protagonists are chance friends, furred and feathered fauna, feisty masters or off-course disciples. Lucid or ludic, iconic or ironic, comic or cosmic, parodic or parochial, the guises of masters and sages are many, and their unsettling variety can be seen as the consequence on the narrative plane of the *Zhuangzi*'s lessons on the pitfalls of pedagogy, the dangers of public recognition and the limits of verbal instruction. Some of these unconventional protagonists in early philosophical literature eventually realize what is restraining them, and sometimes they manage to break free without trying to improve the world or manage others' lives. In all these tales and parables, the authors of the *Zhuangzi*, unlike their contemporaries, do not seek to command assent, or to present themselves as moral authorities imposing a single line of conduct. Aside from a few ideas and aphorisms from the *Laozi*, in the *Zhuangzi* there are no positive instructions based on a repository of texts or a set of codified norms and patterns of conduct. Relationships between masters and disciples are characterized by a systematic tendency to ignore or to disparage education centered on the rote learning of texts, the memorization of moral precedents, and the acquisition of ritual manners. Zhuangzi's fictional Confucius bemoans his failure to instruct and transform people through writings from the past and ritual manners. Enlightenment flows forth from puzzling narratives or indecorous situations. Ordinary circumstances are intertwined with the most unlikely fantasy. And yet, the fictional encounters presented in the book are true dialogues, in that the characters engage in exchanges that are not dictated by any established authority that would only use interlocutors as mere interchangeable messengers or mouthpieces. These dialogues that often tack and swerve are an opportunity for an opportunity for an authentic discussion that sometimes demand harsh treatment of the other. Jean-François Billeter observed that the *Zhuangzi* is the only work from early China in which the reader can witness one character suddenly undergoing a deep change in the middle of a conversation, and sometimes experiencing a spiritual conversion after a moment of debate or of solitary seclusion.[1]

There is a predictable risk involved in extracting a remark from the *Zhuangzi* and considering it as a piece of an underlying doctrine that the commentator would have to reassemble through a merry cherry-picking expedition across the Taoist orchard of the thirty-three chapters. Nothing is systematic: every position, situation or conclusion finds an opposite that is equal in dignity: exclusive concentration on one thing can be fruitful or fatal, a full dedication to others can be a form of holiness or just a self-destructive way of life; following a master for years can be the sign of an immature mind or the evidence that you have the right stuff and smarts to become a sage. If one of the primary functions of literature is to expand and enrich the scope of what words can express about the subjective experience of the world, then the *Zhuangzi* has no equal in early China, with its inventive capacity to hustle the language away from certainty and stasis. The uncanny ability of certain masters or sages to strike or change people who come to question them is less a question of delivering words of wisdom and soothing truths than of finding the right words for the right person at the right moment. Many sayings in the *Zhuangzi* are contextual, adapted to a specific situation: the speaker (a sage, a hermit, a master, a craftsman) adjusts his words according to the aptitudes, temper, and needs of the listener. Old sparring partners, ephemeral coteries, informal meetings, chance encounters, travelers' talk: all these different contexts of speech converge towards the ideal of a merry fellowship that stands clearly aside from the sphere of the state and the strictures of an orthodoxy. Into the oppressive atmosphere of the court and in place of the relationship between the sovereign and his courtiers, Zhuangzi and his followers ventured to introduce a form of mutual entente liberated from ritual manners, protocol and precedence, conflict of interests, ulterior motives for profit or promotion. In the story of the four friends taking an oath, Master Yu and Master Lai's dauntless assent to life was pushed to its limits in the experience of deformity and death; in the crass funerals led by the flippant cronies, we observed the clash, unbearable for Confucius' disciples, between a heedless parody of funerary lament and the dutiful observation of grievance conforming to ritual norms; in the striking story of Butcher Ding chopping up an ox, read from a political standpoint, we watched the rehabilitation of the most servile gesture as a motor of personal emancipation, as the butcher enjoyed the efficiency of a spiritual energy (*shen*) in his dancing motions, thereby abolishing the long and rigid chain connecting and differentiating the menial task of killing an animal and the privileged intake of ritualized meat partaken with the Spirits. The only common thread that runs across these various tales and dialogues is the sometimes therapeutic sometimes light-hearted use of literary imagination, freed from any pretense to historical truth. Indeed, the *Zhuangzi* makes full use of literary imagination, not for shaping but for distorting the images provided by perception, memory and habit. By resorting to brief pieces of fictions, the *Zhuangzi* disregards the implicit demand of verisimilitude in discourse, the better to reject the conventional judgments and norms embedded in the uncritical use of language. The *Zhuangzi* appropriates characters and events famous from early historical texts, and reshapes them in unorthodox ways. It puts subversive speeches in the mouth of imaginary characters, and unlikely speeches in the mouths of historically attested individuals. It may be argued that Zhuangzi has diverged so extravagantly from canonical and historical writings and their predetermined form that he ends up straying into a hitherto uncharted territory, one which today we would call *fiction*.

The only true teaching that deserves our veneration, is not made of a master's sayings, is not made of a ruler's speeches or a wise minister's sermons, it is what we manage to draw from the rapt listening to the deep forces working within us. This kind of learning fully achieves the state of adjustment of our personal existence to the impersonal process of life, and in passing eliminate the reactive and resentful meddling of consciousness. It is this idea which is encapsulated in the title of Chapter 6 *Dazongshi*:[2] the Way, the Great ancestor, is the only authentic master, and other human beings, whether we call them sages or masters, can at best be friendly but ephemeral monitors who alert us to the fact that we are off-tracks or disoriented.[3] In his long unfinished novel *The Man Without Qualities*, Robert Musil writes in a very similar vein of the optimal state one is led to experience once one has managed to get rid of one's conscious faculties and abilities, and dive deep in the space within, to the very root of life:

> "You must keep quite still," her inspiration told her. "You cannot leave room for any land of desire; not even the desire to question. You must also shed the judiciousness with which you perform tasks. You must deprive the mind of all tools and not allow it to be used as a tool. Knowledge is to be discarded by the mind, and willing: you must cast off reality and the longing to turn to it. You must keep to yourself until head, heart, and limbs are nothing but silence. But if, in this way, you attain the highest selflessness, then finally outer and inner will touch each other as if a wedge that had split the world had popped out!"[4]

The tales about free roaming animals, the stories of agony and death, with their strong destructive potential against moral and political institutions reveal men's common blindness, their predatory harshness, even when the somber realism of the philosopher-storyteller is highly colored by bursts of parody and burlesque. The various lifestyles invented in the *Zhuangzi* adumbrate what kind of tradition could have taken shape in Chinese society: a tradition giving prevalence to diversity over unity, to equality over hierarchy, to individual liberty over central authority. This philosophical strand was rapidly buried throughout Chinese imperial history by an unanswerable political paradigm of Unity binding together once and for all monism and monarchism.

One of the core ideas that has guided this book is that our human failure to conduct our life free from worries and violence can be ascribed to what we find at the very foundation of political societies: "a hopeless mess of contradictory forces" as John Dewey puts it, and this is a quasi-incurable condition for most human beings. Hence the need to figure out and reassess our instinctual drives, social compulsions, and cultural norms. Rather than establishing the conditions of an absolute sovereignty, as did most thinkers of the Warring States, the *Zhuangzi* advocates a radical withdrawal from institutions (ritual, sacrifice, government), while also making critical charges against apparently far less suspect practices, such as the simple acts of speaking, naming, and organizing the world. Zhuangzi resolutely sets himself apart from the didactic styles of court advisors, strategists or self-proclaimed experts in all sorts of state business. If his characters—all those obstreperous disciples, cantankerous hermits, outstanding artisans, perspicacious cripples, and astute outlaws—show an irreconcilable variety of profiles and lifestyles, we should certainly not see in this the symptom of an inconsistent doctrine fraught with contradictions; this motley of interacting characters represents possible types of personal accomplishments and individual flourishing, and their stories recount emotional episodes, successful attempts or paroxysmal attitudes running afoul of normal everyday experience "in the human world."

In the manifold representations of these imagined lives, what arises is a fundamental doubt concerning the power of language itself, which is spelled out repeatedly when the authors enquire how they can go on alongside the suspicions that they uncover as they progress. "Now that I have said something, does what I have said not belong to the same category as what I have criticized? I do not know. Whether it belongs to the same category or not, in any case, because categories constitute themselves reciprocally, nothing differentiates them for me. This being so, allow me to say something about it."[5] Authentic men in whom the dimension of the spirit, the *shen*, exists without hindrance, do not write; infants, animals or seasons do not gloss on things, and do not go so far as to waste their breath. Man is held back by restraints, curbs or shackles that prevent him from truly holding on to his vital powers. The ideal would be to write without having to break the silent workings of things, to write as if one had managed to concert the Heavenly and the Human mode in the same spring. We may conjecture that writing became for the authors of the *Zhuangzi* a way of reconciling the artifice of any human enterprise with the attempt to overcome the myopic effects of language on our perception. The host of characters and situations featured in the book are so many literary exercises aiming to bridge the gap between the world as lived experience and the world as a linguistic construct (a construct that is consistently dissected in Chapter 2, "All things on a par").

The fragments, the episodes, and erratic considerations sometimes segue into the next and sometimes just follow on from each other with a link that is nothing but a spider's web or a "autumn hair" (*qiu hao*) to use a common expression from Zhuangzi's time. One may reasonably see in this skein of small fragments and longer stories a direct consequence of the book's editorial vagaries, and yet, these are not the ruins of a completed work that was subsequently lost, nor are they the planned notes of a book that never came to fruition. A reader attuned to contradiction and complexity may observe that the discontinuous mode of composition mirrors the overall sense of dislocation that is almost theorized in many passages, the sense of a crack running through the traditional order of discourse, underlain by the late Zhou structure of political authority and ritualized domination. Juggling the Human and the Heavenly perspectives while featuring a dizzying riot of characters, the book also fathoms the deep or sudden changes in their moods and mindsets, and these effects of discontinuity are fully brought to bear on the way these texts were written and juxtaposed. The reader feels constantly whisked up and down, flung to and fro, passing as in a dream from the dark side of a satire to the blissful rapture of the spirit enchanted by the tide of unknown forces. Perhaps Zhuangzi the moralist and Zhuangzi the mystic become finally one in the awareness of the tiny interstice that separates the wise and the wild, and nature in its raw simplicity from the simpleton's naturalness.

NOTES

Introduction

1 Haun Saussy, *Translation as Citation. Zhuangzi Inside Out* (Oxford: Oxford University Press. 2017), 60.

2 Chapter "Lie Yukou," *Zhuangzi jishi*, 32.1049–1050

3 "Un homme qui pense par lui-même et consulte avant tout sa propre expérience, médite aussi ce que disent les autres et fait un usage réfléchi du langage": see Jean-François Billeter, *Leçons sur Tchouang-tseu* (Paris: Allia, 2002), 41.

4 A mythical figure, minister to the Emperor Yao, often quoted for his uncanny longevity; he is said to have lived for 800 years.

5 Chapter 6, "The Primordial Master," *Zhuangzi jishi*, 6.275.

6 *Tian ji*: literally the mechanism of Heaven.

7 It may have been partly inspired, perhaps unashamedly plagiarized—this remains a moot point—from Xiang Xiu's own and now lost commentary.

8 Some sinologists, including, in France, Jean-François Billeter and Song Gang, have put forward the idea that Guo Xiang's commentary allowed him to put forward an opportunist reading of the *Zhuangzi*. He would have done so in order to give himself a store of nocturnal escapades far from the burden of public office and at the same time to guarantee, with a certain cynical detachment, the occupation of his post, in the manner of a certain number of scholars in early medieval China (3rd-6th centuries), during the Chin and Wei dynasties, who found themselves under the rod of ephemeral princelings and barbarian courts who they scorned, at a time of political disunity, moral crisis and the decay of the imperial order established by the Han dynasty.

9 This artistic technique by which something familiar is rendered suddenly strange and difficult to perceive, thereby renewing our everyday apprehension of common things, was coined by the Russian formalist Viktor Shklovsky (1893–1984) "ostratenie" or "defamiliarization."

10 *Zhuangzi jishi*, 19.646.

11 Henri Michaux (who had the *Zhuangzi* as one of his bedside books) in *Les Grandes épreuves de l'esprit, et les innombrables petites* (Paris: Gallimard, 1966), 27.

1 Carving up a Myth in the Kitchens of Power

1 The question of the identity of the character will be considered below.

2 According to commentators who refer to the explanations of the Han scoliast Zheng Xuan (127–200), this is a passage from the song *Xian Chi, Lake of All Things*, or *Reservoir of the Universe* allegedly dating from the time of the legendary Emperor Yao and mentioned in *The Book of Rites* (*Liji*) and in *The Rites of the Zhou* (*Zhouli*). As no trace of this composition has survived, the translation of the title is only tentative.

3 *Zhi jing*: this appears to refer to the network of horizontal and vertical arteries and veins called *jingluo* in Chinese medicine.

4 This phrase does not appear in the current usual accepted historical editions of the *Zhuangzi* but has been rehabilitated by the contemporary publisher and commentator Chen Guying, who takes it from the work of the philologist and compiler anthologist Chen Jingyuan—aka Bixu zi, or Jasper-Empty-Master—author of an *Errata and Lacunae in the Zhuangzi* (*Zhuangzi quewu*). Chen quotes two versions of the *Zhuangzi* where this phrase appears, Wen Ruhai's and Liu Deyi's. I have to admit that this phrase could be a note by a commentator—added between the lines of the main text and later included as part of it—because it does not fit neatly with the prosody of the passage. However, it does clearly reflect the meaning of the story of butcher Ding, which is, as we shall see, under the cover of a joyous lesson for wellbeing, also a critique of the moral teachings of Mencius on the subject of an ox frightened by the prospect of its sacrifice.

5 R. Sterckx has produced a remarkable analysis of the paradigm of food in early China, "Food and Philosophy in Early China," in R.Sterckx. ed., *Of Tripod and Palate. Food, Religion and Politics in China* (New York: Palgrave Macmillan, 2005), 34–61.

6 The myth of the cook-minister Yi Yin probably began circulating at the end of the fourth century, as the *Mencius* (5.A8) was already

refusing to see culinary talent as the cause of Yi Yin's success, attributing it entirely to his virtue.

7 It should be emphasized here that Ding, unlike Yi Yin, is not a cook but a lowly butcher, as the description of his work makes clear. There is nothing to show that he plays a part in the preparation of dishes for the sovereign.

8 For a biographical note about King Hui of Wei-Liang, I would suggest the reader consult the *Comprehensive Dictionary of Chinese History* (*Zhonguo lishi da cidian*), eds. Zheng Tianding, Tan Qixiang et al., Shanghai cishu, vol. 2, p. 3262. For a more general idea of the geopolitical situation in the seven great rival States of the period, the most comprehensive reference is the classic *History of the Warring States* (*Zhanguo shi*, Shanghai: Shanghai renmin, 1955, ed. rev. 2003) by Yang Kuan, where the author describes the situation in Wei in Chapter 7, p. 300 in particular. In a Western language, the finest analysis is without a doubt Mark Lewis's "Warring States Political History" in the *Cambridge History of Ancient China. From the Origins of Civilization to 221 BC* (Cambridge: Cambridge University Press, 1999); on Wei and King Hui, cf. pp. 619–20 and p. 634.

9 This interview supposedly took place during the thirty-fifth year of the reign of Hui, about 334 BCE. The discussion quoted in this paragraph is found in the *Mencius* IA. 1–3 (*Mengzi zhengyi*, 35 et seq.)

10 *Mencius* IA.3, *Mengzi zhengyi*, 51.

11 The scene described by Zhuangzi is clearly pure invention. Not only is it historical fiction, but it is also entirely unlikely. To underline one of the singularities of Zhuangzi's style, it should be noted that in ritualistic literature, it would have been unthinkable to portray a lowly servant with such a strong individual character: he freely recounts his experience, his slow acquisition of skills, his incomparable talent compared to other butchers, and the degree of pleasure he derives from the mastery of his craft. Nor can the characters portrayed here by Zhuangzi be formally identified. However, if Prince Wenhui is a sort of fictional recreation of a historical personage, then he was probably based on King Hui of Liang. He is less likely to be an allusion to the King of Zhao, Hui-wen, who probably died too late (266 BCE) to coincide with the writing of the internal chapters, and even less likely to be an echo of King Hui-wen of Qin (356–311 BCE), given the considerable distance between Qin and Song, Zhuangzi's country. This historical identification is far from definite, as it is almost certain that Zhuangzi or the anonymous follower was acquainted with Mencius' writings and that in order to respond to them, he used the characters Ding and Wenhui to construct a set of resemblances which match and

contrast with various characters from memorable, historical or mythical episodes, such as Mencius and King Hui of Liang; King Xuan of Qi and the ox being led to slaughter; or the mythical figures of the minister-cook Yi Yin and King Cheng Tang.

12 This comparison, which has been the focus of scholarly discussion in China, does have its limits: the knife is a tool which, like the brush, uses a dynamic of the hand, but cannot occupy a place within the framework of the psychology governing an unpremeditated gesture, or a gesture unencumbered by the external resistance of a concrete obstacle. Ding's activity exists in the context of weightiness, opacity, and encumbrance. The psychology of the actor differs according to the type of materiality confronting him but also according to the sort of tool he wields.

13 Commentators note that the tune of Mulberry Grove is a victory song associated with the foundation of the Shang dynasty by King Cheng Tang. This may well be be another indication in favor of the idea of a re-writing of the myth of the minister-cook Yi Yin, because the latter was in the service of the first Shang king.

14 Cf *Mencius* IA.7 (*Mengzi zhengyi*, 80 et seq.).

15 In this respect the *Mencius* says: "The gentleman is so disposed towards animals that when he has seen one alive, he cannot bear to see it die" (*Mengzi zhengyi*, 83).

16 *Junzi yuan pao chu* (*ibid*). This expression became commonplace and is found in many early texts.

17 This expression, first used by King Xuan, is then repeated adroitly by Mencius in his response.

18 On this point I would refer the reader to the analysis by Billeter, *Leçons sur Tchouang-tseu*, 15–20. Although our interpretive perspectives differ greatly, the phenomena of attention to the self that he notes and reveals in the *Zhuangzi* have been a powerful and enduring intellectual stimulation.

19 Wang Fuzhi (1619–92) comments on this passage in his *Explanations of Zhuangzi* (*Zhuangzi jie*, 120–5) by saying that the large bones of the ox represent the principal dangers in life. The spaces between the joints symbolize the means of avoiding troubles and difficulties; the dexterous use of the ever sharp knife represents the possibilities for protecting oneself from the perils and plagues encountered on the hazardous path through life while maintaining vital energy intact.

20 *Zhuangzi jishi*, 15.535.

21 It says in the *Han Feizi* : "None of the sovereigns of antiquity were more saintly than T'ang the Victorious, no vassal was more sagacious than Yi Yin, and yet the most wise of ministers spoke seventy times to the most saintly of kings before his voice was heard. It was not until he had joined the kitchens as cook for his king, that, having become familiar, the king discovered his virtue and gave him employment" (see chapter "Dangers of Discourse," *Han Feizi jijie,* "Nan yu," I.3.22).

22 The story of the commoner Chen Ping is typical in this respect. The way he carves the meat reveals his measured action and impartiality, gaining him a promotion to the post of prime minister. On this point see *Balanced Discourses (Lunheng jiaoshi,* 27.1122, chapter "Ding xian") by Wang Chong (27–100).

23 See for instance, *Nicomachean Ethics,* Book Ten, in particular sections 7–8, in which Aristotle explains that a well-good life (*eudaimonia*) is coextensive with contemplation (*theoria*).

24 On Aristotle's discussion of slavery and his embarrassment, see Haun Saussy, "A Backstage Tour of the Palace of Culture," *History of Humanities,* vol. 4, no. 1 (2019): 64–5. http://dx.doi. org/10.1086/701985

25 Gaston Bachelard appositely quotes the philosopher Alain's *Twenty Lessons on Fine Arts*: "One doesn't sculpt what one wants. I would say rather one sculpts what the thing wants" ("On ne sculpte pas ce que l'on veut; je dirais qu'on sculpte plutôt ce que la chose veut"), *Vingt Leçons sur les Beaux-Arts,* 1931, e-version based on the 1931 edition published by Gallimard, Seris nrf, p. 84. See http://www.uqac.uquebec. ca/zone31/Classiques_des_sciences_sociales/index.html. The philosopher is pointing to the intuition of the inherent order of a thing, of the naturally present internal structure, that is the notion of its natural outlines, or *tian li* mentioned by the *Zhuangzi.* Anyone who has tried to make a little sculpture in wood understands this idea of a design inherent to the material, which organizes itself according to its pre-inscribed power-lines.

26 Sarah Bakewell, *At the Existentialist Café* (New York: Other Press, 2017), 37. This confession is recounted by Emmanuel Levinas who heard it from Husserl, and then was passed to the editor of the Husserliana. Husserl's analogy between his sharpening away the blade and his endless conceptual fine-tuning comes from a version heard and noted by Simone de Beauvoir in her diary, November 18, 1939 (Simone du Beauvoir, *Wartime Diary* trans. Anne Deing Cordero, eds, Margaret A. Simons and Sylvie Le Bon, Urbana and Chicago, University of Illinois Press, 2008, 161).

2 Zoocide: Zooming out for the Wild in the Zhuangzi

1 Respectively, an inscription engraved on a stele on Mount Lang Ye dating from 219 and an inscription on the gate at Jieshi from 215, described in the "Annals of the First Emperor" *Historical Records* by the great Han dynasty historian, Sima Qian (cf. *Shiji* "Qin shi huang benji," Zhonghua shuju, 6.245 and 6.252). Roel Sterckx, to whom we owe these references, has noted many texts mentioning the transmission of virtue by the sovereign to insects, horses, cattle, etc., dating from the Warring States period and from the Han era (cf. *The Animal and the Daemon in Early China* (Albany: SUNY Press, 2002), 291 n. 113).

2 Using a wealth of textual sources, Roel Sterckx has parsed these early Chinese conceptions concerning animals. His pioneering study carefully examines the ideological phenomenon of the extension of moral and political order to the reign of nature, and that of the constitution of a model of sovereign authority by the textual use of the animal kingdom. These points are discussed in the critical review of his book that I delivered at the behest of the journal *T'oung Pao*, no. 89 (2003): 178–92.

3 Chapter "Responding to Emperors and Kings" ("Ying di wang"), *Zhuangzi jishi*, 7.287. This should probably be understood as a heavily ironic allusion to the famous debate on human nature in the *Mencius*, between the eponymous philosopher and his obdurate adversary Gaozi, the former trying to prove that man's nature can in no way be understood in the sense that this word bears when talking about "the nature of an ox." In other words, although whiteness indicates an identical quality in the expressions "whiteness of jade" and "whiteness of a feather," the word "nature" (*xing*) is modified by the realities to which it refers in the two foregoing cases.

4 Chapter "The Way of Heaven," *Zhuangzi jishi*, 13.482–483. Compare this reply from Laozi with Mencius' admonition in the eponymous book: "Mengzi said to King Xuan of Qi: 'If a ruler treats his subjects as his hands and feet, in return they shall treat him as their heart and belly. And if he treats them as his hounds and horses, they shall treat him as a mere commoner!'" (*Mengzi yizhu*, chapter "Li Lou, xia" 8.3: 186).

5 The artistic genius of the Shang era around 2000 BCE was perhaps most finely expressed in the admirable and inventive representation of

animals, particularly in the shapes and decorative motifs of their bronze vessels, on which are depicted mostly imaginary beasts and not the usual hunting game.

6 Jade axes decorated with animal masks have been unearthed in tombs dating from the Longshan culture. Burned and crackled scapular bones of deer have also been found and there is little doubt that these are connected with the practice of divination by fire.

7 The number 72 is highly symbolic in Chinese numerology and has an important value in the classification system. It is also Confucius' supposed age when he died, and the number of disciples he is said to have trained.

8 *Zhuangzi jishi*, 26.933–934.

9 Léon Vandermeersch makes the comparison in "L'imaginaire divinatoire dans l'histoire en Chine" (*Bulletin de l'Ecole Française d'Extrême-Orient*, 79.1 (1992), 1–8. See also Jean Levi's etc. superb introduction to his translation *Book of Lord Shang* (Paris: Flammarion, 2005), 12–13 and 42–5). See also Albert Galvany, "Le stratège comme maître des signes: art de la guerre et art sémiotique en Chine ancienne," in *War in Perspective: History and Military Culture in China* (Galvany and Graziani eds., *Extrême-Orient Extrême-Occident*, no. 38, Presses universitaires de Vincennes, 2015).

10 The author uses the term *zhi* whose multiple meanings require different translations: a little *zhi* (*xiao zhi*) can mean a weak awareness of things and beings, a poor knowledge, a petty intelligence, a narrow conscience. In contrast to this, the great *zhi* lauded by the author means simultaneously a wide conscience, a vast knowledge or high intelligence. If the fish does not see the pelican, as in Confucius' example, it is because it has a *xiao zhi*, a narrow perception of what stands in front of its eye, because its mind is muddled by plans and projects, or riveted to further goals.

11 The *Hundun*, who has no holes, cavities, or orifices on his body is traditionally called in English 'Humpty-Dumpty', the egg-shaped nursery rhyme character who once broken could not be put together again.

12 Cf. Jean Levi, *Propos intempestifs sur le Tchouang-tseu* (Paris: Allia, 2003).

13 Jean Levi is referring here, without saying so explicitly, to René Girard's principal thesis of the scapegoat, set out notably in *Things Hidden Since the Foundation of the World* (Redwood City: Stanford University Press, 1987).

14 The French philosopher Jacques Rancière uses the phenomenon of the autonomous acquisition of language to explain Joseph Jacotot's pedagogical ethic and the importance of such an intellectual adventure at the beginning of the nineteenth century. Here is an enlightening passage running parallel to the thought of the *Zhuangzi*: "The *words* that a child learns best, those whose meaning he comprehends most clearly, that he best appropriates for his own use, are those he learns without explanation from a teacher or before any explanation by a teacher. In the unequal returns of various intellectual apprenticeships, what all children of men learn best is what no teacher can explain to them, their mother tongue. They are spoken to, and around them people speak. They hear and remember, imitate and repeat, make mistakes and correct, succeed by luck and start again with method, and at too tender an age for the explainers to begin their instruction, are all or almost all—whatever their gender, their social status or the colour of their skin—able to understand and speak the language of their parents" (*Le Maître ignorant. Cinq leçons sur l'émancipation intellectuelle*, coll.10/18, (Paris: Fayard, 2004), 13–14).

15 *Zhuangzi jishi*, 17.552–553.

16 *Zhuangzi*, Chapter 6. The last chapter of this essay provides a translation and commentary of the whole passage dedicated to "the true men of yore."

17 *Wen*, which by extension represents culture, and more precisely the literary and aesthetic refinements of a civilized society.

18 *Zhuangzi jishi*, 14.515.

19 *Lüshi chunqiu*, V.5.

20 See *Han Feizi*, III.10, chapter "The Ten Errors."

21 *The Book of Rites* (*Liji*, 38.1117).

22 "He fu" or "Rhapsody on the cranes" in Fei Zhengang et al. eds., *Complete Rhapsodies of the Han Dynasty* (*Quan han fu*), (Beijing: Beijing daxue chubanshe, 1997), 41.

23 It is not altogether impossible that this toady acclamation of royal virtues, like many epic poems (*fu*) of the same type, has a veiled satirical intention. It sounds like the fustian of a flatterer but it may well be pure irony. In which case, this verse is even more cogent in its parody, and can be seen as reminiscent of the *Zhuangzi*.

24 Leaving out of consideration here the moot point of knowing who among literati actually believed this discourse. The important thing is that such edifying scenes exerted a strong ideological traction.

25 *Zhuangzi jishi*, 18.621, chapter "Supreme Joy." A shorter version of this story can be found in Chapter 19, "The Full Comprehension of Life."

26 On this point, cf. Sterckx, *The Animal and the Daemon*, 170.

27 The air that carries the germs for transformation of beings can only be likened to the sublime and terrifying music mentioned by the Yellow Emperor in Chapter 14 of the *Zhuangzi* ("On the movement of Heaven").

28 The theme of pacific conciliation with the animal world is studied in a detailed discussion in Chapter 5 in R. Sterckx, "Transforming the Beasts" (cf. *The Animal and the Daemon*, particularly from page 148 onwards).

29 "(. . .) qu'il se trie soy mesme et separe de la presse des autres creatures, taille les parts aux animaux ses confreres et compaignons, et leur distribue telle portion de facultez et de forces que bon luy semble." For the original text, cf. *Les Essais*, II.12, eds. Pierre Villey and V.L. Saulnier (Paris: PUF [1924] 1965), 452, and for Florio's superb pioneering translation: http://www.luminarium.org/renascence-editions/montaigne/2xii.htm

30 This passage summarizes in substance the analysis of Mark E. Lewis in *Writing and Authority in Early China*, in the chapter "Writing the Past" (Albany: SUNY Press, 1999), 127 et seq.

31 Confucianism is partly a retrospective creation dating to the Western Han dynasty (206 BCE–9 CE), but in Zhuangzi's time (fourth and third centuries BCE) there were definitely ritualists who claimed to belong to the school of Confucius, though they probably knew little about the historical Confucius.

32 See the *Book of Rites*, *Liji* I.1, chapter "Minor Rituals" ("Qu li"). The *Book of Rites* is a collection of writings by Confucius' epigones, recording in detail the codes of behaviour and manners to be observed in family and social relations as well as detailed liturgies for funerals and sacrifices.

33 Cf. Mark. E. Lewis, *Sanctioned Violence in Early China* (Albany: SUNY Press, 1990), 171. The reference to Mencius is found in *Mengzi zhengyi* (ed. xinbian zhuzi jicheng, Taibei: Shijie, 1974), 219.

34 *Lunyu yizhu*, 9.14: 91.

35 The label "primitivist" was proposed in 1981 by A.C. Graham to designate the cluster of Chapters 8–12 in the *Zhuangzi* (see A.C. Graham, *Chuang-tzŭ. The Inner Chapters* (Indianapolis, Cambridge: Hackett Publishing Co., 2001).

36 *Zhuangzi jishi* 24.8919.

37 See *Zhuangzi jishi*, 9.330.

38 *Ibid.*

39 *Chuxue ji,* edited by Xu Jian (659–729) (Beijing: Zhonghua shuju, 1962), 29.703. I owe this reference to Roel Sterckx.

40 *Zhuangzi jishi,* 24.833

41 In the Guo Xiang edition, this paragraph (*Zhuangzi jishi,* 6.272) has been moved to become part of a story in dialogue form and is spoken by Confucius. As the first passage mentioning the fish out of water calls for this development, the editorial correction suggested by A.C. Graham has been followed here; the two passages are thus placed next to each other (cf. "Textual Notes to Chuang Tzu: The Inner Chapters," in Harold Roth, ed., *A Companion to Angus C. Graham's Chuang Tzu,* edited by Harold Roth (Honolulu, University of Hawai'i Press, 2003), 26).

42 As regards the theme of cosmic rambling and the imagination of space, I refer the reader to my specific study of this topic in *Les Corps dans le taoïsme ancien,* Chapter 5, "Chaos ou Cosmos" (Paris: Les Belles Lettres, coll. Realia, 2011).

43 *Zhuangzi jishi,* 5.217.

44 I am quoting here Henry James' remark about Anthony Trollope's novels, reproduced by Adam Gopnik in his article "Trollope Trending"(see *The New Yorker* (May 4, 2015): 28).

45 We do not know enough about the pre-Han recensions of these texts, so labeling these passages as "overtures" may be a risky gesture in the context of their production. But ever since the Han they have occupied the position of incipits, and their part-to-whole correlation with the remainder of the works they inaugurate is unquestionable.

46 Translation Burton Watson, *The Complete Works of Chuang Tzu,* p. 30.

47 Many commentaries suggest that the term *nu* refers here not to anger but to ardor and impetuousness. For my part, I support the idea of an inaugural fury and would refer the reader to the stimulating study by Song Gang, "La fureur du Zhuangzi," *Cahiers Marcel Granet,* "Du pouvoir," no. 1 (Paris: Presses universitaires de France, 2003).

48 Chapter 10, "Robbers and Burglars" (*Zhuangzi jishi* 10.359).

3 One Monster, Two Mortals, and Myriad Metamorphoses

1 *Si j'estoy faiseur de livres, je feroy un registre commenté des morts diverses. Qui apprendroit les hommes à mourir, leur apprendroit à vivre* Montaigne, *The Complete Essays,* translated by M.A. Screech, Book I. 20 (London: Penguin Classics, 1991), 100. "To philosophize is to learn how to die." The subsequent quotations from Montaigne are from the same chapter.

2 *Lunyu yizhu*, 11.12:113.

3 There are however eloquent moments of pathos in Confucius, as seen in certain scenes of death recorded in the *Analects* or in the *Book of Rites* (chapter "Tan gong") about the death of Yan Hui, Bo Niu, or about his own imminent death. See Amy Olberding, "The Consummation of sorrow: an analysis of Confucius' grief for Yan Hui," *Philosophy East and West*, vol. 54, no. 3 (2004): 279–301.

4 See Marcel Granet, "Le Langage de la douleur, d'après le rituel funéraire de la Chine classique," *Journal de Psychologie* (February 1922): 425–34.

5 *Zhuangzi jishi*, 6.258–62.

6 Montaigne, *Essays*, 103. In French: "C'est la condition de vostre création, c'est une partie de vous que la mort; vous vous fuyez vous mesmes. Cettuy vostre estre, que vous joüyssez, est également party à la mort et à la vie."

7 *Xin zhai.*

8 The image of the well, where one would certainly have difficulty making out one's reflection in the water at the bottom, has above all the metaphorical value of its dark depths and the return to the shady origin of all things.

9 To be more precise, Zhuangzi replaces the first exclamation *wei zai!*: "Wonderful!" or "Marvellous!" by another, *jie hu!* to represent a heavy deep sigh, a plea or a cry of consternation. It is not difficult to imagine that Yu's physical confrontation with his own reflection in the well troubles him for an instant and that his concluding tirade is an act of bravura in immediate reaction to the shock. In other stories, the *Zhuangzi* refers to the luck befalling deformed or mutilated individuals; the chapter "In the World of Men" includes a portrait of a certain invalid and crippled Chou, whose physical appearance is identical to Master Yu's, and who, thanks to his condition, escapes forced labor and military conscription; he is even given free firewood by the authorities. Such are, this time on a political level, the advantages of being crippled and deformed.

10 "La seule différence que je connaisse entre la mort et la vie, c'est qu'à présent vous vivez en masse, et que dissous, épars en molécules, dans vingt ans d'ici vous vivrez en détail" (Diderot, letter to Sophie Volland, October 15?, 1759, in *Lettres à Sophie Volland* (Paris: Gallimard, 1984). The translation of this passage is by Charles T. Wolfe and is taken from his study "Sensibility as Vital Force or as Property of

Matter in Mid-Eighteenth-Century Debates" in Henry Martyn Lloyd (ed.), *The Discourse of Sensibility: The Knowing Body in the Enlightenment* (New York: Springer, 2013).

11 See, for example, the passage of the *Analects* (*Lunyu yizhu* 3.4:24.) in which, when questioned on the foundation of ritual, Confucius recommends sobriety rather than lavishness, and declares that in mourning he prefers there to be deep affliction rather than a thorough attention to the minutiae of decorum. Confucius also emphatically exclaims : "Wearing mourning without any sorrow, how could I bear the sight of that?" (*Lunyu yizhu*, 3.26: 3–4).

12 A retraction of a similar nature is betrayed by the behavior of the eponymous hero in Ibsen's *Peer Gynt*. On the road, Peer meets the Button-moulder who maintains that the time has come for him to be melted down in the giant ladle of nonentity. Peer is horrified and baulks at this idea: "I do not wish to lose an iota of myself." He begs the Button-moulder—who can afford to be conciliatory for he is sure of victory—to be allowed "to borrow myself on credit" and on several occasions he manages to delay the melting down "until the next crossroads." These stolen deadlines naturally prove useless. The *Zhuangzi* employs similar imagery to describe the experience of passing away but his characters behave with a stolid or amused resolve that Peer Gynt obviously wants.

13 This images is also inspired by the cosmic aura the Laozi gave to the bellows of Heaven and Earth, which, by being vacuous, provide an unending supply. The more you work them, the more they produce (*Laozi zhuyi ji pingjia*, 5.78).

14 Yu the Great, the founder of the Xia dynasty, his son Qi who inherited the throne and the Yellow Emperor were all masters in the art of forging.

15 See Marcel Granet, *Danses et Légendes de la Chine ancienne* (Paris: Presses Universitaires de France [1926], rpt. 1959), 503.

16 Granet, *Danses & Légendes*, 498–9.

17 *Ibid.*

18 On the topic of outcasts and pariahs created by legal mutilation, see Albert Galvany and Romain Graziani, "Legal Mutilation and Moral Exclusion: Disputations on Integrity and Deformity in Early China," *T'oung Pao* 106 (2020): 8–55.

19 The term for corporal punishment (*xing* 刑) is nearly identical to the one denoting the visible and external form of things (*xing* 形). They are homophones and are frequently interchanged in the ancient literature.

20 It is worth recalling that Zhuangzi and Diderot, who were both
fascinated by monsters and deformity, make metamorphosis their
keyword and rival each other in imagining strange bodily shapes
bearing unknown organs (see *le Rêve de Julie de Lespinasse*). "For
Diderot disorder conditions Nature's power," writes Annie Ibrahim,
who quotes the following passage from *Letter on the Blind* (*Lettre sur
les aveugles*), which is so in tune with Zhuangzi's thought on nature:
"What is this world? A complex whole, subject to endless revolutions,
all showing a continual tendency to destruction; a swift succession of
beings who follow one another, press forward and vanish." (cf. "Le
matérialisme de Diderot: formes et forces dans l'ordre des vivants," in
Annie Ibrahim (ed.), *Diderot et la question de la forme* (Paris: PUF,
1999).

21 The reader interested in the procedures concerning the ritualising of
death which Zhuangzi was criticising may like to consult the chapter
"Questions from Master Zeng" in the *Book of Rites*. This chapter
contains a fastidious casuistic discussion between Master Zeng and an
imaginary Confucius on the protocol to observe at funeral ceremonies.

22 Although in the *Analects* Confucius tends to avoid the question of
death, in certain dramatic circumstances he can cry out his anxiety and
despair. When his dearest disciple Yan Hui dies, the master howls in
sorrow and twice he exclaims "Heaven is killing me!" (*Lunyu yizhu*,
11.9: 112). When he visits another disciple, Bo Niu, who is
succumbing to an illness, he laments out and loud: "He is lost! Such is
Heaven's will. But such a man, for such an illness, such a man, and
such an illness!" (*Lunyu yizhu*, 6.10: 58).

23 *Liji zhengyi*, 7.206–207. Although prone to shed tears, in the same
chapter Confucius disapproves the excessive show of sorrow.

24 Montaigne, *Essays*, 102.

25 The fictional nature of the story of the four masters is mischievously
reinforced by the names chosen for them. The character *yu* in Chinese
means driver, a carriage, or chariot. Master Yu imagines the
transformation of his backside into a wheel and his mind into a horse.
As mentioned earlier, the character *si* means sacrifice. Is Master Si not
helping his friend to offer himself to Heaven without reticence and to
return his bodily form to the invisible? Master Lai's name is also
eloquent: *lai* means to come, to arrive or become. Master Lai is the one
who talks of going where the authors of the world, the Yin and the
Yang, align us to join with whatever is becoming. *But if we consider
the universe as a huge furnace, and the play of transformations like a
Master founder, where couldn't we go?* And, *li* in Chinese means
plough. The function of a plough is to turn the soil, to mix seed into

the soil so that life can spring up. Before he dies, Master Lai says quite rightly to his friend: *The earth—this great clod—burdens me with a body, then tries me with life, relaxes me with age, rests me with death.* Finally, it should be added that the *Zhuangzi* associates the symbolism of the four names taken individually with a numerological allegory: the four friends represent the four seasons, the two dying Masters correspond to the "full" seasons of summer and winter, while the two others represent spring and autumn, which are the intermediary seasons.

26 A chapter extracted from *Signs*, reproduced in *Michel de Montaigne*, ed. Harold Bloom, Modern Critical Views (New York, New Haven, Philadelphia: Chelsea House Publishers, 1987), 60.

4 Fun at the Funerals

1 The *Zhuangzi* is exploiting here the ambiguity of the character *fang* meaning, in the context of ritual, principles, rules, instructions, and limits to be observed; but the author also plays with the geographical sense of *fang*: a region, country or area, and particularly in Chinese cosmology the squares that divide space, or angles and directions. In opposition to the sphere of Heaven, *fang* refers to the square representing the earth. By respecting social rules, Confucius is tied to this earthly world. The two sassy boon companions described by the master are characterized by movement, freedom to roam in the Heavens, and scorn for vulgar conventions. Ritual transgression appears to represent free crossing of earthly frontiers.

2 The word *dao* is here translated by 'flow' and 'ebb' in order to maintain the continuity and the parallel between what fish and what humans do. The dynamics and pervasive action of the Way (*dao*) compares to water in the *Laozi*.

3 *Zhuangzi jishi*, 6. 264–73.

4 The various authors of the *Zhuangzi* like to use historical characters who will be familiar to readers of Confucian memorabilia: above all Confucius, then some of his disciples like Zigong or Ziqin, and, in some crucial dialogues the most talented and touching of them all, Yan Hui. The authors of the *Zhuangzi* give them various roles to play, put in their mouths words of their own invention, and use them in such a way as to reveal (what they think is) their true character or the stuff they are made of. Confucius and his disciples make about forty appearances in the *Zhuangzi*.

5 A good example is provided in the chapter "Tan gong, 1" of the *Book of Rites*: "Meng Xianzi, after the service which ended the mourning period, still kept his instruments of music hung on their stands, and did not use them; though he could also return to his women's chambers, he abstained from entering. The Master said: 'Xianzi is one degree above other men'" (*Liji Zhengyi*, 6.190).

6 The relevant articles of the etiquette regarding the story under consideration can be found in the chapter "Rules on hurrying to the mourning rites" (as James Legge translates) of the *Book of Rites (Liji)*.

7 See the story analyzed in Chapter 3.

8 *Analects*, 3.26.

9 See Sima Qian's *Historical Records (Shiji)*, 67.2195–99.

10 *Analects*, 5.13.

11 *Analects*, 5.27.

12 In this, the Zigong portrayed by Zhuangzi is a fairly faithful rendering of the Zigong in the *Analects*, often the subject of Confucius' jibes. Wanting to know the master's opinion of him, Zigong asks him directly: "What do you think of me?" Confucius retorts: "You are an instrument." Zigong, who doesn't understand why his master is reducing him to the level of an object, insists: "What sort of instrument?" The master replies: "A vessel for offerings (*hulian*)" (5.4). In another passage Confucius makes an ironic remark concerning Zigong, who is allowing himself to criticise others: "Ah! No doubt he has reached the state of a sage . . . Alas! For my part, I have no leisure for this" (14.29).

13 Peter Sloterdijk, *Im selben Boot. Versuch über die Hyperpolitik* (Frankfurt: Suhrkamp, 1995).

14 In his perceptive monograph on Confucius, Jean Levi shows the negative effects of the appropriation by the forbiddingly dour, supercilious and strait-laced Zengzi of Confucius' sense of ritual, through his devoting an "exclusive and narrow-minded cult to filial piety" *Confucius* (Paris: Pygmalion, 2003).

15 *Analects*, 19.17.

16 *Analects*, 5.9.

17 *Book of Rites* chapter "Tan Gong, 1." Zengzi pours reproach on Zixia: "When your parents died, and you held the funeral ceremonies, the inhabitants of your country hardly heard word of them (i.e., you did not give your parents the honours they deserved). That is your second fault" (*Liji zhengyi*, 7.202).

18 Montaigne, *Essays*, "On restraining your will" 3.10: 1143.

19 Twelve years after this chapter's initial publication in French, Paul d'Ambrosio and Hans-Georg Moeller forged the oxymoron "genuine pretending" to characterize this attitude in many a character in the *Zhuangzi*. It fits exactly Mengsun Cai's frame of mind as explained by Confucius in this story (*Genuine Pretending: On the Philosophy of the Zhuangzi* (New York: Columbia University Press, 2017).)

20 This argument for modern Chinese readers sounds pretty much like those developed in Buddhist schools later on, though the Buddhist doctrine on death is in fact very different from the visions sketched out in the *Zhuangzi*. Yet, historically, the *Zhuangzi* acted as a powerful interface between Chinese civilization and Buddhism and many literary references paved the way for Buddhism's triumph among the upper classes over the course of the early medieval period (known as the Six Dynasties period, roughly between 300 and 600 CE). On the Zhuangzi as a means of accommodating Buddhism on Chinese soil, see Saussy, *Translation as Citation*, chapter 4.

21 Chapter "Supreme Joy," *Zhuangzi jishi*, 18.614–615.

5 Ascesis and Ecstasy

1 Chapter, "The Primordial Master," *Zhuangzi jishi*, 6.252–256.

2 In Chinese, this protagonist is called Nü Yu, literally "Dame-Twist" or "Hunched Woman" or, perhaps, "Dame Lonely." The term *nü*, woman, can also be read as a family name, recorded in certain early Chinese sources (the *Chronicles of Zuo*, or *Zuozhuan*, for instance, mention two people with this name in the state of Qin, Nü Hou and Nü Kuan). At the beginning of Chapter 24, Xu Free-of-Demons ("Xu Wugui"), the minister of Marquis Wen of Wei, bears the name Nü Sang, but his surname is probably pronounced Ru. In the present story, the character Nü Yu is fictional, and the connotative function of the name seems to take precedence over the denotative: in other words, although the name of the person featured by the author can also refer to a male character, in this tale the name *Nü* is adduced to represent a woman. As we shall see a bit later, the author has good reasons to give this character female form in keeping with Laozi's identification of the Tao with "the mother". The deathbed tales in Chapter 3 provide other examples of the facetious use of names in the *Zhuangzi*.

3 It is worth noting that most of the "authentic men" in the *Zhuangzi* are never portrayed as masters; they have no disciples, nor do we hear

them preach, they do not recite, teach or study any texts. At best they give someone a piece of their mind and only speak of their art of life in passing, as an aside. On this topic I refer the reader to my study "Elusive Masters, Powerless Teachers and Dumb Sages: Exploring Pedagogic Skills in the *Zhuangzi*," in Karyn Lai and Chiu Waiwai eds., *Skill and Mastery: Philosophical Stories from the Zhuangzi* (CEACOP East Asian Comparative Ethics, Politics and Philosophy of Law, Rowman and Littlefield International, 2019): 61–84.

4 As a single word, *nü* means "woman" and thus stands in direct opposition to the traditional title of master *zi,* also meaning a child of the male sex. If we are to believe Zi Kui's admiring compliment, the curve evoked by her name (*yu*: bent, hunched, crooked), is not so much the symptom of the condition of a shrivelled and aged woman as it is the intimation of an inward and bowed posture running foul of the ethical and moral values that prevailed in society: rectitude, straight, and aligned posture, correctness (notion of *zheng*). The *Analects* also clearly signal that a master should see that everything is *zheng*, positioned correctly, straight and regulated, be it a seating-mat or a pupil. Falling foul of the bodily manifestations of moral authority inculcated since a very young age, the *Zhuangzi*'s twisted and hunched beings are often endowed with true moral understanding, an enviable destiny and an abundance of vital potency, like Master Yu, who on his deathbed has "his chin buried in his navel, his shoulders overlooking his head," or Uncle-Distorted (Zhilishu) (*Zhuangzi jishi*, 4.180) or Yin-Qi-Zhi-Li-Wu-Shen, the Dislocated-Hunchback-with-Twisted-Feet-and-No-Lips, favorite councilor to King Ling of Wei (*Zhuangzi jishi* 5.216.)

5 Cf. Jon Elster, *Sour Grapes. Studies in the subversion of rationality* (Cambridge, London, New York, Melbourne: Cambridge University Press & Paris: Éditions de la Maison des sciences de l'homme, 1985), 48.

6 Henri Michaux, *Passages* in *Œuvres complètes*, vol. 2, Bibliothèque de la Pléiade (Paris: Gallimard, 2001), 285.

7 The name of this character is almost identical to the name of the ignorant disciple in the present story, Nanbo Ziqi. It is tempting to think that, as a result of various and faulty transcriptions, they are one and the same, one being impermeable to the intuition of the Way and the other, a master accomplished in the techniques of ecstasy. In Chapter 27 ("Yu yan"), a certain Yancheng Ziyou retraces for his previous master—another Ziqi but this time "from the Eastern walls" (*dong guo*) and not from the South (*nan guo*)—the nine states he experienced during his spiritual transformation. This number

corresponds to the number of days spent in meditation by
Buliang Yi. Here is the translation of this episode: "Yancheng
Ziyou said to Ziqi of the Eastern Walls: 'One year after I had
begun to listen to you, I returned to a native and rough state; after
two years, I did nothing but follow, offering no resistance; the
third year, I was free of all shackles; the fourth year, I was once more
a simple thing; the fifth year, everything flowed towards me; the
sixth year, the Spirits entered me; the seventh year, the natural
action completed itself; after eight years, I lost awareness of life
and death; and the ninth year, I attained the vast mystery." Here
we have a description of successive levels or ascending degrees.
The ultimate realization begins with abandonment, forgetting
and regression as a prelude to a more radical dehumanization
of the worldview. The description ends with an expression, "the
great wonder" or "the supreme mystery," which cannot be qualified
otherwise than by its own incommunicability, and, like the "One
and Only (*du*)" or "the diaphanous dawn" in the main story under
consideration, signals a qualitative leap, opening onto a new
dimension.

8 *Wu sang wo*, literally: "I have lost my own self," "I am mourning
myself." The expression figures at the beginning of Chapter 2.

9 An exemplary expression of this conception of the Tao or the
Principle can be found in "The Inner workings" ("Nei ye"), a long
meditative poem probably dating from the early fourth century BCE,
so almost contemporary with the *Zhuangzi* and considered by many to
be the original text of Taoism: "The 'Tao' is thus/That which the
(mouth) cannot speak/That which no eye can see/That which ears
cannot hear/By it the mind is nurtured and the body ordered/Men lose
it at death/And gain it with life/Losing it, things and actions
disintegrate/Obtaining it, they are accomplished" (*Guanzi jiaoshi,*
16.49: 399).

10 A.C. Graham, in his philological notes on his translation of the inner
chapters, notes that the meaning of encroachment or intrusion is
attached to the term *ying* in the discourse of the Mohist school. The
Mohists, in their enquiry into the logic of propositions, examine the
conflict between, or the overlap of, the different senses within an
individual reality (see "Textual Notes to Chuang Tzu: The Inner
Chapters," 27). Zhuangzi is one of the most forceful detractors of the
Mohists and of their senseless efforts to shape their lives according to
logic weighed down by sterile paradoxes.

11 This story comes at the end of Chapter 13, "The Course of Heaven."

12 A passage in Chapter 2 of the *Zhuangzi* expresses in the same facetious manner the problematic status of the hypothesis on the beginning of the universe, the absurdity of the very notion of an origin, and the fallacy of all cosmogony: "Let us say that there is a beginning. But in that case there was a time when there had not yet begun to have a beginning. And so there was a time when there had not begun to have a time when there had not yet begun to have a beginning. There is the there-is, there is the there-is-not. There was a time when there had not begun to have the there-is-not. There was a time when there had not begun to have a time when there had not begun to be the there-is-not. And suddenly there was the there-is-not. But in the end I still do not know concerning the there-is and the there-is-not which of them there is and which of them there is not. Just now, I have spoken, but I still do not know whether what I say speaks of something or not" (*Zhuangzi jishi*, 2.79).

13 Chapter "The Mountain Tree," *Zhuangzi jishi*, 20.694.

14 Dame-Twist says in this respect that initially she had "taught" (*jiao*) Buliang Yi, but the term is abandoned once the relationship is established, to give way to the recurrent term *shou*, to maintain, guard or protect, just as in the second part the notions of speech and discourse ("Auxiliary-Inks" and "Chain of Recitations") are resorbed and replaced by vision, listening and careful attention to the silent transformations within all things.

15 Elsewhere, in a fictional dialogue between Yan Hui and his master Confucius, concentration of the mind on internal power takes the form of listening to vital energy. "Do not listen with your ears, listen with your mind, Do not listen with your mind, listen with your breath (*qi*)" (*Zhuangzi jishi* 4.147).

16 Friedrich Nietzsche, *Beyond Good and Evil* (New York: Cosimo, 2006) 10, para. 9.

17 For an outline of the development of the idea of nature in Western literature, and in German Romanticism in particular, the reader might like to consult the last work by Pierre Hadot, *The Veil of Isis: An Essay on the History of the Idea of Nature*, translated by Michael Chase (Cambridge MA: Harvard University Press, 2006). See also Ernst Robert Curtius, *European Literature and the Latin Middle Ages* (Princeton: Princeton University Press, 1953), esp. "The Goddess Natura" and "Invocation of Nature."

18 *Hyperion*, translated by Ross Benjamin, Archipelago Books, 2008 (quoted by Hadot in *The Veil of Isis*).

6 The Way of the True Men

1 With the exception of a short passage, a sort of eulogy in verse, which poses several textual problems. I have intentionally left this aside in my commentary; a conjectural translation is however included as a footnote.

2 Chapter "The Primordial Master," *Zhuangzi jishi*, 6.224. All the following quotations about the true or authentic men of the past are extracted from Chapter 6 unless otherwise indicated.

3 In Chapter "Signs of complete virtue" ("De chong fu"), an instructive passage on the way of life of a sage describes the ability to remain in a state of naturalness called the "provender and nourishment of Heaven" (*tian yu* and *tian shi*; see *Zhuangzi jishi*, 5.217).

4 This refers to the notion of *dang*, the coincidence, matching or adequacy of names to things. In many passages the authors of the *Zhuangzi* take evident pleasure in outwitting the Mohists at their own hair-splitting arguments. The reader may be interested by A.C. Graham's outstanding study of Mohist thought, *Later Mohist Logic, Ethics and Science* (Hong Kong: Chinese University Press, London: School of Oriental and African Studies, 1978), or alternatively consult the shorter essay in his masterly account of early Chinese intellectual history: "From Mo-tzu to Later Mohism: Morality Re-grounded in Rational Utility," in *Disputers of the Tao. Philosophical Argument in Ancient China* (La Salle, IL: Open Court, 1989), II.2, 137–70.

5 *Analects*, 1.4.

6 Cf. Plato's *The Apology of Socrates*. Montaigne refers to Socrates in his *Essays*, III.12, 1192 "On Physiognomy," *passim* (i.e., "We shall not lack good professors to interpret that natural simplicity. Socrates for one").

7 Maurice Merleau-Ponty, *Résumés de cours. Collège de France 1952–1960* (Paris: Gallimard, coll. tel, 1968), 67.

8 Jean-Pierre Diény, "Le Saint ne rêve pas: de Zhuangzi à Michel Jouvet," *Études Chinoises*, vol. XX, no. 1–2, (2001): 142.

9 *Analects*, 17.21.

10 The prescriptions concerning food in funeral rites are even more significant. See for example the chapter "Treatise on Subsidiary Points [in Mourning Usages]" ("Jian zhuan") in the *Book of Rites*: "In the mourning rites for a parent, when the sacrifice of repose has been presented, and the wailing is at an end, (the mourners) eat coarse rice and drink water, but do not take vegetables or fruits. At the end of a year, when the smaller felicitous sacrifice (*xiao xiang*) has been offered,

they eat vegetable and fruits. After another year, when the greater sacrifice (*da xiang*) has been offered, they take pickles and sauces. In the month after, the final mourning sacrifice (*dan*) is offered, after which they drink the must and spirits. When they begin to drink these, they first use the must; when they begin to eat flesh, they first take that which has been dried (in order not to flatter the tongue)," *Treatise on Rites and Usages*, trans. James Legge, *The Sacred Books of the East, vol. 18, The Sacred Books of China*. The Texts of Confucianism Part 4, *Li Ki* XI–XLVI (Oxford: Clarendon Press, 1885), *Shisanjing zhushu, Liji zhengyi*, 57/37, 1549.

11 "tous contraints et amoncelés en nou" (Montaigne, *Essays*, I.26: 176).

12 Montaigne, *Essays,* "On Physiognomy," III.12: 1198.

13 In Chapter 7, a sage by the name of Master Calabash (Huzi) mystifies his entourage by recounting how he decided to present his "inner self" to the evil guru Ji Xian: "I was showing him the fertile soil of Heaven, showing that neither names nor things had hold of me, and that the spring of Heaven was rising and unfolding from my heels" (*Zhuangzi jishi*, 7.301). Jean Levi has written an ingenious commentary on this parody of the jargon used by adepts of physical training techniques. (See Levi, *Propos intempestifs sur le Tchouang-tseu*, 35–7.)

14 Montaigne, *Essays*, "On Experience", III.13: 1258.

15 "Vivre à propos," *ibid.*, 1108. See François Jullien's apt commentary on this expression from Montaigne in *Du Temps. Éléments pour une philosophie du vivre* (Paris: Seuil, 1998).

16 Above this paragraph features a dubious and obscure passage omitted from my commentary (cf. note 1). I offer here a tentative version taking into account the numerous textual corrections suggested by scholiasts:

> In the past, authentic men
> Rose like peaks that never crumbled;
> They seemed in need, but would receive nothing.
> Roaming the world alone, without ever recoiling,
> Blossoming in the void with neither pomp nor pride,
> Radiant, they seemed to find joy at their ease,
> To act only following necessity.
> The strength they absorbed was so concentrated
> That it spread outward, suffusing their countenance.
> Having their contentment, they contained
> Their Potency at rest.
> In that how vast they were, in the image of the world!
> So eminent that nothing could restrain them.

Elusive! as if they longed to seal themselves off;
Taking leave of themselves, forgetting their own words.

17 It should be noted that this paragraph is preceded by another problematic passage that addresses issues of rites and punishments and represents authentic man as being in a position of power, seen from the perspective of legal Reformers (traditionally called the Legalist school) There is ample justification for considering it as spurious and I agree with the scholiasts who have removed it (Fukunaga and Chen Guying).

Conclusion

1 Jean-François Billeter, *Etudes sur Tchouang-tseu* (Paris: Allia, 2004).

2 Literally, "the Great Ancestor and Master."

3 In spite of the profusion of pedagogic dialogues, in the whole *Zhuangzi* there are only nine regular relationships between masters and disciples, among which a good many are just alluded to but never described or represented.

4 Robert Musil, *The Man Without Qualities*, vol. II, translated from the German by Sophie Wilkins and Burton Pike (London: Picado, 2017), 531–2. This proximity in not happenstance, as is evinced for instance by one remark in the *Posthumous Papers*: "Important: the argument with Lao-tsu, which makes Ulrich, but also my task, comprehensible, carried out afterward by Ulrich" (*ibid.*, "General Reflections," 1844).

5 Chapter "All things on a par" ("Qiwu lun"), *Zhuangzi jishi*, 2.79.

BIBLIOGRAPHY

Editions of the *Zhuangzi*

I have based my reading and translations on the edition and annotations made by Guo Qingfan 郭慶藩 (1844–96), *A Collection of Commentaries on the Zhuangzi* (*Zhuangzi jishi* 莊子集釋), which was first published in 1894 and ever since regularly reprinted. The most commonly used edition is that published in 1961 in the series devoted to the ancient masters (*Xinbian zhuzi jicheng* 新編諸子集成) published by Zhonghua shuju 中華書局.

Abiding by the sound philological principle which stipulates that a scholar should be aware of maximal lexical variations and interpretations with a minimum of cross-examined editions, I have also followed all along Chen Guying's 陳鼓應, *A New Translation with New Explanations of the Zhuangzi* (*Zhuangzi jinzhu jinyi* 莊子今注今譯), originally published in 1975 in Taipei by Shangwu yinshuguan 商務印書館 and then republished in three volumes in 1983 by the Zhonghua Shuju Press, and regularly reprinted since then. Chen's edition is less erudite than Guo's, but more accessible and more popular.

Guo's and Chen's editions comprise numerous commentaries, glosses, and notes from the past centuries. The former has the advantage to reproduce in an unabridged form the three most authoritative commentaries on the *Zhuangzi*, from Guo Xiang 郭象, third—fourth centuries BCE), Cheng Xuanying 成玄英, (fl. 630–660), and Lu Deming 陸德明 (556–627), who compiles disparate observations in his *Textual Annotations of the Classics* (*Jingdian shiwen* 經典釋文).

Whenever I encountered a particularly abstruse or puzzling passage in the *Zhuangzi* for which the aforementioned editions were of no help, I consulted Wang Xianqian's 王先謙 (1842–1918) edition, published in 1909 and since completed by Liu Wu, *Collected Explanations on the Zhuangzi*, (*Zhuangzi jijie, Zhuangzi jijie neipian buzheng* 莊子集解, 莊子集解內篇補正, Beijing: Zhonghua shuju, 1st ed. 1987; repr. 2004). This edition offers a plethora of philological notes and commentaries from the Qing era

(1644–1911) for each sentence in the first seven chapters (traditionally revered as the "Inner Chapters").

Several other annotations and glosses culled in the editions listed hereafter helped me to gain a clearer picture of the general exegetical context on a handful of specific stories and dialogues in the *Zhuangzi*:

Zhuangzi 莊子: *Daozangben nanhuajing* 道藏本南華經 / *Zhuang Zhou zhuan* 莊周撰, *Zhuangzi baijia pingzhu* 莊子百家評註, annotated by Gui Youguang 歸有光, and edited by Wang Kaiyun 王闓運, Taibei: Zhongguo zixue mingzhu jicheng bian yin ji jin hui 中國子學名著集成編印基金會, 1978.

(Zhuangzi) *Nanhua zhenjing yihai zuanwei* 南華真經義海纂微, compiled by Chu Boxiu 褚伯秀, Shanghai: Shanghai guji 上海古籍, 1989.

Zhuangzi juanzhai kouyi jiaozhu 莊子鬳齋口義校注 (1235), *The Zhuangzi: Commentaries by Juanzhai (Lin Xiyi)*, annotated by Zhou Qicheng 周啟成, compiled by Lin Xiyi 林希逸, Beijing: Zhonghua shuju 中華書局, 1997.

Zhuangzi yizhu 莊子譯註, edited by Yang Liuqiao 楊柳橋, Shanghai: Shanghai guji chubanshe, 2006.

Finally, among the hundreds of complete editions of the *Zhuangzi*, I should mention the one that remains to my eyes the best work in textual criticism ever carried out on the *Zhuangzi*, the *Zhuangzi jiaoquan* 莊子校詮, authored by Wang Shumin 王叔岷, published in three volumes in Taibei in 1988 at the Academia Sinica's Institute of History and Philology Press (Zhongyang yanjiuyuan lishi yuyan yanjiusuo zhuankan 中央研究院歷史語言研究所專刊).

Unlike Wang Xianqian's edition, Wang Shumin's is based on a clearly identified and reliable version of the original text. It examines and compares variations, culls many commentaries from the Qing, reconstructions of now lost fragments or other indirect traces of the *Zhuangzi*. For simple reasons of convenience, I have not used it as the edition of reference in this book, but I recommend it as the most trustworthy companion for those who set out to examine the *Zhuangzi* with a philosophical mind and a philological expertise.

Recommended translations of the *Zhuangzi*

Graham A.C, *Zhuangzi, The Seven Inner Chapters*, London and Boston: George Allen & Unwin, 1981, repr. 1986.

Watson, Burton, *The Complete Works of Zhuangzi*, New York: Columbia University Press, 1968.

Ziporyn Brook, *Zhuangzi: The Essential Writings with Selections from Traditional Commentaries*, Indianapolis and Cambridge: Hackett Publishing Company, 2009.

Primary sources

The following list only mentions primary sources quoted or discussed in the previous chapters.

Guanzi jiaoshi 管子校釋, compiled by Yan Changyao 顏昌嶢, Changsha: Yuelu shushe, 1996.

Han Feizi jijie 韓非子集解, compiled by Wang Xianshen 王先慎, Beijing: Zhonghua shuju, 1998.

Huainan honglie jijie 淮南鴻烈集解, edited by Liu Wendian 劉文典, Beijing: Zhonghua shuju 1989.

Laozi zhuyi ji pingjia 老子注譯及評介, edited by Chen Guying, Beijing: Zhonghua shuju, 1983; rpt 2003.

Lunheng jiaoshi 論衡校釋 by Wang Chong 王充, edited by Huang Hui 黃暉, Beijing: Zhonghua shuju, 1990.

Lunyu yizhu 論語譯注, annotated by Yang Bojun 楊伯峻, Beijing: Zhonghua shuju, 1980, rpt. 1998.

Liji zhengyi 禮記正義 in *Shisanjing zhushu* 十三經注疏, edited by Li Xueqin, Beijing, Beijing daxue chubanshe, 1999.

Mengzi zhengyi 孟子正義, compiled by Jiao Xun 焦循, annotated Shen Wenzhuo 沈文倬. Beijing: Zhonghua shuju, 1987.

Quan han fu 全漢賦, edited by Fei Zhengang et al., Beijing: Beijing daxue chubanshe, 1997.

Shangjunshu zhuyi 商君書注議, Beijing: Zhonghua shuju, 1974.

Shiji 史記, by Sima Qian 司馬遷, Beijing: Zhonghua shuju, 1959; rpt. 2002.

Secondary sources

Bachelard, Gaston, *La Terre et les rêveries de la volonté*, Paris: José Corti, 1948.

De Beauvoir, Simone, *Wartime Diary*, trans. Anne Deing Cordero, eds. Margaret A. Simons and Sylvie Le Bon, Urbana and Chicago: University of Illinois Press, 2008.

Billeter, Jean-François, *Leçons sur Tchouang-tseu*, Paris: Allia, 2002.

Billeter, Jean-François, *Etudes sur Tchouang-tseu*, Paris: Allia, 2004.

Cook, Scott, "Zhuang Zi and his carving of the Confucian ox," *Philosophy East and West* 47.4 (1997): 521–53.

Curtius, Ernst Robert, *European Literature and the Latin Middle Ages*, Princeton: Princeton University Press, 1953.

Defoort, Carine, "Instruction Dialogues in the Zhuangzi: An 'Anthropological' Reading." *Dao: A Journal of Comparative Philosophy* 11.4 (2012): 459–78.

Diderot, Denis, *Lettres à Sophie Volland*, Paris, Gallimard, Folio classiques, 1984.

Diény, Jean-Pierre, "Le Saint ne rêve pas: de Zhuangzi à Michel Jouvet," *Études Chinoises*, vol. XX, no. 1–2 (2001): 127–99.

Elster, Jon, *Sour Grapes. Studies in the Subversion of Rationality*. Cambridge, London, New York, Melbourne: Cambridge University Press & Paris: Éditions de la Maison des sciences de l'homme, 1985.

Galvany, Albert, "Distorting the Rule of Seriousness: Laughter, Death and Friendship in the *Zhuangzi*," *Dao* (2009) 8:4959. DOI 10.1007/s11712-008-9098-1.

Galvany, Albert and Romain Graziani, "Legal Mutilation and Moral Exclusion: Disputations on Integrity and Deformity in Early China," *T'oung Pao* 106 (2020): 8–55.

Gentz, Joachim, "Transcultural Perspectives on Pre-Modern China," in *China and the World—The World and China*, vol.1, Deutsche Ostasienstudien 37, Ostasien (2019) 1–24.

Graham, A.C., *Later Mohist Logic, Ethics and Science,* Hong-Kong: Chinese University Press, London: School of Oriental and African Studies, 1978.

Graham, A.C., *Disputers of the Tao*, La Salle, IL: Open Court, 1989.

Graham, A.C., "Textual Notes to Chuang Tzu: The Inner Chapters," in *A Companion to Angus C. Graham's Chuang Tzu*, edited by Harold Roth, Honolulu: University of Hawai'i Press, 2003.

Granet, Marcel, "Le Langage de la douleur, d'après le rituel funéraire de la Chine classique," *Journal de Psychologie*, February 1922.

Granet, Marcel, *Danses et Légendes de la Chine ancienne*, Paris: PUF, 1st ed.1926, rpt. 1959.

Graziani, Romain, *Les corps dans le taoïsme ancien. L'infirme, l'informe l'infâme*, Paris: Belles-Lettres, coll. Realia, 2011.

Graziani, Romain, "Optimal States and Self-Defeating Plans: The Problem of Intentionality in Early Chinese Self-Cultivation," *Philosophy East and West*, no. 59 (4) (October 2009): 440–67.

Hadot, Pierre, *The Veil of Isis: An Essay on the History of the Idea of Nations*, trans. Michael Chase, Cambridge MA: Harvard University Press, 2006.

Ibrahim, Annie, "Le matérialisme de Diderot: formes et forces dans l'ordre des vivants" in Annie Ibrahim, ed., *Diderot et la question de la forme*, Paris: PUF, 1999.

Ibsen, Henrik, *Peer Gynt*, New York: Dover Thrift edition, 2003.

Levi, Jean, *Propos intempestifs sur le Tchouang-tseu*, Paris: Allia, 2003.

Levi, Jean, *Le Petit monde du Tchouang-tseu*. Paris: Philippe Picquier, 2010.

Lewis, Mark Edward, *Writing and Authority in Early China*, Albany: SUNY Press, 1999.

Lewis, Mark Edward, "Warring States Political History," in *Cambridge History of Ancient China. From the Origins of Civilization to 221 BC*, Cambridge: Cambridge University Press, 1999.

Liu, Chengji 劉成紀, Wuxiang meixue 物象美學. Zhengzhou: Zhengzhou daxue, 2002.

Merleau-Ponty, Maurice, *Résumés de cours. Collège de France 1952–1960*, Paris: Gallimard, coll. tel, 1968.

Michaux, Henri, *Les grandes épreuves de l'esprit*, Paris: Gallimard, 1966.

Michaux, Henri, *Passages*, Paris: Gallimard, 1950, reprinted in *Œuvres complètes*, bibliothèque de la Pléiade, Paris: Gallimard, 2001.

Moeller, Han Georg, "Liezi's Retirement: A Parody of a Didactic Tale in the *Zhuangzi*," *Dao*, September 2016, Vol. 15 no. 3: 379–92.

Montaigne (de), Michel, *Les Essais*, édition critique Villey-Saulnier, Paris: PUF, 1978.

Olberding, Amy, "The Consummation of sorrow: an analysis of Confucius' grief for Yan Hui," *Philosophy East and West*, Honolulu: University of Hawai'i Press, vol. 54, no. 3 (2004): 279–301.

Puett, Michael, "Violent Misreadings: The Hermeneutics of Cosmology in the Huainanzi," *Bulletin of the Museum of Far Eastern Antiquities* 72 (2000): 29–47.

Rancière, Jacques, *Le Maître ignorant. Cinq leçons sur l'émancipation intellectuelle*, Paris: Fayard, coll.10/18, 2004.

Roel Sterckx, "Food, Sacrifice and Sagehood in Early China" Cambridge: Cambridge University Press, (2011).

Saussy, Haun, *Translation as Citation. Zhuangzi Inside Out*, Oxford: Oxford University Press, 2017.

Sloterdijk, Peter, "Im selben Boot. Versuch über die Hyperpolitik," Frankfurt: Suhrkamp, 1995.

Song, Gang, "La fureur du Zhuangzi," in *Du Pouvoir*, in *Cahiers du Centre Marcel Granet*, no.1, Paris: PUF, 2003, 49–70.

Sterckx, Roel, "Food and Philosophy in Early China," in Roel Sterckx (ed.), *Of Tripod and Palate. Food, Religion and Politics in China*, New York: Palgrave Macmillan, 2005, 34–61.

Sterckx, Roel, *The Animal and the Daemon in Early China*, Albany: SUNY Press, 2002.

Vandermeersch, Léon, "L'imaginaire divinatoire dans l'histoire en Chine," *Bulletin de l'Ecole Française d'Extrême-Orient,* 79.1, 1992.

Vandermeersch, Léon, "Le rationalisme divinatoire," in Léon Vandermeersch, *Études sinologiques*, Paris, PUF, 1994, 159–89.

Wang, Baoxuan 王葆玹, *Laozhuangxue xintan* 老莊學新探, Shanghai: daojia wenhua yanjiu congshu, Shanghai wenhua, 2002.

Wang, Fuzhi 王夫之, *Chuan Shan quanshu* 船山全書, vol. 13 in *Zhuangzi jie* 莊子解, annotated by Wang Xiaoyu 王孝魚, Changsha: Yuelu shushe, 1993.

Yang, Kuan 楊寬, *Zhanguo shi* 戰國史, Shanghai: Renmin, 1955, rev. ed. 2003.

Zheng, Tianting 鄭天挺, and Tan Qixiang 譚其驤 éds., *Zhonguo lishi da cidian* 中國歷史大辭典, Shanghai: Shanghai cishu, 2000.

INDEX